# Virgin

## By

## Angela Sherwood

This book is a work of fiction. Names, characters, places, and incidents are either products of the authors imagination or used fictitiously. Any resemblance to actual events or locales or persons, living or dead, is entirely coincidental.

Virgin

Copyright © 2012 by Angela Sherwood

All rights reserved. Printed in the United States of America. No part of this book may be used or reproduced in any manner whatsoever without written permission except in the case of the brief quotations embodied in critical articles and reviews.

First paperback edition, 2012

ISBN-13: 978-0615623573 (Custom Universal)

ISBN-10: 0615623573

**For Ken Kilkuskie**

## Chapter 1

Days that begin, when I run so late that I have to slip on my nylons during red lights, while in the car, never bode well for me. I should have known better than to have any hope of the rest of the day going well.

Sure enough, upon hurtling into Cedars Memorial Hospital's parking lot, my little VW bug did a slip and slide on the icy pavement, and nicked a giant SUV that was just pulling into a space. I quickly threw my car into reverse and took off to another parking spot about three spaces down. Usually, I would have stopped on the spot and spoken to the other driver but the waist band of my nylons was wrapped around my thighs, and I wanted to finish pulling them up before confronting my victim.

I had just finished hoisting the nylons up and was pulling my skirt back down, which was not and easy feat in the confines of my beloved bug, when there was a knock on my window. I finished tucking my skirt around my legs and quickly threw open the door. It thumped into the man who'd just knocked. He was holding a paper cup of coffee, and the coffee went flying into his chest, where it spilled down his overcoat in rivulets. I stared at his coat in horror for a moment, and then pulled my gaze to his face. The man who stood before me had blond hair that shone in the wintry sun, a profile to match that of Adonis, and green eyes, which were fixed on me with a certain...well I'm not sure hate is quite the right word, but maybe a strong dislike?

I opened my mouth to speak, but the man held up a hand to stop me and spoke instead. "You do realize it's against the law to hit someone else's car and then make a run for it? Don't you?"

"What are you? A cop?" I asked.

"No. I'm a concerned citizen, who's brand new Cadillac SUV, was just whacked by your little...what the heck do they call those things anyway?"

"A bug." I answered, glancing at my watch. I had exactly ten minutes to report for my new job, which I needed desperately.

"A what?" He answered.

"A bug," I retorted. "I whacked your brand new, *gas-guzzling,* Cadillac SUV, with my poor, little bug."

"You don't seem very sorry," he replied.

"I am sorry. I'm very, very sorry, but I'm really late too. And I wasn't just going to run off. I was going to park and come talk to you, but you jumped the gun, and so now you have coffee spilt all over your nice overcoat, which I'm really, really sorry about too. There. Satisfied?"

"No."

"Well, could you please tell me what you want me to do so I can get to work?"

He just stood there and stared at me with astonishment. I guess I didn't sound sorry enough or something, but staring at him, staring at me, was getting me nowhere. Plus, the man was so beautiful to look at, he was making my eyes hurt.

I ducked into my car, grabbed my bag, pulled out a pen, and grabbed his hand. Before he could protest, I scribbled my name on his palm along with my phone number. "When you figure it out, call me. I'll give you all my insurance information, whatever you want, but right now I've got to go.... see ya!"

I took off and headed for the entrance of the hospital as fast as my legs would take me. I hoped he wouldn't follow me, and as I reached the door, I glanced back. He had disappeared.

I arrived at the Human Resource office with one minute to spare and was told by the receptionist to have a seat. I took the moment to get my breath and try to re-assemble myself into some state of calm, all the while wondering how much the green-eyed Adonis back in the parking lot was going to gouge me for. As for my little bug, it already had so many dings and dents, that I doubted whatever damage I'd inflicted would even be noticeable.

The receptionist returned and asked me to follow her to the Emergency Department.

"The Emergency Department?" I asked.

She nodded. "Dr. Caudill requested you meet him in the Emergency Department. He said you were to start there today." She led me out the door and we started down a long corridor.

I was starting to feel a little nervous. "But this is a desk job right...I'm not expected to take care of patients or anything am I?"

The receptionist just kept walking and shrugged. "I really don't know. I don't assign the jobs. I just lead people around and file paperwork all day. I do know, given I filed your paper work, that you're making more money than me, and that just kind of irks me, you know?"

I didn't reply. I was too busy remembering my mother and the countless Sunday dinners she'd destroyed with the gruesome tales she told about volunteering at the local nursing home. Although my mother had a nursing license, she choose to volunteer in order to set a good example for the congregation of the church where my father had preached.

Mom's volunteer work involved things like bathing patients, rubbing their feet and brushing their teeth. The things she discovered while doing these things could curdle the stomachs of the heartiest eaters.

I remember one story in particular, where she had to pry a glob of rotten food out of the mouth, of a woman named Mrs. Patterson. At the end of the story, Mom had thunked a jar containing Mrs. Patterson's glob on the table. This had delighted my younger brothers, but had left an anything but healthy impression upon me. In fact, I had heard enough horror stories about bed sores, mile long toe nails, matted, louse ridden hair, plugged noses, and don't even get me started on what vaginal areas could contain...that I decided I would never, ever, ever want to be involved in the medical profession. Which is why I was confused and somewhat horrified, to find myself being sent to the Emergency Department.

My guide led me to a small anteroom just outside the E.R. doors and told me to wait on a small couch. She closed the door behind her as she left, and I became engrossed in studying the plaques on one wall. They were all in memoriam to doctors and nurses who had all seemingly met an untimely demise. Losing interest in the plaques, I turned to study my reflection in the etched mirror on another wall.

My short, blonde hair was beginning to lose some of its lighter streaks due to the winter months, and I wiped at an errant smear of mascara under my dark, brown eyes. The skirt and shirt I wore were well used, but looked passable; besides, I knew my best features were my long legs. Most people forgot about the skirt after seeing the legs. I looked delicate at first glance (Mom's features), but I was a tomboy and could pack a punch, thanks to my two brothers, who were currently career air force men, living overseas. I gave up on the mascara smear and sat back down.

Before too long, a forty-ish, bearded male entered the room and introduced himself as Dr. David Caudill, Manager of the E.R. at Cedars. His hair was dark and peppered with gray. He was thin, almost to the point of gaunt, and had a slightly distracted air about him, as though he had several internal lines of thought running at once.

"Welcome," he said as he shook my hand. "We're pleased to have you onboard our staff. I'm sorry to have kept you waiting, but one of my resident physicians had some sort of altercation with a crazy woman in the parking lot this morning. I was trying to help him decipher the name she'd scribbled on his hand."

I gulped. I was pretty positive the crazy lady had been me, even though I didn't consider myself crazy. "Where you able to?" I asked wondering if I was about to be fired before I even started my job.

"Able to do what?" He asked distractedly. He was looking down at a clipboard he'd carried in with him, which had my resume attached to it. My name was highlighted in bold yellow, right at the top.

"Decipher the crazy lady's name."

"Oh that. No. His hand was wet with coffee when she'd written it. The writing ended up just a smeared mess."

I sighed in relief, but then my stomach clenched, as I realized that Dr. Caudill had said the man was one of his resident physicians. I knew I'd run into the guy somewhere. I decided to worry about that later and deal with the business at hand.

'Um, Dr. Caudill," I began, "I think there might be a mistake?"

"Mistake?" he asked.

"Well yes," I answered. "I was led to believe I'd been hired for a desk job, in an office."

Surprisingly, he threw his head back, laughed, and said, "I bet you did. I just bet you did."

This did not ease my unease one, little bit.

At my confused, and probably slightly, terrified look, he went on. "The position you're entering here is brand new. I'll wager whoever interviewed and hired you wasn't exactly sure of the job description themselves. However, I've looked at your resume and am pleased with your disaster response history, as well as your education."

He was referring to 2 years of Disaster Assistance work with the National Emergency Response Team, otherwise known as NERT, and 4 years of college, resulting in a Bachelors degree in Psychology.

"I think Human Resources made an excellent choice. So, if it suits you, we'd like to get you started today."

I hesitated, my stomach in knots. Memories of Sundays, danced through my mind's eye. "What exactly will I be doing, Dr. Caudill?" I asked, hoping against hope, he'd tell me I'd sit in a cute little office somewhere, taking phone messages.

"Wow!" he answered with a big grin. "You really are clueless. Aren't you?"

Normally, I would have been insulted by a comment like that, but the way he said the words, with a childlike glee, made it okay.

"Yep. Clueless. That's me," I answered, trying to muster a smile. I already had a sneaking suspicion I'd keep the job. I liked my boss. That alone was a huge plus. I really couldn't afford not to take the job anyway, as I'd just been laid off from NERT, due to a serious lack of horrific, U.S. disasters. My checkbook was feeling the pinch. It was nearing Christmas, which meant spending money on presents. I already had Alfred, my slightly, slimy landlord, breathing down my neck, and the electric company was threatening to cut off my power.

Dr. Caudill went on to describe his vision of the role I'd play at Cedars Memorial Hospital. At first it didn't sound too bad. I would greet the walk-in patients and their families, coordinate visitors with patients, help patients with no family, friends, or money with rides home, coordinate shelters for the homeless. The list went on. I was beginning to think the job might be okay after all.

That thought disappeared with his next words. "When patients come in dead or trying to die, you will be expected to be present in the resuscitation room. You'll be in charge of recovering their belongings, assisting in identifying the patient if necessary, contacting the hospital chaplain, and comforting any grieving family members. Oh, and do you, by the way, have any aversion to blood or emesis?"

Dead people? I thought. Even Mom hadn't mentioned many dead people. I had almost no experience with dead people. I realized he was waiting for an answer of some kind, but couldn't remember the question.

"Umm, what was that?" I asked. "I was still stuck on the dead and dying people."

"Blood and emesis, can you work around it? Or do you gag and faint?"

"What's emesis?" I asked.

"Vomit." There was that huge grin again.

I considered what working with dead people, blood and vomit would be like. I thought of my checkbook. I thought of Alfred. I thought about Sunday dinners. I thought about my checkbook again. I thought about Christmas happening next week.

"No problem," I answered. "Bring on the blood and vomit."

And that was how I, Charlene, Charlie for short, Ross Meadows came to work at Cedars Memorial Hospital.

## Chapter 2

I discovered my tolerance for vomit later that day. A perky, little nurse had stationed me at a desk in the Emergency Room, waiting room. The desk sat in front of the doors separating the waiting room from the rest of the Emergency Department. A lone, miniature, Christmas tree adorned my desk, and piped in Christmas carols permeated the air.

My instructions were to sign in newly, arriving patients on little sign-in slips and hand the slips to the triage nurse, who resided in a little office to my right. The slips were to be handed to her through an opening cut in the bulletproof glass that surrounded her desk. I wanted to know why the triage nurse needed bulletproof glass. If she needed it, why didn't I have it?

So far, I had signed in a woman with abdominal pain, a man with a migraine headache, and a screaming infant with a fever of 102 degrees. There were already at least eight assorted other patients in various states of moaning discomfort, milling around the waiting room, when I'd arrived.

The nurse who'd shown me my desk, had handed me a stack of pink, rectangular tubs and said, "Here, it's flu season, you'll need these." She'd also told me that if I had any questions to ask the triage nurse. I wanted to know what the pink, rectangular tubs were for, but my first encounter with the triage nurse had made me hesitant to ask. I decided to add it to a list, along with the bulletproof glass question.

The triage nurse, whose name was Katy Dee, was in her late 30's and built like a linebacker, with hair dyed a gothic black, and hung to her shoulders. She had piercing, blue eyes, a harsh voice, and an even harsher manner. Actually, Katy Dee was just plain scary in general.

After I signed in the patients, Katy Dee would prioritize them. This involved calling them into her office, talking to them about their symptoms, and getting their vital signs, such as blood pressure, temperature, and weight. Then she'd give the patient an armband and send them back out to the waiting room. This is where the other aspect of my waiting room tasks would come into play. According to Katy Dee, I was to observe the patients and talk to them now and then, so they wouldn't feel like they had been forgotten.

"Why would they feel like they'd been forgotten?" I asked.

Katy Dee had smiled. "You'll figure that one out eventually, Ms. Charlene." She gave me a once over and said, "Do you really think those shoes are a good idea in here?"

I looked down at my favorite, black pumps and asked, "These? What's wrong with these?"

Katy Dee laughed and didn't answer. She looked me over again and said, "I think you ought to know, if you're here to snag a rich doctor, you can forget it. Do you know how many nurses, fresh faced and just out of nursing school, have come here thinking the same thing?"

I wasn't sure of a good answer, so I thanked her for the advice and left her little, glass enclosed office. I hadn't considered the rich doctor angle. Actually, I hadn't given much thought to my love life at all, probably because I didn't have one to think about.

I spent the first hour observing the patients in the waiting room and intermittently signing in new patients. It seemed for every four patients I signed in, a nurse would come and call one patient back, to be seen by a doctor. At this pace, the waiting room was filling at an alarming rate.

I noticed a slightly, overweight woman in the back corner rocking herself back and forth in her chair. She had her arms wrapped around her knees, and as she rocked, she quietly muttered to her self. I wasn't sure what she was there for, as she had already been signed in when I arrived. As I watched, she lifted her head, and appeared to start conversing with someone next to her. The problem was, no one was there to talk to.

I decided I probably ought to check on her, so I left my desk and started walking toward her. As I approached, her one-way conversation became more animated, and I was able to make out some of the words. "I won't! mutter, mutter. No! mutter, mutter. Bastard! mutter, mutter." She started thumping her fists on her knees and her face scrunched up in a ball. "I won't, I won't, I won't."

"Miss?" I asked. "Can I help you with anything?"

The woman ignored me and continued thumping her legs, "I won't, I won't, I won't."

I noticed other patients staring at her in alarm.

"Miss?" I asked more firmly this time. "Is there something I can do for you?"

The woman swung her head toward me and fixed me with a point blank gaze. "Henrietta here says I need to kill you, but I told her I won't." The woman turned to the empty seat next to her. "You hear that Henrietta, I won't and you can't make me, Bitch!"

"Huh," I answered, and started backing away. I wondered who Henrietta was and what I had done to upset her.

The woman didn't appear to notice my gradual exit and continued to stare at the spot where I'd just been standing.

I pushed into Katy Dee's office. She was taking advantage of a break in incoming patients, and had her nose buried in a Harlequin Romance.

"Ahem." I cleared my throat, and Katy Dee looked up at me with raised eyebrows.

"Anything wrong?" she asked.

"Do you see the lady in the back corner there?"

Katy Dee looked and shrugged. "Sandy? What about her?"

"She says her invisible friend, Henrietta, wants her to kill me, and I was kind of wondering if I ought to be concerned. Like maybe we should call Security or something?"

Katy Dee laughed. "Sandy is on the homicidal rant today, is she? Bless her heart."

I stood staring at Katy Dee and felt like slapping myself to make sure I was awake. I'd just been issued a death threat and she was blessing the heart of the woman who'd issued it.

Katy Dee sighed and turned to her computer, hitting a few keys. "This is Sandy's file. Today is her 298th visit to Cedars Memorial Hospital, Emergency Room. She's a homeless schizophrenic with homicidal thought patterns. Some days, she comes in for a snack and to get out of the cold. Other days, like today, she comes to us hoping we'll make the voices stop. Don't mind her. She's harmless. "

I looked dubiously at Katy Dee who was now getting crackers and juice from a mini-fridge under her desk "Give her the juice and crackers. It'll settle her down for a bit."

I was still hesitant. After all, the person telling me not to worry, was sitting behind bulletproof glass, now wasn't she?

I took Sandy the juice and crackers. I was still nervous, but Katy Dee's absolute lack of concern had bolstered my courage, somewhat. Sandy was back to rocking back and forth, along with the unintelligible muttering. I placed the juice and crackers in her hands. Without looking up, she said, "Henrietta says thanks for the juice, but she's still going to find a way to stick a knife in you." Then she looked up at me and smiled the most angelic smile imaginable.

"Tell Henrietta she's welcome, but if she comes near me with a knife, her juice and cracker days are over," I answered, and turned back to the rest of the waiting room. I didn't have time to dwell on the Sandy situation though, because that was when the emesis, a.k.a., vomiting, began.

It started with the baby with the fever. Mother was leaning over her child, gazing adoringly into her infant's eyes. Baby had her mouth open in a little O, and as I watched a geyser of yellow vomit erupted from the little O mouth, rising and swelling over the mother. When the geyser subsided, baby started grinning and giggling, and Mom's mouth was formed into an O of stunned surprise.

"Um, hang on. I'll get you a towel," I said. Vomit no problem my ass, I thought as I started toward the triage office for a towel. Who would of thought such a little baby could *hold* that much? I grabbed a towel and hurried back out to the waiting room. The sight before me stopped me in my tracks.

A man sitting two seats down from the mother and baby had his head buried in a trashcan, retching and acking out his breakfast. A little old lady, two seats away, couldn't seem to look away from him, and as I watched, she covered her mouth with her hands, and her throat began to work. As I stood watching, about every third patient started gagging in a grisly domino effect. I grabbed the pink, rectangular tubs from under my desk. I knew what they were for *now*, and ran around passing them out as quickly as I could. I ran to the triage office for more towels, back to the waiting room, then back to the triage office. "Katy Dee, everyone's throwing up and I'm out of tubs and…"

Katy Dee slowly looked up from her book. "Call housekeeping." Her gaze returned to her book. "By the way, looks like your shoes could use a little cleaning too."

I looked down at my favorite, black pumps and sure enough, they'd become the casualty of someone's breakfast.

I called housekeeping and escaped to the restroom to clean up my shoes. Remembering Katy Dee's comment about them, I wondered what kind of shoes would be better for the job; rubber galoshes? Thigh-high waders? Maybe, I should just wrap them in cling-wrap and call it good. I was still mulling this over as I headed back to my little desk, when I stopped cold. There, leaning his perfect butt on my desk, was the Adonis from the parking lot. I couldn't be sure, but I was pretty confident he was waiting for me.

## Chapter 3

I frantically looked around for an escape and ducked into triage. Definitely not a good hiding place given all the glass, but I had do try to do something to avoid him. Unfortunately, Adonis had seen me and somehow managed to follow me right through the triage door. Katy Dee looked up from her book.

"Finished cleaning those shoes?" She asked with a smirk, but didn't wait for an answer. "Charlene, this is Dr. Sam Macgregor. He's here to give you a tour of the patient treatment center of the Emergency Department."

I turned to fully face Dr. Macgregor. He stood there with a wide grin on his face, seemingly thrilled at this turn of events. Once again, I felt my eyes hurt. No one, but no one, should have teeth that perfect, a dimple that cute, or eyes that wicked.

"Well, now," he said. "It's *so* nice to meet you Miss? I'm sorry. I didn't catch your name."

I suddenly felt like a mouse between the paws of a playful cat, and decided Dr. Macgregor was probably the type to play a long time with his prey before he finished it off. Well, if that was how it was to be, I was game.

"No, no," I replied. "The pleasure is all *mine*, I assure you Dr. Macgregor. I'm Charlene Meadows, but my *friends* call me Charlie."

Katy Dee watched this exchange with some interest until a patient knocked on her window. "Well, if you two, *very pleased*, individuals will leave, I have work to do." She opened the door and ushered us out. Dr. Macgregor wrapped his hand around my arm as we left, probably because he was afraid I'd take off again. The heat of it there was doing very strange things to other parts of my anatomy. I found this quite disturbing, given the circumstances, and tried to disengage my arm, but he held on firmly, propelling me through a set of doors that led to the patient treatment area of the Emergency Room.

"I'm not going to run off on you, you know. You can let go of my arm now," I gritted between clenched teeth. This had no effect. He continued to propel me down a hall and around a corner, out of sight of the busy nurse's station we'd just passed. Here, he finally came to a stop and dropped my arm.

"Well?" He asked.

"Well, what?" I replied.

"What am I supposed to do with you now?"

I put my hands on my hips and stuck out my chin defiantly. "What do you want to do with me? Fire me? Sue me?" Go ahead."

"Now, why would I fire you?"

"Because I hurt your big, new Cadillac."

"Don't you mean my big, new, *gas-guzzling*, Cadillac?" He asked, then shook his head. "No, that's why I'd sue you."

"Well, then because I spilled coffee on your nice, new over-coat."

"No. That only happened because I was too busy watching you pull your skirt down to step away from the car."

I flushed. I had no comeback for that one, and some of the fight went out of me. "Well if you're not going to fire me, and I hope you don't sue me, why don't we just exchange insurance information and call it good. Then you can give me a tour of the Emergency Room and life can go on."

Dr. Macgregor was regarding me with a bemused expression and a wicked look had come back into his eyes.

"I don't care about the car, really. There's not even a scratch on it. The only reason I approached you in the parking lot was to make sure *you* were okay. Watching you pull your skirt down was worth the bump, anyway."

I flushed again. "Are you flirting with me, Dr. Macgregor?"

He shrugged and grinned. "Maybe. Do you want me to?"

"Maybe," I shot back. "Do you want me to want you to flirt with me?"

He didn't answer right away, but when he answered he left no doubt.

"Absolutely."

A nurse came around the corner and interrupted us. "Dr. Macgregor, there's a code about five minutes out, and they wanted me to check to see if you were available to handle it."

Dr. Macgregor snapped into professional mode. "What's the code?" he asked.

The nurse who was a petite brunette, wearing blue scrubs, didn't miss a beat. "50-ish male, apparent cardiac arrest. CPR has been in progress for 5 minutes. EMS picked him up at the mini-mart on Euclid."

Dr. Macgregor nodded. "I'll take it."

I started to turn to go back to the waiting room, figuring I'd just lost my tour guide, when Dr. Macgregor called me back. "Charlie, where are you going?"

"Back to the waiting room," I answered.

"Oh no you don't. This is part of your job responsibilities...being present in the resuscitation room, gathering the patient's belongings and identifying them. Didn't Dr. Caudill go over that with you?"

I hurried after Dr. Macgregor who had started walking at a fast pace through the halls. "He did, but I thought I'd get a little mock run through or something first."

Dr. Macgregor pushed through double doors marked RESUS and I followed him through the doors. "The best way to learn in an E.R. is hands on."

At that moment, blue lights started flashing overhead and a synthetic voice called, "Code Blue, Code Blue, Code Blue," from overhead speakers. Dr. Macgregor winced and said, "No time like the present, right?"

The double doors flew open and what seemed like an army of people swarmed in, all surrounding a gurney with a rather bluish looking gentleman laying on it. The nurses and techs heaved, and slid the man to the resuscitation room stretcher. The gurney he came in on was quickly wheeled out.

The man looked rather familiar at first glance, but I didn't get to linger on that thought, because one of the nurses asked if I was the new employee who would be identifying the John Does and could I please get the patient's pants off?

Maybe, it was the woman's tone or my inbred need to please, but without thinking, there I was, working at the man's belt buckle. One of the techs slapped a pair of latex gloves at me and said, "Here lady. I think he wet himself."

I cringed, realizing now what the dark stain was on the crotch of the man's trousers, and quickly slipped on the gloves that ended up being at least two sizes two big. Fumbling through the too large gloves, I finally managed to get the buckle undone and the pants unzipped. I tried to tug the pants down, but the man's weight was too much. I was stuck. The same tech slapped a pair of scissors in my hands and said, "Cut them."

"What?" I asked.

"Cut the pants off and be quick about it, why don't you?"

I looked at the unconscious man and said, "I'm so sorry sir, not my idea, okay?" I started cutting. All around me the crisis team was working with a frenzy I'd only see on television. Each had a specific task and each was doing it with a fine cut precision while Dr. Macgregor directed. I felt like a bumbling idiot in their midst and wondered what the heck I was doing there. The vomit-filled waiting room was starting to look good at this point.

I finally had the pants off, and much to my dismay, discovered our patient didn't wear underwear. I studiously tried not to look at the man's penis, but it was right there looking so small and limp and well, so *pathetic*. A gloved hand grabbed the penis startling me from my reverie. The nurse attached to the hand gave me a knowing, sideways look, and said, "I need to insert a urine catheter. Perhaps you'd like to look through what's left of his pants for some identification?"

I smiled weakly at the nurse and started searching the front pockets. I found a handful of change, a toothpick, and a single key. I wrapped them in a paper towel so I could rinse them off later and stuck them in my shirt pocket.

I pulled on the wet pieces of pants still under the patient, finally cleared them of the man's body, and began to go through the back pockets. I found his wallet.

"Do we have an I.D. yet?' Dr. Macgregor called out over the din of activity centered over the stretcher.

"Almost," I called back. I folded the wallet open and pulled out the man's license. "It's, umm, wait I can't read it." The license had been in the wallet so long that it was corroded with crusted gook. I grabbed a paper towel and scrubbed at the name area. "His name is Alfred Tenny." I looked at the face portrayed on the license in disbelief. The lights in the room seemed to flicker and a white-hot heat flooded my face.

"Good," barked Dr. Macgregor. "Carla, call records for any and all past medical records on Alfred Tenny."

"Yes, Doctor," the nurse answered and went to the phone.

I continued to stare at the face in the picture and checked the address. Just as I had suspected, the address showed Alfred lived on Crown Circle. Alfred Tenny was my landlord. It dawned on me that I'd just cut my landlord's pants off. The lights in the room began to dim, and I was suddenly very dizzy. The voices from the crisis team started to fade against a roaring in my ears.

## Chapter 4

I was swimming in a pool of darkness, and my head was pounding with a dull thump, thump rhythm. Voices swirled around me while brilliant specks of light appeared and started twirling beneath my eyelids. "I think she's coming around, Doctor."

"Charlie? Charlie? Charlie?"

I wanted to keep watching the pretty specks of light, but the insistent voice kept calling my name. I felt something warm patting my cheek. I managed to pry at least one eye open, and found Dr. Macgregor's face hovering above mine. I decided his face was even prettier than the specks of light and forced my other eye open. He was gently patting my cheek, but stopped when he saw I'd come to.

I was lying on the little couch in the anteroom I'd started out in, with Dr. Caudill, that morning. Dr. Macgregor was leaning over me, and I felt myself flush at once. He seemed to have that effect on me. The moment his body was near mine, my core temperature seemed to want to shoot up ten degrees, or more.

Dr. Macgregor placed a hand on my forehead, looking concerned. A nurse I hadn't met yet, stood behind him with a pinched look on her face. I got the sense that she was rather annoyed.

"How are you feeling, Charlie?" Dr. Macgregor asked.

I decided Dr. Macgregor's hand on my head felt entirely too good, and afraid I'd tell him so, I pushed it away, and sat up. The pretty specks of light returned and started dancing through the air in front of my eyes. "Wow! What are those pretty specks of light?" I asked, trying to pluck one out of mid air. It disappeared, so, I tried to grab another one.

Dr. Macgregor stepped back and looked at the annoyed nurse. "I think she may have a concussion."

The nurse, a blonde twig of a girl with way too much eye makeup, sniggered. "I think she may want to start looking for a new job."

"Joyce!" Dr. Macgregor admonished. "It's my fault she passed out. It's her first day. I should never have let her stay when that code came in."

I stopped trying to catch specks of light and rubbed my aching head. "I passed out?"

Dr. Macgregor nodded. "Unfortunately, right in the middle of the resuscitation room."

"Oops," I said, then remembered Alfred. "Is Alfred going to be okay?"

"Alfred?" Dr. Macgregor asked.

"The patient. His name is Alfred Tenny," I answered.

"Oh yes, Mr. Tenny. We lost him to cardiac arrest." He looked at Joyce. "Did we ever get in touch with his family, Joyce?"

"Not yet. We're still trying the phone numbers from his old file."

Poor Alfred, I thought. He was so young. What 48, maybe 50? He was slimy and creepy, yes, but too young to die of a heart attack. The image of his tiny penis tried to surface and I struggled to push it back down. The room twirled and steadied again, but at least the specks of light had disappeared. "You won't be able to reach any family," I told them.

"What do you mean, how would you know?" Joyce shot at me.

"Um, he's...well, he was my landlord. He was always complaining about how he only had himself left in this world."

Dr. Macgregor swore under his breath then said, "You knew him? No wonder you passed out. Rule number one of the resuscitation room is that no one ever works on someone they know."

Joyce looked a little less annoyed but it didn't ease the pinched look on her face. I was beginning to think that the pinched thing she had going on was just her normal look. "Well why didn't you say anything, Charlene? We would have told you to leave."

"I didn't know it was Alfred, at least not until I finally managed to get his I.D. out of his pants." I shuddered a bit at the memory.

"I think you've had enough of Cedars Memorial Hospital today, Charlie," said Dr. Macgregor, as he leaned forward and took my hands to help me to my feet. With his hands in mine, a tingle went straight to regions uncharted. I flushed and decided I should be ashamed of myself. I was practically standing on poor Alfred's grave, and here I was rediscovering my libido.

Dr. Macgregor noticed the flush. "Do you feel okay?"

What a ridiculous question. My head hurt, my pride hurt, and my hormones were singing so loudly I was surprised no one else could hear them. I wasn't okay by a long shot.

"I'm fine," I answered.

Dr. Macgregor stepped closer, his emerald eye's searching mine. "I'm afraid you hit your head pretty hard. Would you like me to do an exam? We could do a CAT scan just to be sure."

I hesitated. I was pretty sure I needed my head examined, but it had nothing to do with the bump I'd received when I passed out, and everything to do with the feelings Dr. Macgregor's proximity was arousing.

As Dr. Macgregor continued to study my face, the clinical nature left his gaze and something much warmer replaced it. For a moment I was sure he was going to kiss me, and I found I liked that idea very much. I felt myself leaning toward him, and the bright specks of light reappeared. They were very pretty.

Joyce cleared her voice, breaking the spell. "So are we going to do a CAT scan or what?" She asked curtly.

Dr. Macgregor blinked.

I blinked.

"No thank you," I replied.

"I think she's fine," Dr. Macgregor announced.

"Apparently." Joyce said sarcastically.

"Is it okay if I go now?" I asked. "I think I just need to go home and take some Tylenol."

"Sure," Dr. Macgregor replied. He pulled out a pad of paper from his lab coat and jotted a number on it. "Call me…I mean if you suddenly feel dizzy or light-headed."

Joyce glared at both of us as I took the paper.

I stifled the urge to laugh. Was he kidding? Just being around Dr. Macgregor made me light-headed and dizzy.

## Chapter 5

Once I reached my car in the parking lot, I was relieved to find that my run-in with Dr. Macgregor's car had left no noticeable, new damage to my bug. I climbed behind the wheel of my car, turned on my cell phone and checked the messages. There was one from Sherrie, my best friend, reminding me to meet her for drinks at Spanky's later that night. There were two from my mother, wanting to hear about the new job, and one from Alfred. I got goose bumps as I looked at his number displayed on my phone. I realized that he'd probably called about the rent. I bypassed the message without listening, turned on the car and made a left turn out of the parking lot and headed home.

When I reached my apartment building, everything looked normal and in place. The building was actually an old two-story post office that had been converted into five apartments—three on the ground floor and two upstairs. I rarely saw my upstairs neighbors and honestly couldn't even tell you their names. I knew one was a car mechanic, divorced and in his 40s, and the other was a middle-aged secretary at the local, elementary school. That was all I knew. The people upstairs didn't socialize with the downstairs occupants.

It seemed odd that everything appeared normal when I knew it should be otherwise. Alfred was dead. I paused in front of his apartment door on the way to my apartment, which was next to his. I looked up and down the hall, and then tried his doorknob. To my surprise the door swung open. I looked up and down the hall again, then peeked inside.

I have always been a little too curious for my own good, so I found myself stepping inside the door. This put me inside Alfred's living room and gave me a view into his bedroom and kitchen. Books, newspapers, pizza boxes and clothes were strewn across the living room floor. I flipped on the light switch, bringing the assorted mess into better clarity, and something went scurrying across the floor. A mouse? A rat? I swallowed hard. I'd conquered my fear of vomit. Why should a little rodent bother me?

I tried to take another step into the apartment, but couldn't do it. I flipped off the switch and stepped back out of the apartment, closing the door behind me with a shiver. I just couldn't muster my courage, and I shivered again at the thought of a rat. Quietly admitting defeat, I turned to go to my apartment and found myself standing chest to chest with my other first-floor neighbor, Haley Smith.

Haley was a very busty woman in her 50s. She practiced Wicca and was a self-proclaimed seer, whose graying, blonde hair was kept in brightly beaded cornrows. She was always garbed in very colorful robes, and adorned in crystal pendants, earrings and rings. Her light-blue eyes were intense as she stared at me.

I had let her "see" for me a year ago and that had been enough for me. She'd said there was no man in my future, no good fortune, no increased wealth and no foreign travel. I mean, what good is a seer if they can't see anything good? Actually, she'd been right. Here it was a year later, and I was still penniless, man less, and hadn't been anywhere other than disaster areas, assigned by NERT.

"I smell the scent of death on you and all around you," Haley stated in a grave, matter of fact voice. "Where have you been today, Charlie? The cemetery?"

"Close," I answered, "Cedars Memorial Hospital. I started my new job today."

Haley was always very dramatic, and today her drama was making my already sore head ache even more. "What are you doing out here in the hall, Haley? Shouldn't you be inside gazing into you crystal ball or something?" I asked curtly. I was miffed at having been snuck up on.

"Oh pooh," Haley answered, waving her heavily be-ringed hands. "You know my visions don't come from crystal balls. They come from here," she said, pointing to her heart. "I need to talk to you. I've had some disturbing visions concerning you lately."

I sighed. The last thing I needed was more bad news. "Haley, I told you after the last time that I didn't want to hear any more of your visions concerning me. They're downright depressing!"

Haley narrowed her eyes at me, unfazed. "Charlie, your life may be in danger and it has something to do with Alfred."

"Alfred? But that's impossible!" I blurted.

"Why is it impossible? Because he's dead?" Haley tapped my shoulder with her index finger. "No, Charlie, it's not impossible. Something to do with Alfred is going to reach out and touch you from his grave."

My mouth hung open. "Who told you Alfred was dead?"

"No one told me, sweetie. I felt him passing this afternoon." She shuddered. "He was screaming all the way like the little wuss he was. Now, shut your pie hole and come into my apartment and have some tea with me. We need to talk."

I realized that my mouth was still hanging open and snapped it shut. I hesitated. It was getting late. I wanted a shower and some aspirin for my still aching head, and I had approximately 45 minutes to get downtown to meet Sherrie at Spanky's.

As though reading my mind, Haley said, "Oh pooh, this will only take 10 minutes of your time, and the longer you stand there deliberating, the more time you're wasting. Besides, you don't want me to tell certain authorities that I caught you sneaking out of Alfred's apartment, do you?"

I sighed. I was a victim of blackmail. "Okay," I said, and followed Haley into her apartment.

Although Haley's apartment had the exact same floor plan as mine, for some reason, it appeared completely different. Haley's place was warm, colorful and inviting. Little glass figurines and crystals gave off prisms of refracted light, and the sound emitted by little water fountains throughout the apartment gave the impression that there was a babbling brook nearby. My apartment still looked like someone was just moving in, even though I'd been there for more than a year. I had no talent in the homemaking department.

I sank into one of Haley's comfy, velvet-covered chairs and sighed. It didn't help that her holiday decorations were phenomenal. I thought of the poor tree I'd purchased last week. It was a runt and had lost most of its needles on the ride home. I'd almost thrown it out, but then I thought of Charlie Brown and how he'd rejuvenated his tree. How could I give up when Charlie Brown hadn't?

Haley placed a cup of tea and two aspirin next to a figurine on the small table next to my chair, and settled into another chair across from me with her own cup. I knew I hadn't mentioned my headache. She probably could tell by my scrunched up forehead that I had one, but sometimes, I had to consider the possibility that she did indeed have a gift. I swallowed the aspirin down with the tea.

"Okay, now Charlie, I know you think I'm just a wacky, old lady with a few loose screws, but what I see is real and what I feel is real. After all, how can you doubt me after the reading I did for you last year?"

"It's not that I exactly doubt you or your readings, Haley, it's just that I don't like them. Now, if you saw something happy, like, oh say, that I was going to meet the man of my dreams or win the lottery; then I'd like you to come talk to me."

"You just won't take me seriously." She looked defeated, and I tried to cheer her up.

"I believe, that you believe, what you think you see."

"Well, I guess that's something anyway," Haley replied.

"So shoot, what's the doom and gloom of the day?" I asked.

Haley took a sip of her tea and regarded me solemnly. "The visions I've been seeing are strange, because it feels as though you are in danger from several sources. Someone truly evil is going to be seeking you out." Haley paused and shivered. "Someone wants something you have. Then I see someone else who wants to harm you. I can't figure out how, but somehow it's interwoven, yet separate. I keep seeing Alfred's face. He's left you in trouble in some way. Am I making sense?"

I looked at Haley, who was bobbing her head up and down as though trying to lead me into an affirmative answer.

"No," I said flatly. "I'm totally confused and really late. Can I go now?"

Haley pouted in disappointment. "Oh pooh." But she sent me on my way, nonetheless. "Yes, shoo, shoo! Go, but please,

please be careful. I don't want a new neighbor. You're so nice and quiet over there. God knows who you might be replaced with, if you are kidnapped or murdered or worse."

What could be worse than being murdered, I wondered? I took a last sip of my tea and stood up to go. "Thanks for the tea and aspirin, Haley." I paused when I saw the concern on her face and tried to placate her. "I really, really promise to be careful, okay?"

Haley nodded and waved me toward the door, looking no less concerned.

I went to my apartment and shed my clothes—hoping that I had also shed the death thing Haley had noticed—and tossed my clothes in the hamper. I then took a quick, extremely hot shower and dressed for Spanky's. My mind kept trying to worry about what Haley had said, but I was just too tired to want to really examine her prediction in any great detail.

I dressed in jeans and a turtleneck sweater, finger-combed my hair, swiped on some mascara and headed out the door wearing my favorite leather jacket. I shivered as I walked past Alfred's apartment and quickly dismissed the image of soiled pants and the other little thing that flashed in my mind.

Spanky's was really within walking distance of my apartment, and I hesitated about driving. I did a mental calorie tally for the day and realized that I'd missed lunch and hadn't had much for breakfast. That meant I was negative as far as calorie consumption for the day, which meant I could opt for the bug guilt-free.

I arrived at Spanky's a few minutes later and picked Sherrie out of the crowd immediately. Sherrie, with her flaming red hair and the usual cluster of men around her, trying to gain favor, was hard to miss. The place was loud and crowded—more so than usual because it was close to the mall and Christmas was around the corner.

I finally managed to elbow my way to Sherrie's booth just as the two men she'd been talking to walked away, looking extremely disappointed. Obviously, Sherrie had already given them the brush-off.

"Hey girl! How was your first day at your new job?" Sherrie asked, as she jumped up to give me a hug. Sherrie was a tall girl, about two inches taller than my 5 feet, 5 inches. She had long, curly, red hair and dark eyes. We'd been thrown together as roommates in college and remained fast friends ever since.

"If I had to choose one word to sum it up," I answered, "deplorable." I plopped down in the booth across from her and heaved a sigh.

"Oh come on, Hoochie girl. How bad could it have been? Did you break a fingernail typing or something?" Hoochie girl was Sherrie's pet name for me from our college days. Only Sherrie could call me Hoochie girl. Anyone else would die if they tried.

"Well, first of all, I don't type at this job. Somehow, I've landed a job in the E.R. that is just about as up close and personal as you can get without a nursing degree or medical license. I didn't find this out until after I rear-ended a totally hot doctor in the parking lot. Secondly, a homeless schizophrenic named Sandy told me that Henrietta wanted me dead, and then practically every patient in the E.R. waiting room threw up on me. Next, I had to cut off Alfred's pants, after which I fainted, and then he died."

Sherrie gave her head a quick shake. "Back up. Who was the hot doctor?"

I burst out laughing. It felt so good to be back in the company of someone predictable.

The waiter appeared and we ordered our usual drinks. Sherrie always had a Grey Goose martini and I always had a vodka tonic. Sherrie had expensive taste. I didn't care. I also ordered a steak salad and extra-crispy fries.

Over the drinks and food, I went on to explain the events of the day. Sherrie listened with rapt attention. Later, as I scraped a last piece of lettuce from the plate, Sherrie asked, "So you didn't listen to Alfred's message?'

"No, it just seemed way too creepy at the time. I mean, the guy just died."

"Yeah," Sherrie countered, "but didn't Haley say he was going to touch you from the grave? A phone message from a dead guy sounds like getting touched from the grave to me. Maybe, we should listen to that message."

"Okay, okay," I said, searching through my purse for my cell phone. "Here it is. Oh crap, the battery's dead. Did you bring your phone?" I asked, thinking I could check my messages remotely from her cell phone.

"No, I left it at home just in case Eddie called." Eddie was one of Sherrie's new boyfriends. I knew from experience that when she didn't want to appear too eager or available to one of her new guys, she would leave her phone at home so she wouldn't answer it when he called. This was Sherrie's logic in its finest form.

"Oh, well," I said, "Alfred's last words will have to wait."

"Soooo," Sherrie leaned toward me with a sly look. "What does this Dr. Macgregor look like?"

I grinned. "Adonis."

Sherrie let out a whoop. "Hoochie girl's got a crush!"

"No, no, I never said that," I protested.

"Doesn't matter," Sherrie teased, "the grin said it all. I know when my girl sees something she likes, and it's been a while since I've seen a grin like that."

I grinned again, looked at my watch and realized it was already past 10 p.m. "I'd really love to stay and debate the issue with you, but it's late and I have day two at Cedars to look forward to tomorrow."

"Yes, it is late," Sherrie agreed. "I've got a full day tomorrow, as well."

Sherrie was a hypnotherapist and a certified Reiki master at the Crystal Air and Light Spa. She took her clients and her work very seriously. If she felt she didn't have enough energy or the right kind of energy, she'd reschedule her appointments for a time when there was a more "positive" influence around her. Personally, I wasn't completely sure the positive / negative thing wasn't just an excuse to take a day off once in a while, but, because she was my friend, I gave her the benefit of the doubt.

We paid our tab, left the pub, stepping out into the frosty air. "Are you walking or driving tonight?" Sherrie asked as she wrapped a gorgeous cashmere scarf around her neck.

"Driving," I answered. "It's cold and calories weren't an issue today."

Sherrie laughed, "I guess not, after your day. Well, since you don't need a ride; I'll see you soon. Call me the minute you listen to Alfred's message, okay?"

"Sure thing," I replied and headed toward my car with a last wave.

## Chapter 6

I didn't check Alfred's message that night. Instead, I waited until I was on the way to work the next morning. I hit the message prompt button on my cell phone and pressed 1. Alfred's message came up, and there was a huge burst of static in my ear. I was so startled that I swerved the car, eliciting angry beeps from the uptight motorists around me. I corrected the steering and waited until I was in the hospital's parking lot before trying to listen to his message again.

"Charlie, it's Alfred," I heard and shivered. Alfred was dead, and there I was, listening to his voice. "There's something you need to know. It's important. Please call me the minute you get a chance. Oh, by the way, the washing machine is out of order today." The line went dead, and I sat in the car feeling perplexed. If Alfred had been calling about the rent, I was sure he would have just said so. Then I realized I was late for work and forgot about everything but getting to the time clock in the next 30 seconds.

I had clocked in and was shedding my coat in the employees' lounge when Joyce walked in. Joyce didn't look very happy. Actually, from what I'd observed so far, Joyce never seemed to look very happy.

Joyce marched up to me and placed her hands on her hips, reminding me of Daphne from the cartoon, Scooby Doo. "I can't believe you came back after that hugely embarrassing scene you made yesterday."

I raised an eyebrow. "Yeah, well some of us are gluttons for punishment, I guess. Is there some special reason you may have been hoping I wouldn't show up today? Or are you just trying to make conversation here?"

Joyce narrowed her eyes at me as she shifted the Daphne stance to the other hip. "As a matter of fact...I do. I lost 20 dollars betting you wouldn't come back. And don't think I didn't notice the way you were flirting with Sam yesterday."

"Sam?" I asked confused. "Oh, you mean Dr. Macgregor!"

"Yes, Dr. Macgregor! It was absolutely shameful the way you threw yourself at him. I wouldn't be surprised if you had fainted on purpose just so he'd have to carry you out of the resuscitation room. I'm going to let what happened yesterday go, because you weren't aware that Sam and I are just about to become an item."

I thought about the conversation I'd had with Dr. Macgregor in the hall the day before. It had seemed to me that Dr. Macgregor had every intention of starting something with me that was beyond the scope of work at the hospital. Maybe he just flirted with everyone that way. I was surprised to find myself irritated at the idea.

"Listen, Joyce, I don't care if you and Dr. Macgregor are or aren't an item. I'm just trying to get through the first week of a very odd, new job. I'm sorry if I offended you in any way, but really, I do need to get to work now."

Joyce shifted the Daphne stance back to the other hip. "Just so long as you and I know what's what around here. Anyway, you're wanted in Dr. Caudill's office. He and Dr. Macgregor are waiting to talk to you."

I left Joyce in the employees' lounge and headed toward Dr. Caudill's office, which was located near the rear of the Emergency Room. I knocked on the door, and Dr. Macgregor quickly opened it. His handsome face lit up with a smile that accentuated his wonderful dimple. "Charlie! Good morning! How's your head?"

I immediately felt my pulse accelerating and my internal temperature rising in the presence of Dr. Macgregor, but I tried to ignore it. I was a professional, after all, and was determined to behave like one.

Miraculously, I hadn't felt any ill effects from my head bump. I smiled brightly and said, "It's just fine today, thanks."

Dr. Caudill was sitting behind his desk, fiddling with a small phone. He glanced up and smiled. "I have a present for you, Charlene."

"A present? Oh, please call me Charlie, Dr. Caudill."

Dr. Caudill pointed to the phone he'd been fiddling with. "This little gadget is going to be your best friend. We want the staff to be able to reach you when they need to. Being this is a rather large department and your duties are so varied, we decided to invest in an in-house, wireless phone for you. It will enable our staff to reach you no matter where you are." He handed the phone over to me.

The phone was tiny and had a small clip so that it could be attached to a belt.

"With this phone you'll be able to take phone calls to patients waiting for disposition, and we'll be able to let you know when you're needed in the resuscitation room. Complaints will be transferred to you as well."

"Complaints? Am I supposed to be able to resolve these complaints?" I asked.

Dr. Caudill nodded. "Yes, if you can. Otherwise, you'll just make a record of them on one of these, and turn them into me." He handed me a stack of complaint forms and went on. "Your extension is on the phone," he said, handing me a small booklet, "and here are instructions on how to place people on hold, transfer calls and so forth. The phone has two lines. Your number will be given to all E.R. staff the minute you leave this office."

I was intensely grateful to discover that the phone was almost an exact replica of the one I had used while I was with NERT.

Dr. Macgregor asked, "Charlie, Alfred Tenny ... can you tell us anything else about him?"

"What sort of information were you hoping for?" I was fiddling with the phone and the instruction book—anything to keep from having to look at him.

"Did he have any close friends or any kind of relative—no matter how distant? Also, what about enemies? Did he have anyone who didn't like him?"

I stopped fiddling and thought for a moment, finally raising my eyes to meet his incredible green ones. "Not that I know of. I do know he did some business with a lawyer at Simon and Simon, because that's who wrote my lease last year."

Dr. Macgregor rubbed his chin, "That could be helpful. Thanks, Charlie."

"May I ask why you want to know?"

Dr. Caudill cleared his throat and gave Dr. Macgregor a stern look, who in turn brushed off my question. "Um, never mind. It's really nothing to worry about, Charlie. If you'll excuse me now I need to start my rounds. I'll see you soon." He made a hasty exit, but not before collecting what looked like a 100-dollar bill from Dr. Caudill.

I looked at Dr. Caudill in disbelief. "You bet *against* me coming back to work?"

He shrugged and flashed a smile. "Let's just say you look a lot more fragile than I'm beginning to suspect you are. How did you feel about your first day, anyway?"

"It was unlike anything I've ever experienced before in my life." I gave him a somewhat accusing glare.

He ignored the glare. "Well, I'm glad you're back, even though it cost me a C-note. Just try to keep from fainting anymore in the future. It sort-of disrupts the crisis team."

I promised to do my best and was dismissed to do my duties. I decided to go to the waiting room, and stowed the complaint forms in one of the drawers in my desk. Joyce was the triage nurse today in place of Katy Dee, who apparently had the day off. I sat at my little desk and thought about the conversation with Dr. Macgregor. He had seemed uptight, and Dr. Caudill's reaction to my question to Dr. Macgregor, had made me all the more anxious to know why they wanted to know if Alfred had enemies. I was also still wondering about Dr. Macgregor and Joyce.

My little phone started ringing and I answered, "Cedars, may I help you?"

The voice on the other end of the line was that of a young male and had all kinds of country wrapped into it. "Yes, Miss, what did you say your name was?"

"My name is Charlie," I answered.

"Charlie, huh? You don't sound like no Charlie I ever heard of. You sound like a woman."

"I am a woman, sir."

"You don't say? Well, okay, maybe you can help me with something."

"I'd be happy to try."

"Well, here's the thing. I was in there a couple of weeks ago—cut off my fingers, don't ya know—and they did their best to put 'em back on but they jus' didn't take. Said who ever picked 'em up shoulda put 'em on ice until we got there."

"Oh my," I answered. "I'm so sorry that happened to you."

"Yeah, I'm a woodworker by trade, and, well, it just seems I ain't got a trade anymore now that my fingers is gone."

"I'm so sorry, sir."

"I'm sure I don't have to tell you how rough it's been."

"No, sir."

"So, here's the deal. I want my fingers."

I sat stunned for a moment. "Excuse me, sir?"

"I said I want my fingers back, Missy."

"Sir, I know it's none of my business, but could you tell me why you want your fingers back?"

There was silence on the other end of the line for a moment. "Well, now, I reckon that *is* none of your business, ain't it?"

I was frantically trying to picture what they do with dismembered body parts in the E.R., and I had a sinking feeling that they weren't kept in the deep freeze anywhere nearby. The other phone line started ringing, and I politely asked if I could put the man on hold.

"Sure thing," he answered.

I answered the other line. It was Joey, one of the techs in the back. "There's a Code Blue en route and they need you in the resuscitation room, STAT."

"I'll be there as soon as I can," I answered, then asked, "Hey, Joey, what do we do with discarded body parts here?"

Joey waited a minute to answer, then said, "You're one sick lady, Charlie," and hung up.

I groaned in frustration and went back to the other line.

"Um, sir, are you there?"

"I'm here."

"Can I take your name and number, and call you back?" I asked, pulling out one of the complaint forms Dr. Caudill had given me earlier.

"When you gonna call back, lady?"

"Just as soon as I find out where your fingers are, sir."

"Well, okay then. My name is Horace Schmidt, and my number is 555-1515. You better call me back or I'll come find you, Ms. Charlie." I hoped this was Horace's attempt at a joke, but I wasn't about to take a chance.

"Don't worry, sir, I'll call you back."

I shut the phone off and felt like thumping my head on the desk. Instead, I stood up and made my way to the resuscitation room.

By the time I arrived, everything was in full swing. This time there was a woman on the table, and I was intensely relieved to see that she didn't have any pants on. Actually, she didn't have any clothes on at all. She was probably around 70 years old, overweight, and definitely blue.

"Charlie, good you're here," said Dr. Macgregor. "This is Lilly Miller. Her belongings are on the counter over there, and her significant other is in the consultation room." He said all this as he busily moved around Lilly Miller's chest with a stethoscope. "Would you log her belongings on the sheet marked 'Personal Items', there on the counter?"

"Sure thing," I said, happy to have to look away at anything other than poor Lilly's naked form being subjected to chest compressions and some sort of tube being stuck down her throat by the busy team that was swarming around her.

"When you're done with that, you'll need to take them to her boyfriend in the consultation room and stay with him until we can give him some news, okay?"

I nodded in the affirmative and started cataloging her belongings. So far, this patient was a breeze compared to yesterday's patient. She had a pink robe, some, um, very interesting lacy underwear (the type you'd expect on a very immodest Victoria's Secret model) and Eva Gabor-style slippers. Her other belongings consisted of a large purse containing a paperback novel and a small change purse. I checked the change purse and found 500 dollars in 100-dollar bills and 45 cents in assorted coins, along with her driver's license and a membership card for the American Association of Retired Persons. The only other item in the purse was a door key from the Moonlight Inn.

Once I had cataloged everything, I placed Lilly's items in a large plastic bag marked "Patient's Belongings" and turned my attention back to the crisis team. The activity around the stretcher had quieted somewhat, and some members of the crisis team were standing around now, shaking their heads.

I went over to Dr. Macgregor and asked him where the consultation room was.

"Oh, that's the room we took you to when you passed out yesterday," he answered.

One of the techs looked up from adjusting Lilly's I.V. "That was you? I heard about that. Too funny."

I ignored him. "So how's Lilly doing?" I asked.

Dr. Macgregor shook his head solemnly. "We managed to get her heart beating again, but I'm afraid she was down too long. There's probably not much left of her brain function. A few tests will tell later on."

"Poor Lilly," I said, and left Dr. Macgregor with his patient.

The gentleman I found in the consultation room was wearing a robe and bed slippers. He was about Lilly's age. He was bald, was wearing silver-rimmed glasses and had a nose that suggested a love of scotch. He was pacing back and forth and wringing his hands.

I introduced myself and asked him his name.

"Matt Stern," he answered. "Did I kill her?"

"Kill who?" I asked.

"Lilly. Is she dead? Oh, how will I tell her family? Please, please tell me I didn't kill her!" He got down on his knees in front of me and grabbed my hand. "What am I going to do, I'm so frightened!"

I tried to gently extract my hand from his grip, but he held on tight. Anyone passing by would have thought he was proposing.

"Mr. Stern, please, please, calm down," I begged. "Here, take a seat over here and let's talk about this okay?" I set the bag of Lilly's belongings on the floor and used my free hand to pry Mr. Stern's hand loose. He finally let go of my hand only to wrap his arms around my knees, pressing his face into my legs.

His sobs were shaking his entire body, and I could feel his tears on my legs. "Mr. Stern! Please!" I begged, but he ignored me.

I attempted to free my knees and lost my balance. My arms flailed wildly as I tried to keep from falling. I almost managed to steady myself, but, at that moment, Mr. Stern shifted, and we both went down in a tangle of arms and legs.

## Chapter 7

I lay on the floor along with Mr. Stern and stared at the ceiling. Mr. Stern continued to sob. Joyce and Dr. Macgregor came into view. They were both standing above us looking down with perplexed looks on their faces.

"Good God, she's fainted again," Joyce rolled her eyes. "And this time she's taken someone down with her."

"I did not," I said.

"Then what are you doing down there on the floor?" she asked.

Dr. Macgregor was silent, though his shoulders were shaking with suppressed laughter.

I struggled to get up, but the weight of Mr. Stern's torso over my legs was too great. "Do you suppose someone could help get me up?"

Dr. Macgregor bent down, shoulders still twitching, and wrapped his arms around Mr. Stern's torso. He heaved Mr. Stern to his feet, where he leaned drunkenly against Dr. Macgregor and sniffled.

Free at last, I stood as quickly as I could and did a quick skirt check—only to find it riding just high enough to expose my underwear. I quickly yanked the skirt down, smoothed my hair and tried to regain my composure—all the while wondering which panties I had put on this morning. I had a sinking feeling it was the pair depicting dancing pigs, and decided to start wearing slacks to work.

"So, what happened?" Joyce wasn't giving up and she was back in her Daphne pose. I looked at Joyce, then looked at poor Mr. Stern. That didn't help matters, but at least his sodden face reminded me of why we were there in the first place. "I think we need to give Mr. Stern an update on Lilly's progress."

Dr. Macgregor placed Mr. Stern on the little sofa, and I sat down next to him. Joyce and Dr. Macgregor pulled the two chairs that remained in the room closer to the sofa, so that they were facing us. Joyce had a clipboard on her lap and wrote a few lines on a pad.

"Mr. Stern," I said, "this is Dr. Macgregor and Nurse Joyce. They've been taking care of Lilly."

Mr. Stern, whose sobs had degenerated into sporadic hiccups, wiped his sleeve across his snotty nose. (I really had to find out where they kept the tissues in this place.) He looked dolefully at Dr. Macgregor. "So, did I kill her, Doc?"

Dr. Macgregor's eyes went up in surprise. "Why would you ask something like that, Mr. Stern?"

Mr. Stern dissolved into tears again, so I stepped in. "Dr. Macgregor, apparently Mr. Stern is terrified that Lilly has died and for some reason he blames himself."

"I see," Dr. Macgregor answered. "Would it help you, Mr. Stern, if I told you that, we haven't lost Lilly, although she's not out of the woods yet?"

"Oh, thank God!" cried Mr. Stern. We all waited a moment while he wiped his nose on his sleeve again and tried to compose himself. Joyce took the opportunity to flash her clipboard at me. She had scrawled "nice panties," on a piece of paper and drawn a sketch of several dancing pigs across the top of the page. I rolled my eyes and turned back to Mr. Stern, who had started talking again.

"You see, Lilly and I were, well, we're on a long weekend away from home, and Lilly and I were, well you know." At Dr. Macgregor's confused look, Mr. Stern continued in a whisper, "We were bumping nasties, Doc."

"I see," Dr. Macgregor replied, "and you think perhaps the exertion brought on Lilly's condition?"

Mr. Stern, though fairly dry-eyed at this point, was wringing his hands and staring at the floor. "Well, maybe, sir. You see I was on top and Lilly was moaning. Really, I thought she was having fun. I mean, if you were with a lady and she was carrying on and moaning, wouldn't you think you were pleasuring her, Doc?"

Dr. Macgregor had the grace to look a bit embarrassed, and I heard a little snort coming from Joyce's direction. "I would certainly hope so, Mr. Stern."

"Well, I thought so too," continued Mr. Stern. "At some point, Lilly got very quiet, but I thought she was just overcome with pleasure, so I just kept going. Not long, mind you, but until I, well, you know."

Dr. Macgregor nodded his head solemnly, but I noticed a twitch coming back to his broad shoulders.

"Well, we lay there real quiet for a little bit and I asked her if it was good for her. She didn't answer, so I asked again. She still didn't answer, so being that I was still on top of her, I lifted my head to look into her eyes and that was when I noticed she wasn't really there, you know? Oh yeah, and she was turning kind of blue."

Dr. Macgregor reached forward and patted Mr. Stern's shoulder. "So I'm assuming you called 911. It's important that we know how long Lilly was out, Mr. Stern. Do you recall how long it took the ambulance to arrive?"

Mr. Stern was shaking his head no. "No, I didn't call 911—well, not right away. I panicked."

Dr. Macgregor echoed, "Panicked?"

"Yes, you see Lilly didn't want her kids to know she was with me and, well, I was afraid if I called 911 right away the ambulance would get there before I could get her dressed. I didn't want them to know we were—well, you know." Mr. Stern looked at us with a pleading look on his face. "Please don't tell anyone."

Dr. Macgregor scratched his head, looking perplexed. "So how long did it take before you called 911?"

Mr. Stern shrugged. "It's not as easy as you'd think to dress someone who isn't cooperating Doc. And it took a little while to figure out how that new-fangled underwear went. I hurried as fast as I could, but it was probably at least oh 10 or 15 minutes, I think—give or take. She's going to be okay, isn't she?" he pleaded.

Dr. Macgregor sighed. "I don't know Mr. Stern."

Mr. Stern looked positively terrified. "Doc, she's got to be okay. I couldn't bear the guilt. And her kids! I know Lilly's 74 years old, but she didn't want her kids to know she has sex and they would lynch me if they knew I'd ... well, if they knew I might be the cause of..." and Mr. Stern broke off and started sobbing again.

Joyce leaned in and patted the shoulder Dr. Macgregor had been patting earlier. "There, there," she said, "at least she was having fun, Mr. Stern. Try to remember that."

I was biting my tongue really hard. She was having *fun*?!

My little phone started buzzing and I answered. "Cedars, may I help you?"

"Yeah, this is Horace Schmidt. I'm still looking for my fingers, Miss."

"I'm still working on it, sir. I'll call you back." I hung up without giving Mr. Schmidt the opportunity to continue the conversation.

Dr. Macgregor and Joyce were discussing Lilly's chances for recovery with Mr. Stern. Things were not looking good, and they were suggesting that Mr. Stern call Lilly's family.

"Please don't make me do it!" he cried. "Can't you do it?"

Dr. Macgregor sighed and gestured toward me. "Charlie will help you contact Lilly's family. It would be nice if you could stay long enough for them to get here."

Mr. Stern nodded in acknowledgment, but I could tell by the look on his face that, as soon as Lilly's family was notified, he was going to cut and run as fast as he possibly could.

Joyce rose to leave and smiled the most sincere smile she could possibly muster. "We're doing everything we can, Mr. Stern. Let Charlie know if you need anything." She was still smiling as she left the room.

Dr. Macgregor got ready to leave as well. He shook Mr. Stern's hand and wished him luck. "I'm going to steal Charlie for just a moment, and then she'll come back to sit with you for a while, okay, Mr. Stern?"

Mr. Stern nodded but kept his eyes on the floor.

I followed Dr. Macgregor out of the room, and he led me around the corner out of sight of the consultation room. "It's going to be a little while before we get Lilly to I.C.U. Are you okay to stay with Mr. Stern until we move her?"

I nodded, wondering if anyone looking into Dr. Macgregor's eyes ever said no. He smiled and leaned a little closer to me, sending goose bumps up my spine. He whispered very slowly in my ear, "They were *very* nice panties." He probably had seen Joyce's doodle as well.

I wanted to blush but willed myself not to. I leaned toward Dr. Macgregor's ear and whispered back, also very slowly. "Whose panties? Mine or Lilly's?" He burst out laughing while I spun on my heel and walked back to the consultation room.

I leaned against the door for a moment before opening it so I could calm my nerves. Take deep breaths, Charlie, I coached myself—deep breaths. Whew, Dr. Macgregor certainly had something I responded to. I took one more deep breath and opened the door. The room was empty except for the bag of Lilly's belongings, which was still on the floor where I'd put it.

I took the bag with me and searched for Mr. Stern in the rest rooms, the E.R. waiting room and the cafeteria, but to no avail. Apparently, the thought of Lilly's enraged children had become too much for him and he'd run for his life.

I decided to go in search of Dr. Macgregor so that I could notify him of Mr. Stern's flight and perhaps get contact information for Lilly. I breezed by the E.R. waiting room again. Joyce was stationed back at triage and was busy with a patient.

I went to the resuscitation room and found a nurse I hadn't met yet and Joey the tech getting ready to transport Lilly to the I.C.U. Lilly was barely visible for the tubes and wires connecting her to assorted machinery and monitors. I asked where Dr. Macgregor was and the nurse told me to check the doctor's lounge. The lounge was next to Dr. Caudill's office and I made my way there.

I knocked on the door and was told to come in. The room that I entered was hardly what I expected. It was tiny and cramped with a cot and a desk squeezed into it. There was barely enough room to walk between the two. Dr. MacGregor was sitting at the desk with a half-eaten club sandwich and an orange fizz soda on the desk next to the computer monitor. The sandwich was sitting on top of a mound of papers. "Missing me already?" he asked, apparently still in a playful mood.

I was determined to keep my focus. "Mr. Stern is missing in action, and I was hoping you had Lilly's contact numbers so that we could reach her family."

Dr. Macgregor sighed and the playfulness left his features. "Damn, I knew he was going to try to leave. I thought he'd at least wait until we made the phone calls." He started ruffling through some of the papers on the desk. "I've got the numbers here somewhere. Why don't you have a seat?"

I raised my eyebrows and looked around. "Where? You aren't exactly set up for company here."

Dr. Macgregor, still looking through papers, waved an arm, motioning for me to sit on the cot. "We keep that here for catnaps because we usually work twelve hour shifts," he explained.

I moved to sit down in the middle of the cot, misjudged the distance and halfway fell into it. The cot rose on both sides and tried to swallow me up. Dr. Macgregor rose quickly and grabbed my hand to pull me back on my feet. "I forgot, that cot tends to try to eat people alive!" he laughed.

At that moment, the door swung open and a nurse poked her head in. Her eyes widened at the sight of Dr. Macgregor and me standing close together with him still holding my hand. "Oh, excuse me," she muttered and quickly disappeared.

"What was that?" I asked.

"That was the end of your reputation at Cedars, I'm afraid." Dr. Macgregor still had a hold of my hand. "In less than five minutes word is going to spread that you and I were in the doctor's lounge doing things."

"Things? What sort of things?" Heat was shooting through the hand he was holding and up my arm and back down to other regions—well, regions less charted of late. Dr. Macgregor smiled. "Things like this," and he leaned in very slowly and kissed my forehead.

He then moved back and studied my face for a moment. I'm sure I looked like lightning had struck and I tried to come up with something witty to say. As it turned out I needn't have bothered, because he leaned back toward me and captured my mouth, silencing anything I would have said—that is, if I could have thought of something to say in the first place.

He released my hand and placed his on the back of my neck, pulling me closer to him. That was the end of all rational thought, as I knew it. My arms, totally of their own accord, wrapped themselves around his back and my hips went up against his while, with utter—and, might I add, somewhat embarrassing—abandon, my body responded in ways I had no idea it knew. His mouth tasted like orange fizz and dill pickles. Pickles had never tasted so good! As the rest of my body spun out of control, my mind faintly registered that Dr. Macgregor's other hand was sliding over my buttocks and continuing down my legs, just reaching the hem of my skirt. Then my phone started to ring.

With a Herculean effort, I wrenched myself back to coherent thought, slid my hands between our bodies and pushed—half-heartedly, I might add—away from Dr. Macgregor's chest, breaking apart enough to answer my little phone. "Cedars, may I help you?" I sounded a bit breathless.

Dr. Macgregor leaned against the desk and folded his arms across his chest, looking satisfied. His gaze was warm and his eyes had turned a deep emerald green.

"Yeah," the voice on the other end replied. "Is this Charlie?"

I cringed, recognizing Horace Schmidt's voice. "Yes, this is Charlie."

"Well this is Horace Schmidt and I still want my fingers."

"And I'm still looking for them, Mr. Schmidt. I'll call you as soon as I have an answer." I once again disconnected the call before he could reply.

I looked at Dr. Macgregor, whose eyebrow was raised, questioning what that exchange was about.

"It was a man named Horace Schmidt," I explained. "He was here a few weeks ago and, apparently, we couldn't reattach his fingers. He says he wants them back. Do we keep things like that here?"

Dr. Macgregor looked thoughtful for a moment. "We might. Sometimes the pathology lab will keep things like that as educational tools for medical students." He picked up the desk phone and dialed a number. "Yes, is Adam around?" There was a pause, then Adam must have come to the phone. "Adam, it's Sam down in Emergency. Great, how are you?" Another pause. "Okay, well here's the thing: We have a guy named Horace Schmidt who wants to know if he can have his fingers back. He was in a couple of weeks ago. You wouldn't happen to have them would you?" Dr. Macgregor looked at me, "He's checking."

I nodded and attempted to use the time to turn down the inferno that had erupted before my phone started ringing. What was I thinking? Only the second day of my new job and I already had a reputation—one that I'd just validated no less. Not that it was all my fault, but if I hadn't liked it so much, I would probably have run out screaming sexual harassment. Apparently, Dr. Macgregor didn't worry about that sort of thing.

"So," said Dr. Macgregor, "what are we going to do about this?"

"This?" I asked. "You mean the fingers?"

"No, you kissing me a moment ago." His look was still warm and I found myself wanting to melt under it.

"I think you must be confused. It was definitely you kissing me a moment ago."

"You kissed me back."

I shrugged. "Well, that's true."

"So, do you want to kiss me again?"

I pretended to think really hard. "Well," I finally answered, "I think further research may be required before I answer that question."

"Research? That sounds as though it could be fun."

Adam must have come back to the phone, because Dr. Macgregor winked at me and started speaking into the receiver again. "You *do* have them? Great! I'll be sending Charlie Meadows down for them. She's our new patient liaison here in the E.R." He disconnected and looked at me. "Do you think you can find the pathology lab?"

I wasn't sure I could find the nose on my face in my current state, but I nodded "yes" anyway. "Are you sure it's okay to give the fingers back to him?"

Dr. Macgregor shrugged. "I don't see why not. Legally they're his."

He had a point. "What about Lilly's contact information?" I asked, trying desperately to control the liquid heat shooting through my body. "I really should get started on calling her family."

"Oh yeah, I'd almost forgotten the original reason for your visit." A smirky little grin appeared on his face and he started ruffling through the papers on the desk again. He found what he was looking for and jotted a few names and numbers on a piece of paper. Handing it to me, he said, "Just tell them to go directly to the I.C.U. She'll be there by the time they get here, and the nurses there will be able to update them on her condition."

I took the paper, thanked him and headed for the door. I was acutely aware of how small the room was and didn't trust myself to stay a moment longer lest I fall at Dr. Macgregor's feet, begging him to ravish me. How humiliating! I had discovered that not only did I have a libido, but also absolutely zilch in the way of control over it.

Dr. Macgregor had other ideas. He caught my hand, and pulled me back to where he leaned against his desk. I ended up squarely against his legs. The contact made my head spin. Jeez, what was it with my body's insane reaction to this guy?

"I want to work on that research, Charlie. Dinner tonight? I'll pick you up at seven?"

Images of an angry Joyce flashed before my eyes. I opened my mouth with the intention of debating the issue but much to my dismay, I said, "Sure," and gave him my address.

With that, I was given another kiss on the forehead—which, I might add, was very anticlimactic after the full mouth kiss and body grind—and released. As I stepped into the corridor it seemed nearly impossible that only 15 minutes had elapsed.

## Chapter 8

I made my way back to the E.R. waiting room and found a stout, gray-haired lady wearing a blue smock seated at my desk. The smock had a Cedars Memorial Hospital logo embroidered on the right pocket, and a nametag reading "Mabel" pinned above that.

Mabel peered up at me from behind her horn-rimmed glasses and barked in a gruff 100-year-old voice, "What do you want?"

I was taken aback by Mabel's rude manner and her uncanny resemblance to a bulldog—made so by a pug nose and a protuberant bottom lip—but I decided to simply introduce myself. "Hi! I'm Charlie Meadows, the new E.R. patient liaison."

Mabel continued to peer up at me, squinting as though she couldn't quite focus. "So?"

"So," I answered, "you're sitting at my desk."

"Your desk, huh?" Mabel poked her bottom lip out even further. "The only desk I see here is *my* desk."

"Oh." I thought maybe I'd better check with the triage nurse before I proceeded any further and excused myself. As I entered the triage office I heard Mabel barking, "What do you want?" at a patient who had just arrived.

Joyce glanced up at me when I walked into the office. She looked even more unhappy than usual. "Didn't I tell you to stay away from Dr. Macgregor?"

Oh boy, I thought, here we go. The rumor mill had already made it to triage. I decided to ignore the question and ask her mine. "Who's Mabel and why is she claiming my desk?"

"Why were you in the doctors' lounge, Charlie?" Joyce demanded.

"I needed Lilly's contact numbers. Now, who's Mabel?"

"Was he really holding your hand?" Joyce had an evil gleam in her eye.

I sighed. "Technically, yes. Dr. Macgregor had his hand in mine. Could you please tell me about Mabel?"

"Technically? What's that supposed to mean? Either he was or he wasn't."

"Not necessarily, Joyce. I mean, intent is a big factor here."

"Oh, do tell, Charlie. What was Sam's intent?"

"His intent," I replied, "was to keep me from falling on my butt again."

Joyce pondered my response for a moment. "Now that's entirely believable."

"So will you tell me about Mabel, please?"

"Mabel," replied Joyce, "is one of our oldest hospital volunteers. She is insanely wealthy and donates lots and lots of money to Cedars every year. She used to be on the hospital's board of directors and essentially she thinks she still runs the place. She's practically deaf, very stubborn, and knows how to use her clout. Basically, if Mabel fancies your desk or anything else, it's hers, and there isn't a thing you can do about it." Joyce looked at the triage slip Mabel had just passed beneath her window and scowled. "Apparently, she can't see well enough to write either."

I looked at the slip. The only thing that had been filled out was the patient's name, and it was illegible.

I left Joyce scowling at the triage slip and decided to use the consultation room as an office so that I could finish my phone calls.

I called Lilly's daughter, Joy, first, being very careful to keep my tone warm but neutral, saying only that Lilly's condition was serious and the family's presence was being requested. I also told Joy that Lilly's personal belongings were in safe keeping with Security.

Joy wanted to know if she was "with that creep Stern." She started to rant, "God, how could she date that *thing* after having a sweet man like my father all those years. I told her he was a frog!" I thought hard about her question and decided that the less she knew, the better.

"I'm sorry," I answered, "I've only been asked to let you know that she's here and that your presence is required."

"Damn, is there anyone there who knows anything?"

I didn't answer immediately and Joy gave up.

"Okay, I'm on my way. Please tell Mom I'll be there as soon as I can."

Given Lilly's present condition, I didn't think that was an option, but I promised I would and hung up.

I called Mr. Schmidt next, but no one answered and he apparently did not have an answering machine. I sighed in frustration. I so wanted to get the delivery of the fingers over and done with.

I checked my watch and realized it was already nearly noon. I decided to go to the cafeteria for lunch. I followed the signs and took the elevator to the garden level, which had a gift shop, a cafeteria, a hospital library and—Eureka! —there was a Starbucks kiosk. I felt like doing a happy dance and headed over for a skinny, toffee nut latte, three shots with light whipped cream. Who needed lunch when brand-name caffeine and empty calories would suffice?

I took the first sip and shuddered with satisfaction. The guy behind the counter sent me a quizzical look. I smiled and shrugged and took another sip, then bought a newspaper from a box next to the kiosk. I didn't actually plan to read the paper. I just like to do the crossword puzzle.

I found a semi-secluded corner in the cafeteria and was trying to figure out 36 down (a four-letter word for a sneakers company), when my little phone started ringing. I answered and Joyce said, "Charlie, we need you up front, there's someone here to see you."

"Do you know who it is?" I asked.

"Two uniforms, on official business."

"Uniforms?"

"You know—police officers. What'd you do anyway?"

I sighed, "What do you mean, what did I do?"

"Well," Joyce answered, "obviously you're in trouble of some kind, so you'd better tell me so I can make sure everyone around here has the story right. You wouldn't believe the gossips in this place."

I rolled my eyes toward the ceiling. "Honestly, I haven't done anything. It must be about one of the patients, Joyce."

"Oh." Joyce sounded disappointed. "Are you sure?"

"Yes, I'm sure. Tell them I'll be up in five minutes."

"Sure thing." Joyce ended the call.

I picked up my paper and refolded it with the intention of finishing the crossword puzzle later, when a headline on page one of the "Area" section caught my eye: "Local Man Collapses at Mini-Mart on Euclid." Underneath the headline was a very bad picture of Alfred holding a trophy of some sort. I skimmed the short article. Apparently, Alfred had just purchased a chilidog with mustard, onions, and sweet peppers and was taking his first bite while heading out the door when he collapsed. The picture was mentioned as having been an archived photo of Alfred from when he'd won an award for an article he'd written in *Coin Collectors' Monthly*.

I stared at the photo. I'd had no idea that Alfred had an interest in coin collecting, much less enough knowledge to write an award-winning article about it. I thought about this information while riding the elevator to the main floor. I was also thinking about how sad it was that Alfred's last meal was a chilidog and that he'd only had a bite of it.

When I entered the E.R., I immediately saw the two police officers who were there to talk to me. They were leaning against what I used to think of as my desk, each holding a cup of coffee in his hand. Mabel was nowhere to be seen. It seemed she was done barking at people for the day and had decided to go home. At least that's what I hoped.

The officer on the right was short and rather stout with big round eyes and a snub nose. His round eyes gave him the air of being perpetually surprised. The other officer was well over six feet tall and had a physique that was obviously developed at the local gym. He had brown eyes and brown curly hair.

Both of the officers straightened up as I approached. I held out my hand and introduced myself. The officer on the right shook my hand. "I'm Officer Oliver Gorman and this," he said, motioning to his tall, good-looking partner, "is Officer Stan Stefansky." Officer Stefansky shook my hand and flashed a hundred-watt smile.

"Pleased to meet you both," I said. "May I help you with something?"

"Well now," Officer Gorman answered, "we're hoping you might. Is there someplace we could go and talk privately?" He raised his eyebrows dramatically, which really enhanced the look of surprise his face carried. I turned and found a good number of Cedars E.R. staff in various states of faked busyness behind me, trying to hone in on our conversation.

"Sure, just follow me," I said, and led them to the consultation room previously occupied by Mr. Stern. "Please, sit down and I'll be right with you." I stepped out of the consultation room and caught Joyce lingering at the doorway. "Can I help you with something, Joyce?" I asked.

Joyce shook her head no. "Um, I was just, um, well I was just passing by and had to pause here for just a moment to…" She broke off and stamped her foot. "Oh shoot, if you won't let me eavesdrop, will you at least tell me what they want when you're done?"

"I really don't think it's any of your business, Joyce." I was getting irritated, and the day was beginning to feel exceedingly long. My phone started ringing and I answered it as I stepped back into the consultation room and closed the door abruptly in Joyce's very surprised face.

I smiled apologetically at the officers as I spoke into the phone, "Cedars, may I help you?"

The voice that came across was full of rich undertones and unmistakably male. "Charlie, this is Adam, down in the pathology lab. Dr. Macgregor called earlier about a Mr. Schmidt's fingers."

"Yes, I remember," I answered. "Is there a problem?"

"Well," answered Adam, "the thing is, I'm one of two people who have a key to the locker where we keep that sort of thing up here. I'm going to be leaving in about 15 minutes to get a head start on preparing for a conference tomorrow and the other person who has the key is going to be on call to come in as needed to unlock the locker. Usually, we only need those items when we're giving lectures, so we're already here when we need to get into the locker. Very rarely, do we have to come in on short notice."

"Oh," I answered, "I see. Did you want to give me the other person's pager number for when Mr. Schmidt gets here to retrieve his fingers?"

"No, actually I want you to come and get the fingers now. I spoke to Collins, he's the pathologist on call, and he lives more than an hour away. He'd prefer it if you would keep the fingers with you so he won't have to come in all that way just to unlock the locker for you."

"Oh," I took a deep breath. "Is it *okay* to keep the fingers outside the locker? They won't spoil or anything?"

Adam laughed. "No they've been preserved in formaldehyde. They're perfectly safe."

"Oh, okay then, can you give me a few minutes? I'm kind of in the middle of something."

"I'll be here for a bit longer, but could you hurry? The conference starts the first thing in the morning and I need to go home to prepare for it."

"I'll be there as soon as I can," I answered.

"Okay, we're on the second floor, Suite 2307B."

"Thanks," I said and put down the phone.

Trying to put aside the thought that I would be the one responsible for Horace's fingers, I turned my attention back to the officers.

"I'm sorry to havw kept you waiting. What was it that you needed to talk to me about?"

Officer Gorman was apparently the talker of the two, because he was the one who answered again. "Alfred Tenny," he stated.

I felt my stomach lurch. Did they somehow find out that I hadn't paid my rent yet this month?

"Alfred?" I asked.

"Yes," answered Officer Gorman. "Our information indicates that you were one of Alfred's tenants."

I gulped and mentally tried to figure out how much money I had left in my checking account. "Yes sir, that's right," I answered.

"Actually, our information indicates that you live in the apartment next to Alfred's. Is that correct?"

"Yes, sir."

"What would you say was the nature of your relationship with Alfred?"

"Huh?" I was drawing a blank on the question. What did that have to do with rent?

"Were you friendly or just strictly business type acquaintances?"

"Um, I'd have to say strictly business acquaintances. What does that have to do with anything, anyway?" I just couldn't see where this was going.

Officer Gorman tapped his pen on a little pad of paper that he'd pulled out of his pocket and looked at me speculatively.

Officer Stefansky finally found his voice and spoke to Officer Gorman. "Hey, Shorty, I think we ought to give her the full story. That way, she might get a better of idea of what we need here."

Officer Gorman—a.k.a Shorty—responded, "I told you never to call me Shorty on duty, Stefansky! It gives people the wrong impression."

"Sorry!" Stefansky looked contrite. For such a big guy he didn't seem to be very bold.

Officer Gorman continued to look upset and neither one of them spoke.

"Listen, gentleman," I intervened, "I have another obligation and only a few more minutes, could one of you please tell me why you're interested in my relationship with Alfred?"

After a bit of hesitation and strained silence, Officer Gorman finally nodded to Stefansky, who cleared his throat and began to explain. "Alfred Tenny apparently had a little more going on than he wanted to reveal to the I.R.S. We've found some evidence of organized crime activities in addition to his landlord activities. He also appears to have been involved in some smuggling of rare coins and gems."

"And this brings you to me because …?"

"Well, of course we need to know if you had any mutual acquaintances or friends, or if you knew if he had any enemies."

There was that question about enemies again. "You're the second person who's asked me that today. Is there anything else I need to know?"

Once again looks passed between the two officers. This time Officer Gorman spoke. "Actually, there is." He paused dramatically and sighed before speaking, "Ms. Meadows, apparently Alfred was the victim of foul play."

"Foul play?" I repeated. "How could that be? He died of a heart attack."

"Yes," answered Officer Gorman, "that's what the initial ruling was, but the lab work showed a form of a very rare and deadly poison in Alfred's blood. The heart attack was most likely caused by this poison."

I felt a little light-headed as I tried to assemble this new information into intelligible niches in my brain.

Officer Gorman continued, "So, we're conducting a full investigation into the matter and need as much information as you can give us or as much as you can remember."

"I see," I answered.

Stefansky cleared his throat and gave Officer Gorman a look. Officer Gorman gave Stefansky a questioning look back. Stefansky made a motion with his hands and nodded toward me. Officer Gorman continued to look puzzled.

Stefansky finally spoke, "Um, Shorty, oops, sorry, I mean Gorman, don't you think maybe you ought to tell her the other thing?" It was becoming apparent to me that, in addition to being timid, Stefansky wasn't the brightest bulb on the block either.

"What other thing?" Officer Gorman asked, clearly annoyed at having been called Shorty again.

At that moment, there was a knock on the door, and I excused myself to answer it. It was a man I'd never seen before. I knew immediately who it was, though, because he was holding a glass jar that was the shape and size that one would usually associate with Vlasic dill pickles. Instead of pickles, however, I could see four very large fingers that were floating in a pinkish solution. I made a mental note to call Horace as soon as possible. Fingers that large obviously belonged on a very large body. In the meantime, Officer Gorman and Stefansky were engaged in what sounded like a heated but whispered debate behind me.

"Sorry to interrupt, Charlie, but I really have to leave. I hope you don't mind my bringing these down to you," said the man holding the fingers.

"You must be Adam." I replied. "How'd you know where to find me?"

"Joyce told me where you were. By the way, it's very nice to meet you."

Adam was dressed in a suit and tie, which were covered by a lab coat. He looked to be in his late 50s and had thick silver hair combed stylishly and impeccably away from his handsome face. He had a distinguished air and his light blue eyes slowly took in the occupants of the consultation room. When his gaze returned to me, his eyes traveled from my face to my legs, then very slowly upward again. The warm, appreciative smile on his face made me flush. He held the jar with the fingers out to me.

I geared up my courage and was happy to see that my hands were shaking only slightly as I took the jar from him. "Thanks for saving me the trip. Do these have any special needs?" I asked.

Adam laughed. His laugh was deep with rich undertones, and it wasn't hard to see how he'd achieved his position in the hospital. "They're not pets, Charlie. All you have to do is keep them somewhere safe until Mr. Schmidt can reclaim them."

I set the fingers on the telephone table next to the little couch, where Officers Gorman and Stefansky were still arguing. Riveted by the fingers in the jar, the two uniformed men fell silent.

I asked Adam if Horace had to sign for the fingers or anything. Adam pulled the paperwork out of his pocket. "After he signs for them, just put the forms in an interoffice envelope and send them to the pathology lab." I took the papers and put them into my own pocket.

"It was a wonderful pleasure meeting you, Charlie," Adam said taking my hand, "I hope I have the pleasure of working closely with you in the future." With a final squeeze, Adam released my hand and made a quick exit.

I closed the door behind him and turned my attention once again to the police officers. Stefansky looked rather pale as he stared transfixed at the fingers. Officer Gorman punched Stefansky on the shoulder and cleared his throat. Stefansky jumped, and quickly refocused his attention on me. "Charlie, we think you ought to know that Alfred had some voyeuristic tendencies as well."

Seeing the confused look on my face, Stefansky he went on. "Um, Alfred had some video equipment in his apartment and, apparently, there are a large number of tapes with your name on them." The paleness started to leave Stefansky's face as it was suffused with an embarrassed red.

"What do you mean, tapes?" I asked. I had a sinking feeling that I knew what his answer was going to be.

"Um, well, um."

Officer Gorman cut in, "The tapes were recorded on video equipment that Alfred had set up between your apartments."

I felt light-headed again and didn't want to ask, but had to anyway. "Where was this camera?"

"Cameras," Officer Gorman corrected me.

"Okaaaay, where were these cameras?" I was breathing a little quickly at this point.

"Your bathroom and bedroom," Officer Gorman answered matter-of-factly.

I tried to speak and couldn't. I was in shock. My stomach was flipping over and over on itself. I could feel my eyes starting to bulge out of my head.

Stefansky and Officer Gorman watched the transformation of a sane professional lady into a scary psycho. Stefansky stood up to leave, saying, "Okeydokey then, I think we're done here."

I held up a hand and found my voice, "Just a minute you two. Where are my tapes and who has access to them?"

Officer Gorman answered, "We have access to them, so does the crime lab and anyone in the police department who is connected to the case."

"I want my tapes."

"They can't be released yet, Charlie," Officer Gorman replied. "They're pertinent to our investigation."

I was flabbergasted. "Of what importance to your investigation are tapes of me in my bathroom and bedroom, Office Gorman?"

Stefansky spoke up, "Actually, there was only one tape of you in the bedroom. Apparently, you don't get much action there." Gorman punched him in the shoulder again.

Unfazed, Stefansky continued speaking, "He had quite a few of you in the bathroom though. He appeared to favor the bathtub." Officer Gorman punched him again.

Stefansky gave Officer Gorman a hurt look, "Ouch, what do you keep doing that for?"

I couldn't believe this was happening and felt like ripping off both their heads. They'd both seen me in my bathtub—naked. I especially wanted to rip Alfred's dead head off his dead body. And to think I'd been respectful of his little weenie and felt *sorry* for him because he'd died with a mouthful of chilidog. I sat down hard on the chair across from the couch and buried my head in my hands.

"Have you dismantled the cameras?" I asked, my voice muffled by my hands.

"Actually, we won't be able to do that until we finish the investigation, Charlie." Officer Gorman said this with as much sympathy as he could muster. I kept my head buried in my hands.

"If it helps, I think you're really beautiful," said Stefansky. "When this is all over, maybe you and me could go to dinner or something. Ouch!"

Because I wasn't looking, I can't be sure, but I think the "ouch" was a response to Officer Gorman's punching Stefansky in the arm again. That arm was probably getting sore by now.

Without picking up my head, I waved an arm at them, "Get out, go away, leave me alone!"

"I'm leaving you my card, Charlie," said Officer Gorman. "Call us if you think of anything that may help us find Alfred's killer."

I raised my head and gave the officers a look of incredulity. "At the moment, gentlemen, I wish I had killed the little prick myself."

"Um, yeah we figured you might feel that way," said Stefansky. The officers took their leave and left me in the consultation room with my wounded pride and a jar of fingers.

**Chapter 9**

I sat for some time, trying to come to terms with the fact that Alfred had been peeping in on me, that he'd been murdered, and that a good number of the city's police force were now intimately familiar with my body and my bathroom. I thought about moving far, far away. I thought about going home and sticking my head in the oven. Neither option suited. I stared at the fingers floating in the pickle jar. In two days my life had become a very, very strange place.

The fingers reminded me that I still hadn't been able to contact Horace Schmidt, so I sighed, picked up my phone and dialed his number. No answer. I sighed again, picked up the fingers and headed to the locker room. After storing the jar safely in my locker, I did rounds through the rest of the E.R., checking on patients to make sure they were comfortable. The E.R. was packed again, so the rest of the day passed quickly, not giving me much time for thought. I tried Horace's number several more times without any answer. As my shift came to an end, I cheered up a little as I thought about my date with Dr. Macgregor.

Joyce cornered me as I put on my jacket. "So what's up? What did the police want?"

I finished buttoning my jacket and pulled my purse out of my locker. "Oh, they were just asking about a patient, Joyce. There's nothing you need to worry yourself over."

Joyce looked disappointed and I almost felt sorry for her. After all, I was getting ready to go to dinner with her "almost an item" man, and now I was depriving her of her gossip, the lifeblood upon which she apparently fed. She wasn't ready to give up, though.

"Well as charge nurse, I need to be aware of all circumstances surrounding our patients. It is your duty to keep me informed of any circumstances that may affect patient care."

"Under the circumstances of this particular patient, Joyce, patient care is no longer an issue and I assure you there is no reason for you to bother yourself over my conversation with the officers who were here. Besides, if you pick up the paper tomorrow, I'm sure you'll be able to read all about it." I picked up the jar of fingers, swung through the doors and walked quickly toward the E.R. exit. I couldn't leave the jar in my locker because I shared it with a night-shift employee. Joyce was close on my heels.

"The paper? You mean it's important enough to be in the paper but not important enough for me to know about? That doesn't make sense!"

I stopped walking and turned to face Joyce—she was so close behind me that she almost smacked into me when I stopped and I shifted for a better grip on the finger jar. "I'm going home, Joyce. Leave me alone."

Joyce refused to be thwarted, but she temporarily lost her momentum when she realized I was carrying a jar of fingers. She stared at the jar for a moment, and then shook her head. "I'm not even going to ask about what you're holding there. Please just tell me this, though. Does the police thing have anything to do with Alfred Tenny?"

I couldn't help being surprised. "Why do you ask that?"

Joyce wouldn't meet my eyes. "Um, well, just a hunch. But it does, doesn't it? I can tell by the look on your face. You have to tell me what they said, Charlie."

I could see that Joyce was upset. Her thin face looked even more pinched, and her eyes had the look of fear in them. "Why do you want to know about Alfred Tenny, Joyce?"

She blanched and appeared to reconsider. "Nothing, just forget I said anything." Joyce turned and walked away as fast as she could without running.

While wondering over the oddness of that conversation, I made my way to my car. I got in after securing the jar of fingers in the passenger seat and pulled out of the parking lot. What possible reason could Joyce have for being interested in Alfred, and why was she so whacked out and acting weird about the situation? I decided to just chalk it up to Joyce being Joyce. Snow began to fall in thick fat flakes, and the weather announcer on WKMJ said we were likely to get four to six inches by morning. A good six inches of the stuff still remained on the ground, from a storm earlier that week.

Once home I took a quick moment before entering the apartment building. The snow around the entrance was broken up by footprints and littered with empty coffee cups. I imagined the police, who must have been there earlier that day, left them. I muttered under my breath as I wandered around picking the trash they had left behind. The snow was beginning to fall more quickly and the wind was picking up, but I didn't want Dr. Macgregor to think that a bunch of slobs lived here, so I continued picking up in spite of the cold.

When I stepped into the building, I noticed the yellow police tape that crossed Alfred's door, and I was relieved that no actual police seemed to be there. I assumed they'd finished for the day. I walked by the door quickly and tried to think good thoughts—not about what a little, slimy jerk Alfred had been.

I entered my apartment, which felt even less welcoming than usual. I went directly to the bathroom and started searching for the camera. It was in the first place I looked—the light fixture. It was just a small tube, the size of a lipstick, and it was placed between two light sconces. No wonder Alfred had included bulb maintenance in the lease. I'd always thought it was strange that he had insisted on replacing the bulbs in the apartment every month even though they were never burned out. I made a mental note to beware of bulb-changing landlords in the future. On the upside, I no longer felt too bad about not paying my rent.

I put utility tape over the little camera lens, then went to the bedroom and did the same with the camera in that light fixture. After that, I felt a little better.

My cell phone started ringing, the caller I.D. display indicating it was Sherrie. I answered, "Hey, Sherrie."

Her voice rang out loud and clear. "Hey, Hoochie girl, how was day two at the hospital? Oh, and you never called me about Alfred's message."

I plopped on my bed and lay staring at the light fixture. "Turns out day one at Cedars was just a sneak preview of day two, and the message was that he needed to talk to me about something important. Oh yeah, and he added that the laundry room was out of order."

"What do you suppose was so important?" Sherrie asked.

"I don't know and I don't really care. At the moment, I'm glad I never have to see the little prick again."

"Little prick? What's with the attitude?"

I sighed. I knew if I told Sherrie about the cameras I would never get off the phone. "I'll have to tell you later, Sherrie. Right now I'm getting ready to go to dinner."

"Dinner? Great! Where do you want me to meet you?"

"I meant dinner with someone else."

There was a pause on Sherrie's end of the line, and then she said, "Cool! Who is it? It wouldn't happen to be the handsome, green-eyed Dr. Macgregor would it?"

"As a matter of fact..." The shriek on the other end of the line cut off my sentence.

"That's too cool! I was just kidding. I mean, I never thought you would go out with him. Oh, this is great! Where are you going? Mind if I show up and just happen to run into you? I want to meet this guy."

"Don't you dare," I was quick to respond. "I'll be nervous enough without you showing up and doing that thing you do." I was referring to Sherrie's run-away mouth and her unerring knack for bringing up the most embarrassing aspects of my past whenever I was with someone I wanted to impress.

Sherrie sounded wounded. "I don't do that anymore."

I laughed. "Yes, you do. Just last month, when Mom came into town, you happened to mention the night that I mixed decongestants and cosmopolitans. You know, the night I thought I was the "dance-dance" revolution queen and ended up tripping and busting my butt on the floor so hard I couldn't walk right for a week."

"It was a funny story!"

"Mom didn't think so and now she's worried that I'm a closet junkie and hang out with the wrong types of people. There's no way I'm ever going to get her to believe I didn't know that decongestants have an adverse reaction when taken with alcohol."

"Okay. Well, I'm sorry about that one, but I promise I'll be good tonight."

"I know you'd try, but I don't even know where we're going. I'll tell you all about it as soon as I can."

"But..."

"Gotta, go! Bye!" I disconnected and struggled off the bed. It had felt really, really good to lie down. I went into the bathroom and rechecked the tape on the camera lens. Positive it was rendered nonfunctional, I felt safe enough to take a shower. I stood as long as I could under the spray of water that I'd made as hot as I could without fear of being parboiled.

Deciding to wear black because it fit my mood, I slipped on my version of the little black dress. It ended just above my knees but with its moderate V-neck and long sleeves it was conservative enough for the occasion. Given that I had thrown my black pumps out after my first day at Cedars, I opted for what I referred to as my Audrey Hepburn boots. They were black leather with a stiletto heel, and zipped up to the knee—very retro 1970s chic and perfect for snowy weather. I brushed my hair, swiped on mascara and called it a done deal with five minutes to spare.

I heard a knock at the door and went to open it, after one last mirror check. Instead of Dr. Macgregor, it was Haley on the other side. "My, my...don't you look nice. May I come in?"

I quickly glanced down the hall for any sign of Dr. Macgregor. "Actually Haley..." She didn't let me finish my sentence.

"I know, I know, you're expecting someone, and I can tell just by looking at you that he must be someone special, huh?"

"Well, I don't know about all that, but yes, I wanted to look nice for him. Can we do this some other time? He'll be here any minute."

Haley waved her be-ringed hand in exasperation, "Fate waits for no one! You must learn to take me more seriously, Charlie."

I didn't respond and stood firmly in the doorway.

Haley gave up, "Okay, okay. But it's important for you to come see me. Strange things have been occurring here." She wiggled her eyebrows mysteriously.

"No kidding," I said and closed the door.

A few seconds later, there was another knock and I lost patience. "Go away! I'm just not into you and your woo-woo stuff!"

I heard a rumble of male laughter on the other side of the door. "I'm not sure what you mean by 'your woo-woo stuff,' but I thought you were maybe just a little into me earlier today."

I did a mental head slap and opened the door. Dr. Macgregor was standing before me dressed in khaki pants and a leather jacket. His cheeks were rosy from the cold outside, and his hair was mussed in a boyishly cute way with thick snowflakes sticking here and there. He grinned and winked while handing me a bottle of wine.

I took the wine. "Thank you. I'm so sorry, I thought you were my neighbor, Haley."

Dr. Macgregor ginned, "No offense taken. Can I come in?"

I felt my cheeks redden again. "Of course, please come in and have a seat."

Dr. Macgregor came in and sat on my little sofa. "You look great, by the way."

I smiled and pointed to the wine. "Would you like a glass?"

"That would be great," he smiled.

I hurried to the kitchen to open the wine and compose myself. "Nice job Charlie," I muttered as I worked to uncork the wine. "Nice way to make a first impression."

I jumped a mile high when fingers started to massage my neck and a voice whispered in my ear, "I think that was about the third or fourth impression, Charlie. And don't worry, I liked all of them."

Somehow, Dr. Macgregor had snuck up behind me and was now sending liquid fire through every pore of my body. His breath against my ear and the feel of his fingers against my neck had me spiraling into a pleasure-induced coma. I could barely function to finish opening the bottle in my hand.

"Ummm," I purred, "your fingers are magic." With that my eyes flew wide open and I shrieked, "Oh no, the fingers!" I ran from the kitchen and bolted from my apartment. I had somehow lost the fingers somewhere between parking the car and opening my apartment door.

## Chapter 10

I flew into the night where total darkness had fallen. The only illumination came from a light above the apartment house door and one light in the parking lot near the cars that were further out in the parking area. I half-ran, half-walked to my car and brushed away the snow so I could look at the passenger seat. No fingers! I looked on the roof and the hood of the car. No fingers! I must have set them down when I stopped to clean up the trash the police had left behind, but where?

At least three inches of snow had fallen in beautiful fat, fluffy flakes already, but it was being pushed around by a steady wind creating mini-drifts here and there. I surveyed the area around the entrance and could see no trace of the jar housing Horace's fingers. I started kicking the snow around, hoping to make contact with the jar, but I was afraid I'd end up breaking it, so I bent over to run my hands through the freezing cold stuff.

Dr. Macgregor emerged from the apartment building, and I could feel his eyes on my posterior as I continued to search through the snow. I had an upside-down, between-my-legs view of him and saw that he was more sensibly dressed in his jacket and wearing gloves. He stood there for a moment, staring at my ass, and I stood up and turned around. "Are you just here to enjoy the view or are you interested in perhaps lending a hand here?"

"I couldn't help myself. What's this all about?" he asked. "The fingers you just shrieked about couldn't possibly be the same fingers we were discussing earlier today, could they? By the way, you have a gorgeous derriere."

I shivered with cold and looked up at Dr. Macgregor. Much to my horror, my eyes filled with tears.

"Oh my," he said wrapping me in a hug. "Let's get you inside where it's warm, and you can tell me what's going on."

Keeping one arm firmly around my waist, Dr. Macgregor led me back inside to my apartment and sat me down on my couch. After pausing to slip out of his jacket and take off his gloves, he knelt in front of me and rubbed my hands to warm them. I continued to cry and snuffle. I pulled my hands from his to swipe my snotty nose, and Dr. Macgregor disappeared into the kitchen. I could hear him opening and closing cabinet doors and vaguely wondered what he was doing snooping around in my kitchen.

It wasn't long before he reemerged with an almost full bottle of brandy that I'd bought on a whim last year, a shot glass, and a hand towel. He gave me the towel, which I used to wipe my nose and hands, and poured out a finger of brandy. "Here, this will settle your nerves a little faster than wine." He smiled and looked very compassionate, and I imagined that Dr. Macgregor's patients rarely complained about his bedside manner.

"Is this doctor's orders?" I sniffled.

"Of course."

I swallowed the liquid in one gulp and handed the glass back to him. "Can I have another?"

Dr. Macgregor raised an eyebrow. "You sure?"

"Yep."

He poured out a second finger, and I tossed it back.

"Whew," I said, "that's better."

Dr. Macgregor sat next to me on the couch and studied my face. "You look a little better. Want to tell me what's up with the fingers?"

"I lost them outside, I think."

Dr. Macgregor looked rather incredulous. "That made you cry?"

"I wasn't crying." I sniffled.

Dr. Macgregor poured himself some brandy. "You weren't?"

"Nope. I never cry."

"Never?"

"Uh-uh. Crying is for sissies." My hands were starting to thaw out, and I started shaking them to ease the prickles. "My nose is just runny because of the cold."

"I see," said Dr. Macgregor. He grabbed my hands in mid-shake and started rubbing them with his own warm hands. The warmth launched itself into every part of my body. Between that and the brandy I was beginning to feel really, really wonderful, despite worrying about what Horace was going to do to me when he found out that I'd lost his fingers.

I watched Dr. Macgregor's face as he massaged my hands. His eyes were turned down toward our hands, and thick golden lashes fanned his cheeks. He had a faint scar above the outside corner of his left eye, and I wondered how he'd gotten it. I pulled my hands away from his and lightly traced the scar with my right index finger and watched the color of his eyes deepen. "How'd you get this?" I asked.

I never got an answer. The next instant, he was covering my mouth in a searing kiss, so delicious, that I decided trying to be modest and act hard to get, wasn't an option. Instead, I grabbed his hair and held on for dear life. He responded by pulling me closer. I slid a hand beneath his sweater and encountered warm, smooth skin. His taut muscles contracted at my touch and I felt goose bumps rise on his skin, despite the heat our bodies were generating. He groaned and his tongue delved deeper into my mouth. This man definitely had a talented tongue. Each time he thrust his tongue against mine, I felt an answering pulse between my legs.

I felt myself start to spin and wasn't sure if it was the brandy or Dr. Macgregor. I felt his hand slide beneath my dress and make its way to my hip. I vaguely realized that now was the time to break things off. That is, if I wanted to go for the 3-dates before sex rule that Sherrie always swore by. Before I could make up my mind, his fingers reached the waistband of my nylons and he broke away with a frustrated sigh. "I've always secretly believed that nylons are the government's attempt to control birth rates."

I seized the opportunity to try to still my spinning head. Leaning back on the armrest of the couch, I regarded him with half-closed eyes. "You have that much experience with them, then?"

Dr. Macgregor smiled slyly, "What, the government?"

I grimaced, "No, ladies' nylons."

He pretended to think, and then his face became more serious. "I've had some experience, yes. I haven't had any interest in a dating relationship for some time, though."

"That's not what I heard from Joyce. You two are about to become an item, aren't you?"

Dr. Macgregor threw his head back and laughed. "Joyce? You're kidding!" Then, because I wasn't laughing with him, he said, "Right?"

I shook my head no. "Uh-uh."

Realizing I was serious, Dr. Macgregor explained, "Joyce is in a very serious relationship with one of the obstetricians at the hospital. Oh yeah, and the obstetrician just so happens to be female."

It was my turn to be shocked. My head had already been spinning for a while, now it felt as though it was spinning in the opposite direction. I wondered why Joyce tried to keep me from pursuing Dr. Macgregor?

Dr. Macgregor's gaze became warm again, and he shifted his position so that he was leaning over my half-reclining, half-sitting, spinning self. He lowered his head and I thought he was going to kiss me again, but, with his mouth hovering just above my lips, he asked, "So what about you?"

My eyes had closed in anticipation of the kiss and I kept them closed while I answered, "I'm an expert on women's nylons."

With a low moan his lips were on mine again and, before I knew it, we were in a heated tangle, doing our best to devour each other through our clothes. I was out of my boots and nylons and had just managed to pull Dr. Macgregor's sweater over his head when a horrible whining shriek cut through the air.

I groaned, "It's the building's fire alarm. We'd better go outside."

Dr. Macgregor ran a hand through his disheveled hair. "You're kidding!"

I shook my head no. "The fire truck will be here within minutes and insist that everyone clear the building until they give the go-ahead to re-enter." Not being able to resist, despite the interruption, I kissed him again.

We still hadn't come up for air when the firefighters knocked on my door. It didn't register at first, but as the pounding persisted, I realized that they had already arrived. I gathered the strength to push Dr. Macgregor away.

Dr. Macgregor groaned and complained, "The knocking stopped, maybe they went away."

I rushed to the door as quickly as I could. "The fact that the knocking has stopped is what worries me." I arrived at the door about 30 seconds too late. The crash that accompanied it splintering was deafening.

"What the...." Dr. Macgregor stood up with his mouth open in surprise.

A firefighter stepped through the splintered door and surveyed the scene—Dr. Macgregor naked from the waist up, my dress askew and hair mussed—and his face lit up with a slow grin. "Sorry to interrupt you, but we were told this apartment was on fire." He gave us a knowing look. "Well, something sure was, huh?"

The firefighter laughed at his own joke and I glared at him. "Somebody called in and specifically said *my* apartment was on fire?"

"That's what dispatch relayed to us, Miss." Another firefighter stepped through the door. He looked perplexed at the lack of flames and smoke. He looked at the other firefighter. "Did they put it out already?"

The first firefighter laughed, "I'd say they hadn't finished building it."

"Did you think maybe you should have tried turning the doorknob to get in, instead of just busting the door in?" I asked.

The first firefighter shrugged. "Could' a, should' a, would' a."

The second firefighter zeroed in on Dr. Macgregor and changed the subject. "Hey, aren't you one of the doctors over at Cedars?" Without giving Dr. Macgregor a chance to respond, the firefighter answered his own question, "You sure are! I see you all the time when I run rescue. Good to see you, Doc!"

Dr. Macgregor winced. "I wish I could say the same."

The firefighters looked at each other. "Sorry about the door. Apparently, it was a false alarm."

"Apparently," I replied.

"Maybe you could put a chair or something in front to keep it closed, since the lock is broken now."

I considered the idea for a moment, and then tossed it out. So many strange things were happening lately that there was no way I could feel secure. "I'll think of something," I told them.

"Well, I'm terribly sorry for the intrusion," said the first firefighter, who looked anything but sorry. I was pretty sure Dr. Macgregor and I were going to be Tuesday night's entertainment at the local fire station. "We've got to get going and do our report. Call us if you need us." Both firefighters shuffled out in their heavy boots and I listened as their footsteps faded down the hall.

Dr. Macgregor and I plopped down on the couch. "Now where were we?" asked Dr. Macgregor with a devilish smile.

I narrowed my eyes at him. "Are you trying to distract me from my door problem?"

His smile widened. "It worked pretty well with the finger problem."

"You just had to bring that up," I groaned. "Mood slayer."

Dr. Macgregor's face grew serious. "No, that would be the two ax-wielding gentlemen who came through your door a few moments ago. Who would make a prank call like that anyway?"

I thought about it. "I don't know. I've never had anything like this happen before. Before I went to work at Cedars my life was boring, boring, boring. Now I lose fingers, have voyeurs; see dead people on a daily basis. And, oh yeah, I'm kind of seeing this hot young doctor."

"Voyeurs?"

"I didn't tell you about that yet. That's the other reason I wasn't crying earlier," I shrugged.

"Oh? Are you going to tell me about it?" He looked concerned.

"Later. It's too much to go into now and I have a door to worry about." I looked over my shoulder at the fractured piece of wood.

"Okay, how about spending the night at my place. I'll even fix you a sandwich to make up for the dinner we didn't have." He took my hand in his and brought it to his lips. I felt the kiss in my groin.

"What kind of sandwich?" I asked, trying to ignore the sensations his lips gave rise to.

"I make a mean tuna fish on wheat."

I grimaced, "I've got one word for you. Ick."

A voice at the door interrupted our conversation. "What happened here?" I turned to look and found Haley standing in my doorway. She walked in and surveyed the scene. Her eyes honed in on Dr. Macgregor's naked torso and my mussed makeup and hair.

She motioned to the damaged door. "Did you do that?" she asked Dr. Macgregor but didn't wait for an answer. "Let me guess. She closed the door in your face too?"

Haley looked like a carnival show reject. Her eyes were heavily lined with charcoal liner and her eyelids were a shocking blue. She was wearing earrings the size of saucers on her ears, and her open jacket revealed a heavily embroidered peasant shirt and skirt. I realized that she must have been hired to do readings at a party and was probably just returning. "I didn't close the door in your face, Haley. We were finished talking."

Haley shook her head, "Oh pooh, *you* were finished talking, I hadn't even started yet."

I ignored her answer. "Haley, meet Dr. Macgregor. Haley is my neighbor."

Haley gave Dr. Macgregor the once-over. "So you're the one my spirit guides have been talking about. They didn't tell me you were so handsome."

Dr. Macgregor stared up at Haley with his mouth open. "Spirit guides?"

"Haley is what you would call a new-ager.' She has spirit guides," I explained.

"Ohhh," he replied. "Nice to meet you."

Haley looked over at the door. "So I guess you'll need a place to stay tonight. My couch is free."

"Actually, Charlie is going to stay at my place tonight." Dr. Macgregor squeezed my hand.

"You can't be serious!" The tone in Haley's voice made me jump.

"It's okay," I said, "he's going to feed me and everything."

Haley narrowed her eyes at Dr. Macgregor. "I don't think Charlie should stay at your place. Have you no respect for her reputation?"

"But he already ruined my reputation," I blurted. "I mean everyone at work thinks...."

"What she means is . . ." Dr. Macgregor didn't get to finish his sentence.

"You put your shirt on!" Haley interrupted. Dr. Macgregor looked incredibly like a chastised child and quickly slipped his sweater back on.

"I liked him with it off!" I complained.

Haley narrowed her eyes at me. "Are you crazy? He could be a rapist, a murderer, or worse!"

I'd had enough. "Who died and made you my keeper and mother superior all rolled into one?"

"Ladies!" The boom of Dr. Macgregor's voice echoed through the apartment. Haley and I both looked at him. He took a deep breath as though he was getting ready to say something.

Instead, he just shook his head, slipped on his jacket and kissed me on the forehead. "I'll see you at work in the morning, Charlie," then he left.

I glared at Haley. "Now look what you've done!"

Haley looked shocked. "What I've done?" She put her hands on her hips. "You should be thanking me for saving your virginity!"

"I didn't want my virginity saved!" I paused with my mouth still open. "Wait, how'd you know I was still a virgin?"

Haley shook her head. "And still she doesn't believe."

'Well, how would you like to be the world's oldest involuntary virgin?" I jabbed my finger at Haley. "I'm looking forward to ridding myself of that status and the sooner, the better! As in, tonight would have been good."

Haley shook her head again. "Charlie, you just don't get it do you? You're meant for much bigger things."

I found that comment rather funny and couldn't keep from giggling. "Um, does that mean you can ... I mean, um, can you predict size?"

Haley's face softened into a smile, but she chose not to answer my question. Instead, she said, "Just come over when you're ready and *I'll* fix you a sandwich you'll like." She left before I could answer.

I still had to wonder how she knew I was a virgin. Maybe she did have a gift. I should probably ask her where Horace's fingers are, I thought.

## Chapter 11

I examined the door. It was a mess on the inside but from the outside it looked like it had barely been touched. I closed the door from inside the apartment and pulled an end table in front of it. I gathered my strength and pushed my stone Buddha statue in front of the door as well. Buddha had been a gift from a friend. She'd sent it via UPS. The UPS guy had tried to sue me for his medical bills, because he'd dislocated a shoulder trying to deliver it alone. I assumed the statue would be heavy enough to deter anyone who might try to open my door.

I changed into my comfiest sweatpants, which happened to be pink, and put on my down jacket, which also happened to be pink. Then I slipped out through my bedroom window, which locked automatically when closed, and trekked to the front of my building through the new snow. The air was fresh and crisp, and the snow cover was untouched by any footprints on this side of the house save mine. As I rounded to the front of the building the contrast was sharp, as a bevy of footprints littered the front walk. The firefighters, Dr. Macgregor, Haley and I had all tramped through the area in the last few hours. I couldn't help doing another visual search for the jar of fingers as I walked into the building. They didn't magically appear.

Once in the building, I knocked on Haley's door. As I waited for her to answer, I walked directly across the hall, and inspected my door. You could barely tell there was damage done from this side. I turned the knob and pushed. It didn't move. The Buddha was doing a great job securing the door.

I heard Haley unlocking her door and I walked back across the hall. She opened the door and did a double take. "Oh my God, you've turned into a Mary Kay sales person on steroids," Haley put a hand to her chest in dismay. "Either that or you're attempting to imitate a bottle of Pepto-Bismol."

"You're one to talk." I cocked my head to one side. "Don't you think it was just a little overkill on the gypsy outfit tonight?"

Haley rolled her eyes and stepped aside to give me room to pass. "Obviously, you've never worked a party for people 75 and over. Those women have very specific ideas about what a true psychic should look like."

I plopped down on Haley's overstuffed couch. "75 and over?" I asked. "Must have been a short party. I mean, pardon my bluntness, but how much forecasting does someone that old need?"

"You'd be surprised," Haley yawned. "You wouldn't believe the sex lives of those women. Why it wore me out just seeing into them. Who would have thought that Shady Elms Nursing Home was really just a commune for swinging seniors?"

I pondered her description. "Is there an age requirement to get into Shady Elms?"

Haley snorted with laughter, "Oh pooh! You're not that desperate."

I punched the pillow she'd put out on the couch for me and flopped onto my back while at the same time taking a bite of the sandwich she'd left for me on the end table. I chewed and thought for a moment. "Probably not," I finally replied.

Haley waited for me to say more but I didn't. I didn't want to get into another argument tonight.

"Here's an alarm clock," she said, handing me an ancient windup model. "Oh, and you shouldn't eat lying down like that. You could choke and die, you know."

I sat back up and took a drink of the Yoo Hoo that she'd set out for me as well. "This is a really great sandwich, Haley. I was starving."

"I'm glad you like it." She smiled with smug satisfaction as I took another drink of my Yoo Hoo. "Good night, Charlie."

"Goodnight, Haley, and thanks again."

Haley smiled and stepped into her room, closing the bedroom door behind her.

I finished the sandwich and thought about taking the empty plate to the kitchen, but I was feeling incredibly tired, as though the effort would just be too much. I reached for the switch on the lamp standing on the end table, missed it twice, and then I must have fallen asleep.

I'm usually not a dreamer. I often go for months without remembering a single one. But that night I dreamed a lot. The first portion of the dream had to do with Sandy, who was once again rocking in the corner of the waiting room, where she had been on my first day at Cedars. As I passed Sandy in the dream, she stopped rocking and peered up at me from beneath her stringy blonde hair. The glazed nothingness left her eyes as she focused on me and lifted a grimy finger and pointed it at my chest. "It's you they want," she said. She turned her eyes to the floor while her fingers played with her grimy hair. "Them's who's been watchin' you ... they want's *you*, Ms. Charlie. You and what you's got."

I felt uneasy in the dream and wanted to know who "they" were, but I couldn't find a way to speak in the dream, which continued on as Sandy peered back up at me, her crooked and blackened teeth showed through her grin. "Nasty bitch, nasty bitch," she started chanting in a singsong voice. Her eyes went vacant again.

In the next part of my dream, I was answering my hospital-issued phone and I heard a raspy voice on the other end of the line. "I want my fiiiiingers! Fiiiiinger lickin' goooooood." Once again, I tried to speak but couldn't. "Fiiiiingers," came the voice, and in the dream a finger came through the receiver and poked me in the ear.

You would think that would have been enough to wake me up but it didn't. I was trapped in a weird dreamscape at Cedars, and the dream relentlessly continued on getting stranger and stranger as it progressed.

I caught a glimpse of Dr. Macgregor walking down a hall and I tried to follow him. When I finally caught up with him, I reached for his hand and grabbed it. He turned and smiled and, still holding my hand, led me down an endless maze of hallways.

In my dream, I was growing tired of traversing the halls, but I was still unable to talk and felt relief when we finally stopped when we found ourselves in a dimly lit room. Dr. Macgregor pushed me into a chair, which resembled a dentists' chair, and I was suddenly somehow strapped to the chair.

That was when Dr. Petrovich appeared and Dr. Macgregor disappeared. Dr. Petrovich started lining up a host of scary instruments on a counter that had magically appeared next to the chair. Finally finished with his task, he turned to me and grinned. I felt a need to scream but once again nothing came out of my mouth. I tried to scream again as he approached the chair, but somehow he suddenly turned into Dr. Macgregor, who leaned in and kissed me. Suddenly, my arms were free and I wrapped them around Dr. Macgregor, who was still kissing me and was starting to explore my body with his hands.

I dreamed that I closed my eyes and pushed my hands into Dr. Macgregor's hair, then froze. Was that a *bald* spot I felt? I groped around on his head with my eyes still closed. Yep. That was a really, really a big and smooth bald spot *right on the top of his head.*

I didn't remember Dr. Macgregor having a bald spot. Surely a bald spot that large would be noticeable. I pulled my head back a little bit and eased one eye open so I could take a peek and make sure it was actually Dr. Macgregor I was kissing. At first my brain didn't want to register what my one eye was seeing in the dream. It appeared that I was actually in a hot lip lock with Dr. Petrovich, who was naked. I pushed him away and put my hands over my eyes. It didn't help. Dr. Petrovich's naked form was seared in my pupils forever.

With my hands over my eyes, I jumped up to run and tripped. An alarm started going off somewhere in the hospital and I sat up, my heart pounding as I looked for the nearest exit.

I was sitting straight up on Haley's couch in the predawn light, and the alarm on the end table was shrilling the 7 o'clock hour. My heart was pounding in tandem with my head. I groaned and reached to shut off the alarm, knocking the half-full bottle of Yoo Hoo off the table in the process.

I hit the off button and sighed with relief as silence enveloped the room. The only sound was the gentle babbling of Haley's miniature water fountains. My head continued to pound as I remembered my nightmare. Eeeew. I felt somehow violated and dirty. Eeeew . . . eeew . . . eeew. I wondered what had brought on such a weirdly twisted dream and thought about the brandy I had the night before. I gingerly shook my head no. I had a hard time believing that two little shots of brandy could have that much of an effect on me, or my head.

I slowly looked around Haley's living room, being careful not to jar my head. I couldn't remember anything past trying to turn off the living room light, and was surprised that I had fallen asleep so fast on a strange couch. I had a sneaking suspicion that I hadn't brushed my teeth last night. I ran my tongue over my teeth and grimaced.

Haley breezed in, colorful silk robes billowing around her, and a cheerful smile on her face. I groaned under my breath. Her bright cheerfulness hurt my eyes and made my head pound even more.

"Did you sleep well?" she asked.

I stared at the woman and considered my nightmare. "I had a ... well ... a somewhat restless night."

Haley frowned, then brightened. "Oh well, I'm sure my couch wasn't quite as comfortable as your nice comfy king-sized bed. Would you like some coffee or tea before I get in the shower?"

I tried to ignore the pounding in my head. "I'm not even going to ask you how you know I have a king-sized bed." As far as I could recall, Haley had never been in my bedroom.

Haley looked startled for a moment. She quickly recovered her usual breezy composure and laughed. "And still you don't believe."

There was something about her demeanor. I couldn't quite put my finger on it. Anyway, my head was pounding too much to think about it.

I accepted the offer of coffee. "Do you have a few aspirin as well? My head feels three times its original size."

Haley nodded and came back in a few minutes with coffee, water and aspirin. "If you're okay, I need to take a shower," she said, "I have a breakfast meeting at my health club today. The food is absolutely awful, but some of those personal trainers ... yum, yum, yummy!" She winked and disappeared back into her bedroom.

I sat for a moment after she went back to her room and hoped the aspirin would start working soon. I remembered the spilled Yoo Hoo and, moving very slowly, I got a wet paper towel from the kitchen and knelt down to clean up the mess. The liquid had pooled under the couch and around one leg.

I pushed the paper towel under the couch to absorb the mess and, as I pulled the towel out, something rolled out with it. I picked up the small object and realized that I was holding a medicinal vial. It looked a lot like the ones I'd seen the nurses in the E.R. use when giving injections. I read the label: benzodiazepine. There was still a small portion of the medicine in the vial. I rolled the vial back and forth between my palms, wondering if I should give it directly to Haley and ask her what it was for, or just leave it on the table, or shove it back under the couch. I was curious about what she used it for but didn't want to appear nosy, even though I evidently I *was* nosy, or else I wouldn't be sitting on Haley's living room floor wondering what she needed the medicine for.

I glanced at the clock and noticed the time, which made me forget all about the debate I was having with myself, and absentmindedly shoved the vial into my jacket pocket. I had to find a locksmith for my door and was going to be late for work if I didn't get a move on.

I stepped out of Haley's apartment, looked at the door to my apartment, and stopped abruptly. I felt my blood pressure surge, and my head and heart started pounding in tandem again. The door was slightly ajar, but I clearly remembered making sure that it was firmly closed last night.

I hesitated and wondered what to do. I turned and tried to reenter Haley's apartment but apparently she had a self-locking door. I knocked to no avail and remembered that she was taking a shower. I was worried that whoever had left my door ajar was still in my apartment, so I decided to go outside and call 911 on my cell phone.

After I explained my situation to the dispatcher, she promised to send someone over soon. To my astonishment, a sedan with a flashing light on its roof pulled up not five minutes later. I don't know whether I was pleased or dismayed when an officer I didn't know exited the vehicle. I was halfway expecting Gorman and Stefansky, because they were handling the Tenny investigation, next door.

I studied the man who emerged from the vehicle as he walked up the steps to where I was waiting. He had dark hair that was just a little on the long side and piercing aqua eyes. It appeared that he'd forgotten to shave for, oh say, days, and the five o'clock shadow gave him somewhat of a rugged look. His faded jeans looked worn to a delicious softness and appeared to hug his lean yet well-muscled body in just the right spots. Even though he wore only a heavy sweatshirt instead of a jacket, he didn't seem to notice the cold, and his eyes honed in on me as he climbed the steps.

"Did you call in the break-in, Miss?" He came to a stop a couple of steps below me and waited for my answer.

I was a bit flustered, as I looked down at him, and felt ridiculously like checking my hair. Instead, I stuffed my hands in the pockets of my parka and nodded. "Do you have I.D.?" I asked.

The man looked confused for a moment, and then he grinned. "What, we just meet and already you don't trust me?"

I shrugged. "Maybe you don't look so much like any cop I know. For all I know you're some psycho wanna be who caught my call on a scanner."

The man flashed a crooked smile. He dug in his back pocket and pulled out a billfold and flipped it open in front of me. "Detective Roman Mendoza, at your service… and you are?"

"Charlie Meadows."

Mendoza grinned again. "Nice to meet you, Charlie. Why don't we go in and have a look around?"

I nodded and turned to open the door to the building. As I swung the door open, I caught my bedraggled reflection on the glass and groaned inwardly. Why was it that on the only day in the history of my life that I'd stepped outdoors without showering or brushing my teeth I had to meet a man who embodied the fantasy man in my adolescent daydreams?

Mendoza followed me to my apartment door. I stood in silence while he inspected the doorframe. He ran his hand inside the jamb and studied the outside of the closed door. "Either the person who broke in here was extremely large, or there were two of them. This is an extremely heavy, well-built door."

"Um, there were two of them." I offered.

Mendoza turned back toward me. I was having a hard time deciding which view of him I enjoyed most. I gave myself a mental shake and tried to focus on what he was asking me.

"How do you know there were two of them? The dispatcher said you hadn't seen any actual suspects." He removed a pen and a little pad of paper from his back pocket and flipped the pad open.

"Well it was the firefighters who actually *broke* the door in," I answered.

Mendoza raised his eyebrows. "Oh? How did that come about? Did you have a fire in your apartment?"

I shook my head no. "It was a false alarm."

Mendoza shook his head in wonder. "You mean to tell me you got your door busted in because of a false alarm? When did that happen?"

"Last night. Somebody apparently called the fire department and reported that my apartment was on fire."

Mendoza tried to get a clearer picture. "So you weren't home when this happened, and you came home to find your door busted in?"

"No, I was home when it happened."

Mendoza rocked back on his heels. "You were home?"

I felt my cheeks turn scarlet. "I was busy," I gulped.

Mendoza stared at me for a moment, and a slow grin spread across his face. "I think I remember hearing about this over the scanner."

I felt myself flush even brighter—if that was possible. "What exactly did you hear over the scanner?"

"Oh, only that some extremely hot woman was busy with a local doctor and, well, never mind…" Mendoza looked thoroughly amused.

I opened my mouth, closed it again, and shrugged. What could I say? It was true.

Mendoza gave me a speculative look. "I guess you … oh, well, never mind."

I narrowed my eyes as I looked at him. "You guess what?"

"Oh, it's not worth mentioning," he kind of hiccupped with a suppressed laugh.

I stomped my foot. "I demand that you tell me what you were going to say."

Mendoza sized me up and decided to talk. "Well, I guess you were a little more put together last night, huh? I mean, nobody mentioned anything about an obese pink person."

"Obese? I've never been obese a day in my life!" I pointed at my jacket. "This is made of down—nice, warm, cozy feathers!"

Mendoza raised a hand, his blue eyes flashing with mirth. "Okay, okay, it's feathers! So if the door was broken already, what makes you think there was a break-in?"

I took some deep breaths and counted to 10. Mendoza waited patiently while I struggled to remain calm. "Last night, I wedged the door shut with my Buddha statue. I checked to make sure the door wouldn't open easily and I couldn't get it to budge. I spent the night at my neighbor's apartment across the hall and, when I checked the door this morning, it was ajar."

Mendoza jotted a few notes on his pad. "What time was it when you checked your door this morning?"

I looked at my watch. "About 15 minutes ago, which means it would have been about 7:15 or 7:20. I'm supposed to be at work by 9:00 a.m. Do you suppose we could speed this up a bit?"

Mendoza ignored my request, studied the door again, and gave it a little push. It swung open. "If you wedged the door from inside the apartment, how did you get out?"

I tried to peer past Mendoza into the apartment. "I climbed out through the window."

Mendoza turned around with a funny little smile playing at the corners of his mouth. "The window?" he repeated.

"The window," I said.

"Okaaaaay, the window." He was still sporting that funny little smile.

I glowered at him. "What's so funny?"

Mendoza pretended to be shocked. "I was just ... um, well, I was trying to visualize the . . . well, you know, the window thing—all those down feathers trying to get through the window. Anyway, I want you to stay out here until I say it's clear in there, okay?"

He was through the door before I could answer, and I felt myself clench my teeth in frustration.

## Chapter 12

I paced up and down the hall, waiting for Mendoza to come out of my apartment. For a guy I found so devastatingly attractive visually, he certainly knew how to push my buttons verbally. I walked over to Alfred's apartment and studied the crime scene tape crisscrossing the door. My thoughts gravitated to who would want Alfred dead and why. I walked back over to my apartment and propped myself against the opposite wall, still mulling over Alfred.

When Mendoza reappeared, I straightened up. He looked grim with the corners of his mouth turned down. The amusement a few minutes before had been entirely wiped away by something else.

"What?" I asked, unable to bear the suspense. "Did they trash the place? Is it still livable?"

Mendoza opened his mouth to speak but seemed to reconsider and turned, then he went back to my door, where he stopped again. He started to turn back toward me, stopped again and stared beyond my door and into my apartment.

"Um, Detective Mendoza?" I asked. My stomach had turned into a hard little knot. I had to know what had happened in there.

My voice seemed to startle him from his reverie, and he turned and walked back to where I was standing. He inspected my face, then turned his eyes to his feet and scratched his head, reminding me of Colombo's mannerisms in the old TV show. .

"Ms. Meadows?" he asked, "Is this your idea of a joke?"

I was flabbergasted and I know the shock showed on my face. "What?! What are you talking about?"

"Okay. I'm afraid I'm going to have to read you your rights before we go any further."

My eyes widened in surprise. "My rights? Are you crazy? What for?"

Mendoza ignored my question and started reading me my rights. I was wondering if I was still asleep. If I could dream up a naked Dr. Petrovich, I was pretty sure I could dream up this craziness.

Mendoza finished reading me my rights and asked me if I understood them. "Yes," I answered. "I understand my rights perfectly. Do you think you could pinch me?"

It was Mendoza's turn to look surprised. "Pinch you?"

"Uh huh. You see, I had a really disturbingly strange dream last night. I mean, at least I think it was last night, but now I'm wondering if I'm still dreaming because, well, things just keep getting weirder and weirder."

I closed my eyes and held out my arm. When the pinch that I expected didn't come, I opened my eyes. Mendoza was staring at me as though I'd dropped in from another planet. "Did you pinch me?" I asked.

"No, I didn't pinch you," Mendoza replied. "How do I know you're not trying to get me for police brutality?"

"Why would I want to do that? Now pinch me this time, okay?" I closed my eyes and held out my arm again.

I felt Mendoza's fingers just above my elbow, and a sharp piercing pain quickly followed.

I opened my eyes and glowered at Mendoza. "Owwww! You didn't have to pinch me *that* hard!"

"You asked me to pinch you, you didn't say how hard." Mendoza had a satisfied look on his face. "Now. You and I have to head down to the station, young lady."

"What for? I haven't even brushed my teeth this morning, much less done anything to get arrested for!"

Mendoza backed up a step upon hearing this new information. "I'm not sure what the crime is yet, but it has to do with fingers that don't belong to you. I found them on the top shelf of your refrigerator."

I was relieved and excited to hear this.

"Cool! Are they in a container that sort of looks like a Vlasic pickle jar?" I asked excitedly.

Mendoza nodded.

"Yes!" I cried out and broke into a little happy dance, humming a victory tune under my breath. I caught a glance of Mendoza while I was in midstep. His sour demeanor stopped me in my tracks.

"You don't understand, " I started to say.

"Obviously," he cut me off, "that's why we're going to run downtown and clear up a few things. I called for backup. They're going to run you in while I take care of the crime scene."

I thought for a moment. "Would that be the crime scene I called you about or the crime scene your warped mind thinks I'm involved in? What were you doing in my fridge, anyway?"

Mendoza narrowed his impossibly blue eyes at me. "You're calling *me* warped? You *danced* because I mentioned some severed fingers in a pickle jar. That's just sick. Are they a trophy? Better yet, are they trophies from several men? How many are in that jar? Four? Five?"

Mendoza stopped his tirade when I started laughing. "Jeez, you've got one hell of an imagination, Detective Mendoza. There's a perfectly logical explanation for those fingers—although I'm not quite sure how they got into my refrigerator, a*nd* you still haven't explained what you were doing snooping in my fridge in the first place!"

Mendoza shrugged. "I was hungry."

At that moment, two uniformed officers came through the apartment building doors. It was Gorman and Stefansky.

I gave Mendoza a last searing glare before turning to Gorman and Stefansky. "Hey guys!" I called cheerfully. "Remember those fingers I was given for safekeeping when you were at the hospital yesterday? Please explain to Detective Mendoza that they are not the result of a murderous urge on my part."

The two officers came to a stop in front of me and gave me the once-over.

Gorman spoke first. "Good morning, Charlie! You're looking very, well, um, *pink* today."

"Yeah," said Stefansky, "and big. Big and pink."

I rolled my eyes. "Do you suppose you could fill Detective Mendoza in on the fingers?" I was getting anxious to get out of my pink outfit, into a shower and on with my day—not to mention that I really had to pee. I hadn't had a chance to take care of that before Haley claimed her bathroom earlier.

"What fingers?" asked Gorman.

I sighed in frustration. "The fingers you saw in the consultation room at the hospital." At their blank looks, I tried again. "You know, they were in a pickle jar, remember?"

"Oh yeah," said Stefansky. "I remember them." Apparently, the thought of the fingers in the jar had the same effect on him as his first sight of them had, and I watched as the blood drained completely from his face.

"Um, do you need to sit down?" I asked.

Stefansky shook his head no.

"You mean to tell me you two already know her?" Mendoza looked like he was either extremely confused or extremely irritated.

Gorman spoke up, "Well, yeah. After all we *were* investigating the Alfred Tenny case until the captain pulled us off and gave it to you. We'd already managed to interview Ms. Meadows here." Gorman glanced at me, and then continued. "By the way, Charlie, as of today, the lead detective on the Tenny case is Mendoza here. I see you've already met."

I looked from Gorman to Mendoza and from Mendoza back to Gorman with only one thought on my mind. "Have you turned the, err, videos over to Mendoza yet?"

Gorman shook his head no. "He was only assigned this morning." He looked at Mendoza. "You're in for a treat, Mendoza, that pink jacket with all those feathers hides quite a bit."

Color suffused my entire body. I'm pretty sure that, along with the scrunched-up look on my face because of my urgent need to pee, wasn't doing my case any good either. "Can I please use the bathroom? I'm sure these two men will be able to tell you about the fingers, Detective Mendoza."

Mendoza looked at Gorman and Stefansky with a questioning look.

Gorman nodded. "She's cool."

I dashed into my apartment and headed straight for the bathroom, noting that nothing seemed out of place, save my Buddha, whose blissful grin looked rather ridiculous now that the statue was tipped over on its side. I slid off my jacket and tossed it on the couch as I cruised by, not missing a step, in my dash to relieve myself.

I closed and locked the bathroom door, and headed straight for the toilet. I took my time. I wasn't eager to continue the conversation I'd exited just earlier.

I brushed and fluffed my hair and brushed my teeth. My headache had receded a bit but I was pale and my eyes looked huge in my face. Too much excitement, I decided, and took a deep breath before stepping out of the bathroom.

Mendoza, Gorman and Stefansky were in deep conversation when I entered the living room, and they didn't appear to notice my entrance. They seemed to be discussing a small object that Mendoza was holding in his hand. As I neared, I could see that it was the medicinal vial I'd found in Haley's apartment.

Mendoza must have sensed my presence, because he broke off whatever he was saying and turned his gaze to me. "Ms. Meadows, are you on drugs?"

I laughed. "Are you kidding? Absolutely not!"

Mendoza looked at the vial he was holding in his hand. "Then how do you explain this?"

"It's not mine," I replied and winced, realizing, that in all the COPS episodes I'd seen on television, that's what the bad guys always said.

Mendoza did the Colombo head scratch again. "When we were in the hall earlier, I noticed that your pupils seemed abnormally large, and your behavior has been a bit strange this morning."

I looked at Stefansky and Gorman, who were both nodding their heads in agreement. Obviously, I would get no help from them.

"So what are you trying to say, Detective Mendoza? That I'm lying?"

Mendoza shrugged, "Maybe. I mean, if the vial isn't yours then why did it fall out of your pocket when I picked up your jacket?"

"Because I found it and put it in my pocket this morning," I explained.

"Oh yeah?" Mendoza raised his eyebrows. "Where'd you find it?"

I hesitated. If I told him the truth, I was afraid I'd get Haley into trouble. "I can't tell you that," I answered.

Mendoza raised his eyebrows. "You can't tell me, yet you insist it's not yours."

I sighed. "I can't prove it, but it's the truth. I don't take drugs."

Mendoza thought for a moment, then a wide grin spread across his face. "There *is* one way."

"One way to do what?" I asked.

"To prove you're not on drugs, of course."

I studied Mendoza. I had mixed feelings about the smile on his face. On the one hand, it was the sexiest grin I'd ever encountered. On the other hand, if I wasn't mistaken, there was something really wicked lurking behind his grin as well. I weighed my options, which were none and none. "Okay," I said. "How?"

Mendoza's grin widened further yet, if that was possible, and his eyes were positively dancing. I knew I was in for trouble. "You could submit to a drug test."

"Hmmm," I squinted up at Mendoza and tried to figure out what he thought was so humorous. "And what exactly would that entail?" I asked.

Mendoza shrugged. "I run you in and you take a simple blood test. The results come back within an hour. If you're clean, you're off the hook."

"And if I'm not?"

"I book you for possession and illegal use of a controlled substance." Mendoza grinned wider.

I had an inkling that the thought of me behind bars was exactly what was lightening Mendoza's mood. I scowled at him. "Okay, I agree." I knew I'd pass the drug test and, when I did, I thoroughly planned on making Mendoza apologize—on his knees if possible.

Stefansky and Gorman had followed our conversation, and Gorman tried to interrupt. "But Charlie...."

Mendoza held up a hand to stop Gorman in midsentence. "Would you and Stefansky finish up the B and E report and call in a locksmith for Ms. Meadows? I'm going to run Ms. Meadows in for her blood test."

Gorman nodded to Mendoza and turned to me. "Would you like to report anything missing?"

"Hold on," I said and walked quickly through the apartment, checking my valuables as I went from room to room. When I returned to the living room, I said, "Everything seems to be here. The only thing that seems to have been disturbed is my refrigerator, and that was in the form of a deposit rather than a withdrawal." I quickly explained that I had somehow misplaced the fingers yesterday and wondered who had brought them back and put them in my refrigerator, no less.

"Is it possible that *you* put them in the refrigerator?" asked Mendoza. "Maybe you just don't remember doing it."

The question left me unreasonably irritated. "What? You mean in my *drug-hazed* state, is it possible that I put them there and just don't remember?"

Stefansky, sensing the tension in the air, stepped in. "Well, I think we've got what we need here. Shorty and I are going to head back to the station now."

Gorman growled. "I told you *not* to call me Shorty!" They were still grumbling back and forth as they headed out through my broken door.

I was left alone with Mendoza, who was dialing a number on the phone. "Yeah, it's Mendoza here. I'm on my way in for a "chain of custody" blood draw. Can you have things ready for me?" He smiled and used a softer voice, saying to the person on the other line, "You always take such good care of me." He listened for a moment, grinned again and said. "Okay then. See you in about 10 minutes," and hung up. He turned to me and was still smiling from his conversation. "You ready to go?"

"Oh, I'll have to call work and let them know I'll be late first. Do we have to go right this minute? If I take a shower first, I can head into work right after the test and...." Mendoza cut me off.

"This is a chain of custody blood draw. That means that, from this moment on, you can't leave my sight until your blood is drawn. That way you can't take anything or do anything that might muddle the results."

I was surprised. "You mean people can actually do that ... fake a blood test or do something to affect the results?"

Mendoza smirked. "As if you didn't know."

I smirked back, brazen with the knowledge of my innocence. "Yeah, that's me, all right. Not only do I take drugs but I also know all the methods for covering up drug use. As if!"

Mendoza handed me my coat. "We'll know soon enough."

I put my coat on and made him wait while I called the hospital. I spoke with Dr. Caudill, who assured me that they would survive without me for an extra hour or so. Needless to say, I didn't disclose my reason for being late. I hung up and thought about Horace's fingers.

"I need to get that jar out of the refrigerator. I don't want to lose the fingers again."

Mendoza raised his eyebrows. "You've got to be kidding me."

"Nope." I started to head for the kitchen. "I lost them once and I don't want to lose them again, and given the state of my door...." Mendoza followed me into the kitchen and leaned against the stove while I opened the fridge.

"I'm not sure I want those things in my car." His tone was playful, but his look was serious.

"That doesn't matter," I countered, "I'm not leaving without them. Besides, what harm will they be to you or your car? Are you squeamish?"

Mendoza narrowed his incredible blue eyes and didn't answer.

I pulled the jar off the shelf and held it in front of me as I studied it and grinned. I was so grateful just to have the fingers back.

Mendoza straightened up and said. "Um, if you're done ogling your prize there, I'd like to get this over with."

I peered at him over the jar. "Squeamish," I stated.

"Am not," he answered.

"Are too," I countered. I had both hands wrapped around the jar as we headed out the door.

He ignored my last retort and closed the apartment door firmly, then checked it. It wouldn't lock but at least it would catch. We walked to his car, and he took the flasher off the roof. He motioned for me to sit in the back. When I balked, he faced me squarely and said, "Police protocol. You sit in the back."

I grumbled and climbed into the backseat. All in all, I was pleased that I did not have to sit next to him and pretend to carry on a conversation. I set the jar of fingers in my lap and stared at the back of his Mendoza's head while he drove. I really wished that I'd just left that medicinal vial under Haley's couch. I also couldn't help worrying about the fact that my apartment door wouldn't lock.

"Hey, Mendoza," I called up to him, "what happens if the locksmith gets to my apartment and I'm not there?"

He looked at me through his rearview mirror. "Don't worry, Gorman and Stefansky are supposed to be coordinating that. They'll make sure it gets done in their presence and as quickly as possible."

"Oh." I lost my train of thought, because I'd suddenly realized that we weren't headed for the police station, which was on the other side of town. "Where are we going?" I asked. "I thought we were going to the police station."

Mendoza sighed and glanced at me again in the rearview mirror. "Although most police officers are able to leap buildings in a single bound and most other things mere mortals can't do, we are not trained to draw blood."

I was about to ask where blood was drawn when my question was answered for me, as Mendoza pulled into the parking lot at Cedars. My mouth dropped open in astonishment. "We're not ... I mean, you're not.... Oh hell. Just tell me we are *not* going to do this in the Emergency Room."

Mendoza parked and turned off the car. He didn't answer until he had gotten out and opened the car door for me. "I can't tell you that because we *are* going to be drawing your blood in the Emergency Room. That's the only agency in town licensed to draw blood."

## Chapter 13

I looked up at Mendoza and ignored his proffered hand. I was *not* going to leave the car. "I work in there. I cannot, will not, be tested for drugs in my place of employment. Might I add that this is only my third day of employment?" I crossed my arms and stared straight ahead. At least now I knew what he'd found so funny earlier when discussing the drug test. He'd *known* I worked at Cedars.

"Come on, Charlie. Get out of the car." Mendoza offered me his hand again.

"No!" I replied. "I changed my mind."

"Charlie..."

"No! No! No!" I smacked his hand away.

Mendoza sighed in frustration and did the Colombo. He looked down at me with irritation rolling through his features.

"Listen, Charlie, I'm going to count to three. If you're not out of the car by then, I'm going to remove you from the car myself."

"Yeah, sure, like that's going to happen." I kept my arms crossed firmly across my chest and continued to stare straight ahead.

"One." Mendoza's voice was quiet but firm.

"Two." I didn't budge.

The next thing I knew, Mendoza was halfway into the car with me. In the blink of an eye, he clicked handcuffs on one of my wrists and was attempting to cuff the other wrist.

"You didn't say three!" I yelled and kicked my legs out to the side, landing a knee squarely in Mendoza's groin.

I heard a whoosh of air escape from Mendoza's lungs, and he went limp, his upper body falling into me. His head rested on the seat, next to me, and I couldn't move for his weight. A high-pitched whine was coming from somewhere deep in his throat.

"You didn't say three." I repeated, this time a little more meekly.

My words seemed to revive Mendoza a bit from his pain debilitated state. He shifted, removing his weight, at the same time moving his hand fluidly beneath his sweatshirt. When his hand reemerged, he was holding a gun. He pointed the gun at me.

I stared at the gun and my mouth formed an O of surprise.

A humorless grin slowly spread across Mendoza's face. "Just try to do that again," he said through clenched teeth.

I managed to tear my gaze away from the gun and looked up at him. "You didn't say three!"

"Are you a broken record or something? Stop saying that and get out of the car," he barked. I got the distinct impression that Mendoza was more than a little miffed. He removed himself the rest of the way from the car and motioned with his free hand for me to do the same.

"You know, you don't have to be such a poor sport," I said. "It's not like I meant to hurt you or anything. You startled me, I mean after all you..."

"Didn't count to three," he finished my sentence.

"Yeah."

"Are you ever going to get out of the car?" he asked.

"No." I stared straight into his eyes. "What are you going to do, shoot me or something? Jeez."

Mendoza pulled the hammer of the pistol back.

"Get out of the car, Charlie, or I'll run you in for resisting an officer."

"As if!" I countered, but I started sliding out of the car anyway. I was almost out of the car when I remembered the jar on my lap. Probably because I heard the crash when it hit the parking lot pavement.

I felt my eyes widen with horror and I stopped cold.

Mendoza still had the gun cocked, ready and aimed between my eyes. His jaw was twitching and I had a feeling his trigger finger was too.

"Um... I'm afraid to look," I said.

Mendoza didn't look down either. He kept his eyes on me. "I think you just busted your jar of fingers."

I nodded, gathered my courage and looked down. Fingers and glass shards littered the pavement near my feet. An index finger lay across the toes of Mendoza's right shoe.

"Uh, Detective Mendoza?" I asked.

"Yeah?" he answered.

I looked back up at him. "You don't have to look, but you might want to give your right foot a little shake."

Mendoza's color heightened a bit. "Why would I want to do that?"

"I'm not sure you want to know. But if you point the gun somewhere else, I'll tell you. Okay?"

Mendoza considered my offer for a moment. "You're right. I don't want to know." He shook his right foot a bit, and the finger rolled onto the pavement.

I stood up, careful to avoid mashing any of the fingers lying on the ground, and stepped around the mess. Mendoza followed every move, gun still in hand.

"You don't happen to have a spare jar in your car somewhere, do you?" I asked. "Maybe that or a plastic baggie or something?"

"You're kidding, right?"

I shook my head no. "I can't just leave the fingers out here like that now, can I?"

Mendoza ignored me. "Turn around and face the car please."

"Now *you're* kidding, right?"

"Nope." Mendoza stared me down and kept the gun trained on my forehead.

Careful to avoid the glass and fingers, I turned and faced the car.

Mendoza started patting me down.

"Hey, cut that out," I yelled. "I'm not a criminal!" I was white hot with embarrassment and maybe, in a somewhat twisted way, from the pat down.

Mendoza grabbed my handcuffed wrist, attached it to my other wrist and turned me around to face him. He had tucked his gun away while I was facing the car. He then opened the driver's side door and leaned in to rummage through the glove box. When he reemerged from the car, he was holding a plastic bag labeled "Evidence" along with a pair of large tweezers.

"Tools of the trade." He said the words more to himself than to me, and I watched while he expertly handled the overlarge tweezers, picked up each finger and dropped all of them into the evidence bag.

I assumed the best pleading expression I could and looked up at him. "The cuffs are so unnecessary, Detective Mendoza. Please, please take the cuffs off. I work in there! I promise to behave."

"You're in my custody, and you're argumentative and uncooperative. You've caused me physical harm. The cuffs stay on." Mendoza took my arm and started marching me toward the E.R. entrance. He was carrying the bag with Horace's fingers in the other hand.

I dragged my heels, but Mendoza kept trudging on ahead. The E.R. entrance was getting closer and closer while I considered my predicament.

"You're heartless," I hissed.

"You're a pain in my ass," he hissed back.

## Chapter 14

Mendoza swung through the doors, dragging me behind him, and led me straight to the triage office. Joyce was sitting at the desk. She had been watching our progress from the moment we'd come through the door. Her expression went from boredom to interest, to astonishment, to glee.

"Hey Joyce," Mendoza greeted her with a wink. "You all ready for me?"

Joyce tried to keep a straight face. "Just as you requested. What are we testing for today, Detective?" Joyce batted her eyelashes at Mendoza and smirked at me. She looked pretty and petite in her royal blue scrubs, which made me feel all the bigger and pinker.

"Hey, Joyce." I tried to pretend nonchalance. She ignored me.

Mendoza ignored me as well and answered Joyce. "Drug screen. Run the gamut." He held up the bag of fingers. "Oh yeah, a jar and some formaldehyde for these, please."

Joyce raised an eyebrow inquisitively and looked at me. "Are those the fingers you were carrying yesterday, Charlie?"

I nodded. "Jar broke."

Joyce sighed. "Apparently." A smug look crossed her face. "I just *knew* there was more to those police officers' questioning you the other day than you were letting on. Sit down."

I sighed, rolled my eyes and sat down in the chair typically reserved for incoming patients.

Joyce picked up the phone and requested a technician's assistance, then turned back to me. "You must have been on a bender last night, huh? First the fire department has to break your door down and now this. Have you looked in a mirror lately? God, you look awful."

"How did you know about the door?"

"That's all anyone has been talking about this morning. You do know that most firefighters are trained paramedics, don't you? Anyway, the firefighters who broke in your door last night made a run in here after they picked up a victim of a motor vehicle accident last night. They shared your story with whoever was on duty last night, who in turn, shared the story with the next shift, and so on. Get the picture?"

I sat there—speechless.

Joey, the tech, came in and Joyce gave him instructions with regard to the fingers. He gave me a few curious looks while Joyce told him what to do. A few minutes later, he left the room with the fingers in tow. I watched as he left and saw him twirl his finger next to his ear, indicating that he thought I was crazy.

"I saw that!" I called after him.

Joyce turned to Mendoza. "You're going to have to take the cuffs off her for me to be able to draw blood. Do I need to call Security for backup?"

"No," he said giving me a look that said, "you'd better behave."

"Damn," said Joyce, "that would have been fun."

I tried to explain, "Joyce, I don't think Detective Mendoza here has explained that I came willingly to prove that I'm *not* on drugs."

Joyce eyed me in the handcuffs that Mendoza was busy removing. "*Right.*"

I sighed and shut up.

Mendoza finished removing the handcuffs and I rubbed my wrists, even though, in all fairness, I had to admit that the cuffs hadn't been tight enough to chaff my skin.

Joyce told me to take off my coat and roll up my sleeve. She then removed a syringe from a box labeled "Police Evidence." She tied a rubber tube around my arm and started poking around with her index finger, looking for a good vein.

I noticed that more and more staff members were finding a reason to go past the window of the triage office. Some were shaking their heads in wonder; others were obviously thoroughly amused at my situation. Apparently, Joey traveled fast.

I felt a sudden sharp pain in my arm as Joyce penetrated it with the needle, and I looked down in time to see my blood flowing into the container attached to the needle. I could have sworn that she was jiggling the needle on purpose to cause more pain. Our heads were fairly close together and I whispered, "Stop jiggling. That hurts."

Joyce whispered back. "Maybe *some* people shouldn't lie about seeing certain doctors outside of work."

"What do you care?" I whispered vehemently. "You're supposedly a lesbian."

Joyce looked up from my arm in surprise. "I'm not a lesbian. I'm bisexual. There's a difference." She then yanked the needle out and pressed a cotton swab hard to my vein.

"Ouch!" I yelped and thought about inflicting bodily harm on Joyce.

She must have seen the look in my eyes, because she quickly rolled her chair away. "You can cuff her again," she told Mendoza.

"Oh, come on!" I protested. "You have my blood. Haven't I been through enough humiliation for one day?"

Mendoza looked unfazed. "You gonna behave?"

I tried to look convincing as I put my coat back on. "Of course!" My voice cracked.

Mendoza laughed. "Did you just squeak?"

A voice from behind me piped up. "I'll vouch for her," I heard him say.

Both Mendoza and I turned to see who was speaking. It was Dr. Macgregor. He looked very respectable and professional with his stethoscope hanging over his white lab coat.

Mendoza's eyes narrowed, as he nodded at him. "Hey, Sam. Long time no see."

I was surprised once again. "You two know each other?"

Dr. Macgregor turned his eyes toward me and nodded. "We played football together in high school. Wish I could say it's good to see you, Detective, but, well, you know." He gave Mendoza a challenging look, and I could sense a definite tension between the two men. Mendoza didn't answer, and Dr. Macgregor turned his attention to me while he took in my appearance. "What's going on? You don't look so good. Are you sick?"

Mendoza answered for me. "I'm told it's the feathers—they make her look bloated. And I really don't think pink is her color."

I sent Mendoza a searing look before turning my attention to Dr. Macgregor. "Mendoza here thinks I'm on drugs."

Dr. Macgregor looked at Mendoza with obvious dislike. Mendoza ignored the look and tried to clarify the situation. "Her pupils are dilated, she's exhibiting some clumsiness, and a drug vial rolled out of her jacket pocket earlier this morning."

Dr. Macgregor considered Mendoza's report. "Well, the clumsiness is nothing new. But drugs?" Dr. Macgregor turned toward me, "So what were you doing with Mendoza this morning?"

I could feel the tension in the air growing and decided it'd be best to separate the two men until I could figure out Dr. Macgregor's obvious hostility toward Mendoza. "I'll explain later," I said. I looked at Mendoza. "Do we have to wait for the results or can we go now? I'm worried about leaving my apartment unlocked."

Mendoza's answer was firm. "We wait."

"Well, as much fun as this is, you're not waiting here," Joyce put in. "I've got patients lining up."

Relieved that the handcuff issue seemed to have been forgotten, I followed Mendoza and Dr. Macgregor out of the office. Mendoza was carrying the evidence box that contained my blood. Joyce closed the door behind us, and I caught a glimpse of a worried look on her face, which surprised me. I thought she'd be lapping up my predicament and making the most of it.

"So what happens next?" I asked Mendoza.

Mendoza did a little wave with the box. "I'm escorting this back to the lab. I'll be back in about 15 minutes. I'd better find you here. Do you understand?"

I nodded.

"I'll keep her company while she waits," added Dr. Macgregor. He leveled a challenging gaze at Mendoza.

Mendoza paused as though he was ready to argue but changed his mind and nodded. "Okay. Please don't do anything stupid like disappearing on me."

Dr. Macgregor and I sat down on the two chairs in the E.R. waiting room that were closest to use. When we were seated, Dr. Macgregor turned to me and said, "Would you like to explain to me what the heck has gone on since I left your apartment last night?"

I sighed. "It's been the weirdest morning. I mean, I woke up from this incredibly bizarre nightmare in which Dr. Petrovich felt me up, then I noticed that my apartment had been broken into. So I called the police, who sent Mendoza there, who in turn decided that I was on drugs, and here we are. Oh yeah, whoever broke into my apartment *returned* Horace's fingers rather than taking anything."

Sam digested this information. " Dr. Petrovich felt you up?"

"It was a dream…more like a nightmare!" I leaned back in my chair and studied Dr. Macgregor. "Jealous?"

"Of a nightmare?" Dr. Macgregor shrugged, but his green eyes glinted. "Maybe. Why does Mendoza think you're on drugs?"

"He already told you that," I answered with more than a little heat in my voice. I was tired having everyone questioning my character.

"Well where'd you get the vial?" He redirected his question.

My tone was sharp. "I can't tell you that right now, but I will tell you that it absolutely is not mine!"

Dr. Macgregor noticed my irritation. "Hey, you can put the claws away, Charlie. I'm not your enemy and I believe you."

I decided to change the subject. "So what's up with you and Mendoza? You both seemed like, given half the chance, you'd like to kill each other."

Dr. Macgregor didn't answer right away. A host of emotions crossed his face before he finally spoke. "Well, you know how you can't tell *me* where you got the vial right now? This will be my thing that I can't tell *you* right now."

"So we're even?" I asked.

"For now. I will tell you this, though. If at all possible, stay away from Mendoza. He's bad news."

I smiled. "Well so far he hasn't been exactly a ray of sunshine."

"I'm serious, Charlie," he warned. "Don't let your guard down with him."

My smiled faded as I realized the intensity of Sam's dislike for Mendoza. "Wow, you really dislike the guy, don't you?"

Dr. Macgregor didn't have an opportunity to answer. Mendoza swung through the doors to the E.R. waiting room with an extremely sour look on his face.

I stood up and faced him as he approached. "So can I go now?"

Mendoza came to a stop in front of me. "As a matter of fact … no."

"No?" Dr. Macgregor and I both blurted in unison.

"No." Mendoza repeated. "Your test came back positive for barbiturates—more specifically, benzodiazepine. Exactly the same medication that was in the vial."

## Chapter 15

I looked from Mendoza to Dr. Macgregor. "Impossible!" I blurted. "I don't take drugs! What's benzodiazepine, anyway?"

"Truth serum," came Dr. Macgregor's quick answer. "I mean, that's what it's typically described as."

"Why would I want to take that?" I asked.

"Exactly my question," answered Mendoza.

"She wouldn't," stated Dr. Macgregor.

"I wouldn't? Why wouldn't I?" I asked.

"Because, all it would do is give you amnesia for a certain period of time," Dr. Macgregor explained. "You don't strike me like someone who wants to lose several hours at a time—much less afford to lose them."

Mendoza was listening while doing the Colombo head scratch thing again. I was beginning to realize that this was his thinking position. "So if she didn't take it and it doesn't sound like she would want to unless she was crazy, which I haven't entirely ruled out yet, how would it get into her system?"

"Well, that's the thing," Dr. Macgregor replied. "The typical way to administer that particular drug is to inject it intravenously. Someone would have had to have given her a shot."

"Why would somebody do that?" I asked.

"The only reason I can think of is to make you tell the truth," answered Dr. Macgregor.

"About what?" I asked.

That question left both Dr. Macgregor and Mendoza with blank looks on their faces.

"How long does this drug usually stay in the system?" asked Mendoza.

Dr. Macgregor shrugged. "Usually no longer than 24 hours."

"Then she had to have been given the drug some time today or yesterday." Mendoza looked at me and frowned. "Have you lost any time in the last 24 hours that you can think of?"

I shook my head no. "As far as I can tell every moment has been accounted for."

"Strange," said Mendoza. "If you'd tell us where you found the vial, we might have clue as to how, what, why, or when."

"I know, and, believe me, if I could tell you, I would," I replied.

"I can run you in for withholding information," Mendoza threatened.

I shrugged. "Like that's supposed to worry me? I'd probably get more and better rest in a jail cell than I've been getting at home lately."

"Good point," Mendoza admitted. "I can't ignore the fact that you're not coming clean with me though."

"Is benzodiazepine an illegal drug?" I asked.

"Well no, not if you have a prescription for it." Mendoza answered. "But, then again, who would have a prescription for a drug like that?"

No one answered his question.

"Listen, Ms. Meadows," said Mendoza. "I'm going to give you 24 hours to 'fess up, okay? If you don't give me answer by then, I'm booking you on possession and use of an illegally obtained prescription drug."

I felt my eyes widen in surprise. "That's almost kind of you, Detective Mendoza, what's the catch?"

Mendoza didn't so much as hesitate before answering, "You cooperate fully with the Tenny investigation."

I studied Mendoza's face. "Meaning?"

"Meaning that, if I need your time or apartment for anything related to that case, you accommodate me. I feel I should also tell you that you are a suspect in the case, being that you told Gorman and Stefansky you wanted to—What were the words you used? —Kill the little prick yourself."

"That's not fair! I meant if I'd known about the hidden cameras, which I didn't know about until *after* he was dead."

"So you say."

I felt Dr. Macgregor's stare, and I knew that he didn't want me to agree to Mendoza's terms, but I was tired and just wanted to take a shower and get on with my day.

"Whatever you want. I'll cooperate." I answered. "Can I go home now so I can shower and get to back here for work?"

"Why don't you take the day off today, Charlie?" Dr. Macgregor suggested.

I looked at him in surprise. "Because it's only like my third day at this job and it just doesn't look good if I take a day off so soon."

Dr. Macgregor smiled. "I'll explain the situation to Dr. Caudill. I mean, after all, we do strive for a drug-free workplace, and the drug should be out of your system by this time tomorrow."

I put my hands on my hips and stared Dr. Macgregor down. "If I don't come back today, it'll probably put betting odds in favor of my not returning to work at all." I dug out a 20-dollar bill from my pocket. "Invest this wisely, and I'll see you tomorrow."

Dr. Macgregor took the bill. "Be careful, Charlie," he warned.

Mendoza answered for me. "She'll be with me, Sam. She'll be fine."

That thought didn't seem to appease Dr. Macgregor, who looked—if anything—more upset by that idea, and he left quickly.

On the way out of the E.R., Mendoza and I stopped by the triage office so I could pick up Horace's fingers. Joey had placed them in a jar that was identical to the first one and had filled it with formaldehyde.

Joyce handed the jar to me with a smug smile. "So it was positive, huh?"

I ignored her question and asked my own, "Isn't dispersing a patient's confidential data without her or his consent a HIPPA violation? I thought you could lose your job for that."

Joyce opened and closed her mouth several times before just shutting it completely. She turned on her heel, closing the office door behind her.

I looked at Mendoza, who looked back at me with amusement dancing brightly in his blue eyes. "Guess you told her, huh?"

"It doesn't hurt to read the employees' handbook." I turned and led the way out of the E.R. to Mendoza's car. I stood by the rear door of the car and waited for him to unlock it.

"You can sit up front now, you know." He flashed a smile, and I found the transformation from tough detective to charming acquaintance devastatingly attractive, in spite myself.

"I think I prefer the backseat. I mean, I don't think its police protocol to have a *suspect* sitting up front with the cop."

"Suit yourself." He unlocked the door and held it while I slipped in. I had the jar with Horace's fingers securely in my grip and was determined that no more accidents would befall the cursed things while they were in my care. I watched while he unlocked his own door and slipped behind the steering wheel.

"Hey, Detective Mendoza, don't you think we should do something about the glass we left in the parking lot? I mean I wouldn't want you to get a flat tire or anything."

Mendoza sighed and turned off the ignition he'd just switched on. "Yes, you're probably right." He picked up a folded newspaper that was lying on the passenger seat and stepped out of the car. I waited while he took care of the glass.

I felt like my mind was going at 100 miles an hour as I tried to sort out the events that had taken place over the last three days. I had a drug in my system and had no idea how it had gotten there. Given that I'd found the vial in Haley's apartment, I had to assume that she'd had something to do with it. I was feeling less and less like protecting her. It would be so much easier to just tell Mendoza where I'd found it and let him question Haley. The only thing that was stopping me was the fact that I wasn't sure if she would admit to owning the drug, or if she'd feign innocence, and then I'd be stuck trying to prove my own innocence. At least this way Haley didn't have to know I knew about the benzodiazepine, and I could try to find something out while her guard was down.

It also occurred to me that the strange occurrences of the last few days seemed to be centered on my apartment building. That was where Alfred had lived and peeped in on me with his hidden camera. It was also where someone had called in the prank fire alarm where I'd found the drug and had probably been given the drug. Something was definitely going on in my neighborhood.

The sound of Mendoza's car door opening brought me back to the present. "I don't know why I just cleaned up the glass from the jar of fingers that *you* busted," he grumbled. He swung himself into the car and turned on the ignition.

I didn't answer, and he didn't seem to mind so we drove back to my apartment in silence. Upon arriving, I opened the car door and stepped out carefully, gripping the jar of fingers tightly. To my dismay, Mendoza got out of the car too.

"Don't you have to go back to the station or something?" I asked.

"What? You don't like my company?"

"Uh-uh."

"I haven't finished questioning you yet."

I cocked my head to the side. "Oh really, then why didn't you make the most of your time on the ride back."

Mendoza shrugged. "I was pondering the evidence."

"Pondering, huh?" I rolled my eyes and started walking toward the entrance to the building. I heard Mendoza following behind me. He followed me to my apartment door.

"Does it look okay to you?" he asked.

"Yep, it looks like we left it," I replied. I was relieved that it appeared that no one had visited while I was away. I pushed the door open and poked my head into the apartment. Everything appeared quiet and undisturbed. I turned back to Mendoza. "Everything looks fine, you can go now."

Mendoza didn't move. "I have some more questions, Charlie."

I sighed, "Can you ask them later? I want to take a shower."

Mendoza nodded. "I'll be back in an hour."

I started to protest, but he held up a hand to stop me. "You made an agreement with me. Would you rather forget the shower and accompany me to the police station?"

I considered the options. Talk to Mendoza in an hour or go to jail. Hmm. "Okay," I said, "see you in an hour," and I shut the door in his face, which made me feel a little better about the whole situation.

## Chapter 16

After depositing the fingers back into my refrigerator, I went directly to the shower and took my time under the hot spray. I lathered my hair slowly and massaged my scalp, where the last vestiges of my morning headache were finally beginning to ease. I then lathered my bath mitt and smoothed it over my skin, starting with my arms, then proceeding to my breasts. I couldn't help thinking about how Dr. Macgregor's hand had felt on them the previous evening.

Just as I was relaxing and remembering that sensation, Mendoza's face popped into mind. I shook my head to clear the image and tried again. The same thing happened. Somehow, Mendoza had wormed his way into my head and was seriously interfering with my Dr. Macgregor fantasy. I gave it one more shot, then gave up. It wasn't that Mendoza's appearance dispelled those lovely warm sensations; it was more like it added an extra tingle, which I found more than a little disturbing. I felt as though I was being disloyal to Dr. Macgregor. I wondered about the tension between the two men and decided to see if I could get anything out of Mendoza about their relationship when he came back.

I quickly finished lathering the rest of my body, ending with my legs and hips. As I was finishing up, I ran the bath mitt over my hip and noticed a very tender spot just above it. I twisted around as far as my body would allow in an attempt to see the area. I saw what appeared to be a nasty bruise, but because of the angle I couldn't get a good look. I couldn't fathom how I could have received it. I hadn't fallen since my shower the night before and it wasn't there then.

I finished my morning routine and pulled on a pair of faded jeans and a warm and cozy turtleneck sweater. When Mendoza came back, I was in the kitchen making a cup of tea.

"I tried to knock, but the door sort of swung open when I rapped." he said, startling me from the calm the hot shower had instilled. "Wow, you sure clean up well. I almost didn't recognize you from behind."

I turned from the counter and my tea and gave him a look that said "drop dead."

Unfazed, he went on, "I mean, now that it's clear that you actually have a behind." He grinned a slow, lazy smile and lounged against the opposite counter, waiting for my retort.

I intensified my gaze, intending to wither his cocky smile but, much to my chagrin, his smile only grew wider. "I brought you breakfast. It's on the table in the living room."

My gaze wavered. "Breakfast? What kind of breakfast?" I suddenly realized that I was famished.

"A cheese and spinach omelet and..." he paused as if he were waiting for a drum roll.

"And..." I repeated, although the thought of the omelet already had my mouth watering.

"Krispy Kremes."

The death gaze really started to fizzle now. "What kind of Krispy Kremes?" I was trying really hard not to be a donut whore.

"Curlers." He waggled his eyebrows.

My death gaze sputtered out completely. "You must be the ultimate ladies' man."

"I have had my fair share of experience." He moved away from the counter, and I followed him from the kitchen to the living room. Not only had he brought donuts and an omelet, but there were also hash brown potatoes and yogurt smoothies.

"Wow," I said. "You must have really thought I could consume some food."

"Actually," he replied, uncapping the lid of his smoothie, "I did." My glare resurfaced and he hurriedly continued, "Not that there's anything wrong with that. It's just that those sweats you were wearing this morning really didn't do you justice."

I didn't dignify that with a reply and dove into my omelet and hash browns. We worked our way through the food in an oddly companionable silence, finally coming up for air after the last curler.

"That was really good. Thanks," I offered.

"You're welcome." He wiped his mouth with his napkin and tossed it on the table. "Are you ready to get down to business?"

I sighed. I'd been admiring that wonderfully masculine, but sensual mouth, and wondering how many women he was currently wooing with Krispy Kremes. I really had to take care of the virginity thing. My hormones were apparently driving me mad. "If we must," I finally replied. "What sort of questions do you have for me?"

"What do you know about Alfred Tenny?" He asked, pulling his notebook and pen out of his pocket.

I shrugged. "Next to nothing, other than he said he didn't have any family. I do know which law firm he uses because of the letterhead on my lease. Speaking of which, do you have any idea whom I'm supposed to pay rent to now?"

Mendoza shook his head, indicating a negative response. "We haven't been able to locate any heirs or family of any kind. We've already checked out the law office you're referring to and found that it doesn't seem to exist. Your building might wind up being put up for auction."

I grimaced. "The thought of my home going to the highest bidder doesn't feel too good. How could the law firm not exist?"

Mendoza shrugged. "I have a feeling Tenny may have drawn up that letterhead himself. I found a ream of it in his apartment."

"Why would he do that?" I wondered.

"So his renters would take him seriously. He gets mileage out of a seemingly legal document without having to ante up the lawyer's fee."

"Good grief! I always felt that he was a little sleazy, but it seems he just gets slimier and slimier. What a pervert!" I was still a little more than angry about the video cameras.

Mendoza knew exactly where my head was. "Yeah, I heard about the videos. Gorman and Stefansky's report states that the tapes are basically of you in the bathroom—very little bedroom footage. I thought you might like to know that, unless anything comes up, I'll probably let their statement stand as is without viewing the tapes myself."

I looked at Mendoza with skepticism. "Really?" On the one hand, I was intensely relieved; on the other hand, I felt mildly insulted that he didn't have the urge to sneak a peek.

"Really," he answered. "Now, the other thing that has me concerned is why anyone would lift, then return those, um, fingers you've been carrying around. Any ideas on your part?"

I pondered his question. "Absolutely none. I feel like someone is trying to mess with my head. I mean, not just with the finger thing but with the drug thing as well. It just doesn't make any sense to me."

Mendoza was silent for a minute. "The drug in your system is used as a 'truth serum. Do you have any deep dark secrets or information that anyone might want to know that you're not willing to share for some reason?"

The only thing I could think of that most people wouldn't know about me was the fact that I was a virgin. Other than that, nothing came to mind. Who'd care about that fact anyway? I sighed and shrugged. "No, nothing."

"I get the sense that you're protecting someone with regard to the drug. Care to share anything on that topic?" Mendoza asked.

I don't know if it was the warm feeling of a full belly or just the quiet, nonjudgmental tone of Mendoza's voice, but I found myself wanting to tell him everything about Haley and where I had found the vial. Even so, I still wanted to check that avenue myself first. "I want to, honestly, but not now."

Mendoza considered my response and nodded. "You have until tomorrow."

I nodded, and then stood up to clear the table. Seeing my intent, Mendoza stood as well and began to help. I leaned over to reach for the empty donut box and accidentally bumped my hip on the table. I must have hit the sore spot I'd found in the shower, because a sharp pain pierced through me. I yelped in spite of myself, dropped the donut box, and rubbed my hip.

"You okay?" Mendoza asked with raised eyebrows.

"Yeah," I answered. "I think I hit a bruise I discovered earlier this morning."

Mendoza set the breakfast debris he'd collected back down on the table. "What sort of bruise?"

I continued to clear the table. "You know, a purplish spot on the skin, usually received as the result of some kind of trauma. It's in a spot that's tough to see, I didn't get a good look at it, and I haven't a clue as to how and when I got it." I turned and walked into the kitchen to deposit the trash in the garbage can. Mendoza followed me.

I tossed the garbage into the can and turned to face him. He had an odd look on his face.

"*What?*" I asked, somewhat uncomfortable with his intense scrutiny.

"I want to see the bruise," he stated matter-of-factly.

"Say what?"

"You heard me."

"Well you can't, I'd have to drop my drawers," I argued. "And for what earthly reason would you want to see my bruise?" My eyes narrowed at a thought that came to my mind. "Unless you're just trying to get my pants off."

I felt my face burn when Mendoza laughed. "You have such a *lively* imagination. Sweetie, if I wanted your drawers down, I'd find a much more creative way to get them there." He paused with an odd little smile. "Not that the idea is unappealing."

Mendoza got back to the subject at hand. "I know it sounds a little nuts, but I think it may be important. You'll have to trust me on this."

I shook my head no. "Uh-uh. No can do."

Mendoza sighed, "Do I have to remind you of our little agreement? Would you rather participate in a strip search downtown?"

My eyes shot daggers at him. "*You wouldn't!*"

Mendoza smiled. "Try me."

I sighed. I knew he meant it. "Oh crap, okay." I turned my back to him and began to unfasten my jeans. I heard Mendoza step closer, and I felt my entire body suffuse with color.

I unzipped my jeans and started scrunching them off my hips a little at a time. I was supremely thankful that I'd worn a pair of my "good" panties. They were made of pale blue lace with tiny side straps. I'd wanted to feel pretty after Mendoza had dragged me around in my sweats earlier.

Mendoza moved closer to me, and I jumped a mile high when his fingers touched my newly exposed skin.

"Calm down," came his quiet voice. I could feel his breath on my neck and, even though for all intents and purposes I knew Mendoza was being totally impersonal, I found that tiny electric sparks were racing and colliding around in my body. Stupid hormones, I chided myself.

I felt Mendoza's fingers move lightly over the affected area. His breath puffed on my neck again, causing goose bumps to erupt over my entire body, when he said, "The entire bruise isn't exposed. I need to push your panties down just a bit."

I felt the heat of his blue eyes on my backside and protested. "Are you sure? I mean, all in all, this is rather uncomfortable."

Mendoza's fingers slipped lightly under the elastic of my panties, and I yelped with the unexpectedness of certain, err, sensations. "Relax," he said, as he moved the panties down a bit. "After all, it's not as though I'm the only man beside your father who's ever seen your backside."

I don't know what possessed me, but without thinking I blurted out the sorry truth. "Oh yes you are."

Mendoza's fingers stopped for a moment, then he continued to explore the bruise. "You're joking."

I didn't answer because Gorman and Stefansky came barging through the kitchen door at precisely that moment.

## Chapter 17

"Holy mole and good grief!" exclaimed Stefansky. "She's at it again! No wonder there wasn't any video action in the bedroom, she uses the kitchen and the living room instead!"

I jumped up, turned around and hitched up my pants, burning with embarrassment. I fumbled with the zipper, and when Mendoza looked like he was going to help, I held up a hand. "Don't you dare!" I finally was able to yank the zipper up, and then I turned to glare at the three men. "Has no one ever heard of knocking?!" I yelled.

Gorman and Stefansky took a step back. "We tried," said Gorman matter-of-factly, "But the door swung open."

I opened and closed my mouth a few times, searching for words, but found none. I marched past the men into the living room, plopped down on the couch and put my head in my hands.

The three men followed and stood over me. "Hey," said Stefansky, "it's cool."

Mendoza looked thoroughly amused, the other officers looked—well—positively gleeful. Gorman looked at Mendoza. "You sure move fast, man."

Mendoza just shrugged. I wanted to smack him for not showing any support.

"What do you guys want?" I asked wearily.

"The locksmith," Stefansky explained, "he should be here any minute to fix your door."

As if on cue, the door to my apartment swung open again and the locksmith entered. "Oops, tried to knock. You guys call for a locksmith?" he asked. He looked 60-ish and was dressed in a navy blue jumpsuit with the name Jack stitched over the left chest pocket.

"Welcome Jack," I said. "You have no idea how happy I am to see you."

"Well," Jack answered, "given the state of your door, I imagine you're about as happy as anyone ever is to see me. Is the front door the only one that needs fixing?"

I nodded. "I only have a front door. How long do you think you'll be?"

Jack looked at the door and thought for a moment. "Probably about an hour or so if you want me to fix the gap in the jamb as well."

"How much do you charge an hour?" I asked.

"Well, given the short notice and all, it'll be a little more. Let's say, oh, about $100 an hour plus parts."

My mouth fell open.

"It *is* short notice," Gorman added helpfully.

I sighed and gave the okay. I made a mental note never to be too involved to answer the door for the fire department again and wondered if the fire department would consider compensating me for the door. Given the entertainment value they'd gotten, it only seemed fair for them to pitch in.

Mendoza drew his coat on and asked Gorman and Stefansky to wait for him outside before they went back to the station house. They said they would and started out the door.

"See you guys later," I called after Gorman and Stefansky as they left. They didn't look back, but I heard Gorman say under his breath, "Now why wouldn't that surprise me?"

I turned back to Mendoza who was regarding me with a quizzical expression. "We're not done talking, but I have to go back to the station for a bit. I'll be back."

He waited for me to agree but I hesitated. "What else could there possibly be?" I asked. I was feeling as though I was losing total control of my life, my home and my schedule. I wanted some time alone not only to regain my sanity but also to allow me to snoop on Haley.

Mendoza must have sensed some of what I was thinking, because his tone softened just a tad. "Listen, there's something I want to show you that I have a feeling may be important, and I have to go back to the station to get it. Bear with me for a while longer, okay?"

I looked at him and almost started to like him—that is, until I remembered our agreement and the fact that, if I didn't agree to cooperate, he'd probably throw handcuffs on me and haul me downtown anyway. "I don't have much of a choice, do I?" I asked.

Mendoza's mouth tightened at my tone, which wasn't very neutral. "Actually, no. You don't," he replied. Without another word, he went through the door, nearly colliding with Sherrie in the process. Sherrie spun around and did a double take, as she watched Mendoza go down the hall with the other two officers until they exited at the end.

She turned back toward me, her eyes wide with wonder. "Who, who, who?"

I plopped down on my couch and motioned for her to sit down. "What's that supposed to mean—who, who, who? You sound like and owl. With your eyes all round and crazy like that, you kind of look like one too."

Sherrie took a moment, recovered her normal expression and sat down. "I know that my first question should be why were the police here and what happened to your door, but all I really want to know at this moment is who was that hunk in the blue jeans that just walked out of here with such a fierce look on his face?"

"Oh him, that's Detective Mendoza," I answered dryly. "He's been *lots* of fun," I added sarcastically.

"Oh, honey," Sherrie replied. "I bet he's a whole lot fun *all night long.*" And she sighed like a lovesick teenager.

"Snap out of it, Sherrie. He's just a man," I said rather irritably. "Who cares if he fills his blue jeans in a way that's absolutely sinful?" I paused and realized that it was the middle of the day on a weekday. "What are you doing here, anyway? Aren't you supposed to be at work?"

"I could ask the same of you," Sherrie replied. "Actually I *was* at work. Then one of my clients decided she was having a stroke while we were doing charka therapy, and I had to accompany her to the hospital." She paused for a moment and glanced at Jack, who was busily repairing my door. She leaned in and changed her tone to a whisper before continuing. "I asked for you at the desk, but they told me you'd been there for a drug test and were arrested for possession. What the heck is going on?"

I groaned. Whatever had been left of my reputation at Cedars was now totally and completely shredded to pieces. Joyce was going to pay dearly for her busy mouth when I got back.

"Well?" Sherrie asked in her normal tone. "Spill it."

I sighed, "It all started with Dr. Macgregor."

"The hottie resident?" Sherrie cut in.

"Yeah, the hottie resident."

I went on to give her a quick and brief description of the sequence of events, with Sherrie interrupting every now and then for more details—especially surrounding Mendoza and Dr. Macgregor.

When I finished, Sherrie sat there speechless, shaking her head.

"Wow, lady," came Jack's voice from the doorway. "You should write for those daytime stories on television. You'd have yourself a hit there for sure."

I rolled my eyes, and Sherrie laughed. "He's right, you know. I think you've stepped into the twilight zone."

"Hey, Jack." I asked. "How much longer?"

"Just finishing up," He replied.

I turned back to Sherrie "Anyway, my plan is to visit my neighbor and see if perhaps I can get some answers without her catching onto the fact that I know something."

Sherrie nodded. Her next question had me wondering if she'd even heard what I had just said. "Why do you suppose Dr. Macgregor dislikes your sexy little detective so much?"

I sighed, "Did you even hear what I just said?"

"Sure, sure," she answered, "it's just that..."

"Never mind," I cut in. "I actually was wondering that myself. When I asked Sam, he didn't want to talk about it. I was going to ask Mendoza, but the impromptu butt inspection threw me off."

Jack meandered over, bill in hand. "Um, here you go, miss. After hearing your story, I decided to give you a bit of a discount."

I looked at the bill. The total was $147, less two bucks, bringing the grand total to $145. I tried to smile. "Gee thanks, Jack."

I pulled out my purse, wrote a check and handed it over to Jack. He took the check and started to turn to leave but hesitated and turned back to me. "Miss, I hope you don't mind, but it was really hard not to hear what you two were just talking about."

"Jack," I replied, "I'm pretty sure just about everyone in town has heard my story by now, along with lots of fun embellishments and fabrications. Don't worry about it."

He still didn't move to go, and I raised my brows in question.

"I can help you," he blurted out.

"Huh?" I asked.

"I can help you with your neighbor, I mean." He looked like an eager child.

"You mean Haley?" I asked. "How?"

"Well, it sounds like what you really need to do is get back into that apartment without Haley being there so you can snoop around a bit, right?" He looked like he was ready to start bouncing up and down with his enthusiasm to help.

"Jack," I held up my hand, "you realize that you're talking about breaking and entering, right?" I thumped my chest with the flat of my hand. "Do I look like the type of person to just break into somebody's home?"

Jack looked hurt. "No, but then again you don't look like a druggie either. Besides, I'm not talking about breaking in. I'm talking about walking in through the front door via a key."

"You have a key to Haley's apartment?" I asked, bewildered.

Jack puffed up with pride. "I've got a key to every apartment in this place."

"How come?" I asked.

"Mr. Tenny," Jack replied. "He had me install the locks and make him a skeleton key to fit every lock in the place about four years ago."

In spite of myself, I was feeling just a little excited by this new development. "If you made it for Alfred, how is it that you still have it?" I asked.

Jack smiled. "I make an extra for every skeleton key I'm asked to make. That way if an owner happens to lose theirs, I don't have to refabricate the thing from scratch."

"Come on now, Charlie," Sherrie butted in, "you can't possibly be thinking of sneaking into...."

"Shhhh!" I said waving her off. I looked at Jack. "How much to borrow your key?"

"Oh, I don't want money," Jack said sheepishly. "I want to know how all this ends up, including the romance stuff."

I laughed and Jack blushed. "Come on," he said, "you probably think the life of a locksmith is really exciting." He paused and looked at Sherrie and me expectantly.

Sherrie and I looked at him blankly.

"Well," he went on, "the fact is, we're only called in *after* everything has already happened, and we rarely get the story behind the busted door or why the locks need to be changed."

"Charlie," Sherrie spoke up again, "I still don't think you should…"

I silenced her with a glare, then turned back to Jack and smiled. "How soon can you get me the key?"

Jack pulled his shirt up above his belt and pointed to a large ring of keys. "Right now."

I wanted to kiss him.

Jack worked the key off the ring and handed it over to me. "Now don't forget, Charlie, I want that key back and I want to hear the rest of the story okay?"

"Don't worry, Jack, you'll get both. Thank you." I pocketed the key in my front pocket of my jeans.

I glanced at Sherrie, who had a stern look on her face that resembled a mother hen and her arms crossed across her chest. I could have sworn she was also tapping her foot just a bit.

Jack handed over the new keys to my apartment, made me promise to be careful and left, quietly closing the door behind him.

**Chapter 18**

I went to the door as soon as it closed and threw the lock. The sound of it sliding into place sounded so sweet that I felt like doing a happy dance. Catching sight of Sherrie's disapproving stare sputtered my steps before I really even got started.

"You are *not* going to use that key to break into Haley's apartment." Sherrie spoke with quiet deliberateness.

"Oh, yes I am." I took the key from my pocket and waved it in the air. "*and* I'm going to use the key to check out Alfred's place too."

Sherrie looked like she was going to have a coronary. "Have you lost your mind? What if you get caught? You're already just a hair's breath away from jail!"

I was silent for a moment, then spoke, "Sherrie, did you understand what I just told you? My life has been turned crazy, upside down! Someone gave me drugs. I feel completely violated both physically and emotionally." I paused and grabbed her hand for either emphasis or strength or both. "I have to do *something*. I have to feel like I have a say in what happens to me."

Sherrie nodded, "I guess I can understand that. Can you let go of my hand though? I can't feel it and I sort of need it for my job."

I laughed. "You mean the one you should be at now?"

Sherrie looked at her watch. "Yep! Gotta go, but I want to be your lookout when you enter your neighbors' homes illegally."

I raised an eyebrow. "Are you sure about that? That would make you an accomplice, you know."

Sherrie shrugged. "Well, hell, maybe we'll end up on the same cell block. The place could probably use some spicing up anyway."

There was a knock at the door, and I grinned, thinking how delightful that people actually had to knock now that I had a lock that worked. I went to answer the door while Sherrie put her coat on.

It was Mendoza. He was holding a rather thick-looking file in one hand and a drink carrier with two lattes in the other.

"My, my! You are good at this aren't you?" I was referring to the lattes. "What kind did you get?"

"Black coffee for me as I don't care for girlie froufrou coffee, and a toffee nut latte for you, with skim milk, of course."

"Hmm, perfect. How'd you know?"

He shrugged. "I'm a detective, remember? I find people tend to gravitate toward expressions of themselves. You're a tough nut with a sugary coating and not much into excess. Toffee nut, skim milk—see?"

I wasn't sure I did, but I let it go. He had followed me in after I closed the door and Sherrie introduced herself. "I'm Sherrie, a very good friend of Charlie's." She batted her eyelashes in a way that made me want to cringe. "So what flavor do you think *I* am?"

Mendoza looked amused and flashed Sherrie a smile that looked genuine. "Oh, I'm sure it's something really sweet, but I wouldn't want to attempt to guess without spending a bit more time with you."

Sherrie gleamed, "That can be arranged."

I felt a flash of something that felt weirdly akin to jealousy. "Well," I interrupted, "too bad you have to go back to work, Sherrie. Are you still coming by tonight—say, eight o'clock or so?" I was hoping she'd remember her offer to be lookout for me.

Sherrie reluctantly turned away from Mendoza. "Sure." Then she turned *back* to Mendoza obviously in no hurry to leave. "I wouldn't mind…"

She didn't have a chance to finish, because I grabbed her arm and marched her to the door. "Gosh, Sherrie! Would you look at the time!"

Sherrie gave me a wide-eyed look, as if to say "What the heck!" as I shoved her through the door, but she was too surprised to say anything. I turned back to Mendoza. He had a look on his face that very strongly suggested that he was laughing at me.

"What?" I asked.

"You sure were in a hurry to get rid of your friend there."

"Yeah? Well, it's actually *you* I'm in a hurry to get rid of. What did you want to talk about?"

He sat down on the couch and motioned to me to do the same. He opened his folder and started going through the contents.

I took a seat beside him and tried to see what he was studying. The papers looked like photocopies of textbooks.

"First of all," Mendoza started to say while still shuffling through the papers, "I need to ask you a very personal question."

"No, you can't see my ass again."

Mendoza smirked at my flippant response and, without missing a beat, asked, "Are you a virgin?"

I felt myself turn three shades of red and break out in a cold sweat. I opened my mouth to speak several times, but nothing came out. I finally gave up and just stared at Mendoza, speechless.

"You know you don't have to speak," Mendoza offered. "You could just nod up and down for yes and side to side for no."

I still didn't move.

"Okaaaay. How about you blink twice for no and once for yes?" he suggested

I felt myself blink by accident.

Mendoza brightened for a moment, then looked perplexed. "Was that a blink, blink, or was that a yes?"

I finally found my voice. "What does my virginity have to do with anything?"

"Ah ha!" Mendoza pounced. "So you are!"

I thought about denying it but decided it wasn't worth the effort. I was wondering at what age my virginity had become a "bad" thing anyway.

"Yeah, so what?" I answered. I stuck my chin out defiantly.

Mendoza didn't even glance up but started ruffling through his papers with a great deal more enthusiasm. "How did that happen?" he asked as he shuffled his papers.

"Oh Jeez," I replied. "You want to know *why* I'm still a virgin?"

Mendoza glanced up. "Well, it's not as though you're scary or anything. And for someone who's never actually had sex, well you just *exude* sexuality."

"I *exude*?" I repeated somewhat lamely.

Mendoza nodded, his attention still on the papers. "The way you eat a donut, for instance…. enough to bring a man to his knees."

Mendoza was so engrossed in his papers that I wasn't sure he realized what he was saying. It was as though his mouth were on autopilot while his brain scanned the work in front of him.

I'd never thought about the way I ate donuts before. I decided to pay more attention next time I had one.

"So, is it religious beliefs, some traumatic childhood exposure, or something else?" He finally looked up from his papers and pinned me with his intense gaze.

I was silent a moment while I tried to put it together myself. "Well," I finally began, "I didn't date much in high school. A lesbian had a crush on me, and she spread a rumor that we were an item. My father was a well-known preacher, and that may have had something to do with it."

"You're dad's a *preacher*?" Mendoza seemed stunned.

"He *was* a preacher. He died three years ago. So what about it?" I asked a bit defensively.

Mendoza grinned. "Oh nothing, it's just I've always had this fantasy about...."

I held up my hand, cutting him off. "Enough said."

Mendoza just kept on grinning. "I'm just saying you can't blame your virginity on your dad. A preacher's daughter, that's the stuff of adolescent male fantasies. What about after high school?"

"I went to St. Mary's Baptist University." I paused for a moment. "I fell for and became engaged to Morgan Townsend, the son of a very up-and-coming state senator, and we got engaged."

Mendoza raised an eyebrow. "I assume you're talking about Senator Skip Townsend's son."

I nodded yes. "I felt special when I was with him, and appearances were as important to him as they were to my father. In my father's opinion, Morgan was perfect. Now that I think about it, maybe he should have been dating my dad instead of me."

Mendoza looked perplexed. "How long were you with him?"

I winced, "Three and a half years."

Mendoza let loose a soft whistle, "And he never managed to get into your pants?" His tone was incredulous.

I shrugged. "He never tried. He said he wanted to wait until we were married." I paused, remembering those days for a moment, and then went on. "I thought I'd go crazy with those hormonal urges and lustful surges. We'd be necking and petting, and I'd get crazier and crazier until I would practically beg him to take me, and still he wouldn't. His vow to wait was that strong!"

Mendoza snorted. "Strong? Uh-uh. Crazy stupid? Yeah. There had to have been something very much amiss with that young man."

I felt a weird surge of gratitude toward Mendoza. Then I remembered whom I was speaking to and did a mental head slap. I was giving *Mendoza* the play-by-play account of my miserable sex life. Yikes!

"So?" Mendoza wanted more.

"So, what?" I was reluctant to go on. I was mortified at what I'd already told him.

"Why aren't you married, living in your senatorial type of mansion and giving birth to little Skips, Biffs, or Buffys?"

I narrowed my eyes and glared at Mendoza. "I had an epiphany."

"Epiphan-what?" Mendoza looked annoyed.

"Epiphany. Look it up, expand your vocabulary a bit."

Mendoza narrowed his eyes at me. "I have a perfectly fine vocabulary."

I decided to let it go and hoped he would too. "So again I ask you, what does being a virgin have to do with anything?"

Mendoza ignored the question. "Wait, there are still a few years to cover here. What kept you from giving it up after the ephin... oh hell, .the 'we may never know what happened episode' with Townsend?"

I took a sip of my now cold latte. "Not much."

"Obviously."

"Very funny. Ha! Ha!" I took another sip of the latte in an attempt to hide my discomfort.

"Okay, sorry." Mendoza did his best to look contrite. The look didn't work on him, and he ended up looking more mentally disabled than anything, which made me laugh out loud.

"What's so funny? I'm trying to apologize here." Mendoza lost the look and went into a guarded glare.

"You shouldn't try to look apologetic," I eked out between guffaws, "It's definitely not a good look for you."

Mendoza sighed and waited patiently until I finished. "So, are you going to tell me about the last couple of years?"

I wiped away tears of mirth and grinned. "The last couple of years I've spent trying to build a life for myself. I worked for NERT for a while, traveling mostly to areas that were ravaged by floods, hurricanes or tornadoes to help the needy. That wasn't much of an atmosphere for fostering any romantic partnerships. In between, I'd land here, regroup and go out again. Then God took a vacation from creating natural disasters, which effectively put me out of work. I waited God out for a while, living on savings, and then was forced to take a real job—if a real job is what you want to call what I've been doing the last few days."

Mendoza digested this information in silence. "Okay," he finally said, "I want you to listen to what I have to say with an open mind. What I'm about to tell you may sound crazy, but I can't help but feel there's a link between your virginity and Alfred's death."

My jaw dropped. "*Please* don't mention anything to do with my sex life and Alfred in the same sentence. That's just plain sick."

Mendoza didn't answer. Instead, he handed me one of the photocopies he'd sorted from the rest. It was a sketch of three coins. Each coin looked like a replica of the others. The coins looked vaguely familiar, and I tried to place them. A caption was printed underneath the sketch of the coins; it read "The Tufalic coins—legend dictates all three must be present for the rite to succeed."

I studied the coins and remembered that Alfred had written an article about some coins. I wondered what coins Alfred had written about. My question was answered in the next instant, when Mendoza placed Alfred's article on my lap. It was entitled "Tufalic Legend: Truth or Fairy Tale?" The article was submitted by Alfred Tenny.

I raised my eyebrows and looked at Mendoza. "This is all very interesting, but what does this legend or these coins have to do with my virginity?"

## Chapter 19

Mendoza tapped the article that was still resting in my lap. "According to this, back in the time when Druids were still hugging trees and fairies were as common as bumble bees, there was a group of people called the Trufalic clan. They had a certain mystic healing ability that was very valuable and sought after by many other people at that time. Though the clan was difficult to find, some seekers did find these people and begged them to teach them their healing arts, but the Trufalics refused. They claimed that the art could not be taught, that it was inherited through this ritual by only a chosen few."

"Hmm, I've never even heard of them." I scanned the article, flipping pages.

"Not many have," answered Mendoza. "However, most museums would pay a fortune to have those coins in their possession. The Smithsonian had one of the coins on display until the day before Alfred died."

"Why did they take it off display?" I asked, still scanning the article.

"More like *who* took it off display."

I stopped reading and looked at Mendoza. "You mean they don't know where it is?"

Mendoza nodded. "The coin disappeared. According to the police report, they think it was an inside job, because no alarms were set off and nothing else was disturbed. Whoever took it was interested only in the coin."

I sat there, silently digesting this new information. It seemed incredibly odd that the coin stolen from the museum had been the very kind that Alfred had written about. Then the next day—bam, Alfred's dead.

"So. I'm still wondering what all this has to do with the fact that I'm a virgin?" I said when I finally spoke again.

Mendoza stood and started gathering his papers. "Read the article. See if you find anything that might give you an idea of an answer to that question."

I looked down at the article that I had been scanning. It was at least 10 pages long or more. I looked back up at Mendoza, who was now slipping his coat on, and I felt oddly disappointed. "Are you finally going to leave me alone for a while?" I asked.

"Yep," he nodded as he spoke. "There are some things I need to do back at the station. Anyway, you look like you could use a nap or something." He reached into his back pocket, pulled out his wallet and extracted a card. He tossed the card on the table. "If anything comes up in the meantime, here's my card. Don't hesitate to call me."

I picked up the card and read "Roman Mendoza, Investigator." It listed the address of his precinct and his telephone and cell phone number. "Thanks, but before I forget, there's something I wanted to ask you."

Mendoza was slipping his gloves on and he paused. "Oh yeah? What's that?"

I cleared my throat. I felt like I was betraying Dr. Macgregor in some odd way, but I really felt the need to know what was going on between the two men.

"Well?" Mendoza seemed anxious to leave.

"I was wondering about you and Sam, I mean Dr. Macgregor," I said. "There's obviously some tension between you two."

Mendoza slipped off his gloves and sat down. He was silent for a moment, then cleared his throat. "Well what did Sam tell you? Did you ask him?"

I nodded. "He didn't want to talk about it. He said it was better left for later."

Mendoza was silent for another moment. "If I was fair, I'd let him tell you his version of the story first. But from where I stand, he hasn't been very fair in the telling in the past."

I waited for him to go on.

Mendoza shrugged out of his coat and stared into space for a moment, as though trying to figure out where to begin. Finally, he began to speak.

"Sam and I were the best of friends all through high school. We played sports together—namely, football. Although we were friends, we were very competitive with each other."

"As friends often are," I commented.

He nodded. "It was a healthy rivalry. It kept both of us on our toes and in peak physical condition. We were the stars of our football team. I was a quarterback and he was a wide receiver." Mendoza paused and was quiet for a moment. "We had a great time all through high school. Our friendly rivalry didn't stop on the football field, though. It poured over into classes, part-time jobs, cars—everything. We were constantly competing. If Sam got a B in science, I had to get a B+. If I bought a used Mustang, Sam would have to get a brand-new one. If I got a pretty girlfriend, Sam would find a prettier one."

"I get the point," I commented dryly. "So where did the trouble start?"

"Where it always does—over a girl, of course," Mendoza said wryly. "Her name was Kimberly Hawthorne. She transferred to our school during our senior year." Mendoza fell silent again, and a wistful look came into his eyes.

I waited for a moment, and then nudged him along. "Detective Mendoza? Are you still with me here?" I teased.

Mendoza pulled himself back to the present. "Sam saw her first. She was petite, maybe five foot three and a hundred pounds soaking wet."

"Let me guess," I interrupted. "She was blonde, blue-eyed, and stacked."

Mendoza's look gave me the distinct impression that I'd overstepped some sacred bounds. I made a note to myself to speak about Kimberly Hawthorne with reverent respect. "Sorry," I said rather lamely.

"Kimberly was a waif. She had long, dark hair—so dark that it looked almost blue in some lights. Her eyes were dark-green and they were huge. She looked so fragile, as though the slightest touch might break her. When Sam told me about her, I thought he was exaggerating, but when I saw her for myself, it was as though Sam had understated her beauty rather than exaggerated it. We were both head over heels in love with her at first sight, but as I'd said, Sam had seen her first. Our rule was if you called something first, you had first dibs."

"Did the girl have any say in the matter?" I asked.

"Actually, no. Sam had first dibs, so I stood back and let him do his thing to try and woo her. I knew that if she didn't go for it, I would get my chance."

"Did you get your chance with Kimberly?" I asked.

Mendoza's gaze was stoic. "No, I didn't. She fell for Sam quickly. She had come from a broken home, where there wasn't much joy or money. Sam quickly became her real family. He was kind and generous, and he came from a very moneyed family—quite the opposite from what she was used to. She looked to him for everything."

"So what happened?" I wondered out loud.

Mendoza went on as though I hadn't spoken. "I spent quite a bit of time with the two of them. We went on double dates a lot. I never seemed to be able to keep a girlfriend for very long, though. When I was in between girls, Sam and Kimberly let me hang out with them. I hate to admit it, but I got pretty jealous. It was impossible for anyone to meet Kimberly and not fall for her. It's funny though, I'm not sure if I was jealous because of her or of the idea of what she and Sam shared. Kimberly was beautiful, but she had some rough edges that bothered me at the time. I thought she might be hiding something, but I didn't have a clue what that might be. When I mentioned this to Sam, he said that she was just that way because she had been raised in a harsh atmosphere."

"Harsh atmosphere?" I asked.

Mendoza nodded. "Sam told me that she'd been abused from a young age, that her stepfather was just as abusive as her real father had been. According to Sam, the abuse was mostly verbal, but some punches were thrown in for good measure, nothing sexual though. Anyway, that's why she was with Sam so much—to escape being under a roof with her stepfather. Not only was I jealous of Sam because I thought I'd fallen for her, but I was also resentful of the fact that I never seemed to get Sam to myself for a guys' night."

"I still don't see the reason you and Sam are no longer friends." I gave him a look that said, "Get on with it."

"It happened the night of the senior prom. Sam, of course, was going with Kimberly, and I didn't have a date. Sam called the day before the prom and told me that he had something important to tell me. I told him to stop over on his way to the prom and teased him about wanting to see him all dressed up like a peacock. He agreed. When he showed up, I razzed him about his tuxedo and told him he looked like a giant penguin. He laughed, but he had a really serious air about him so I told him to tell me what was up. Sam pulled a small box from his pocket and opened it so I could see what was inside. It was an engagement ring. I'd fallen hard for Kimberly and it wasn't easy to appear overjoyed for Sam, the man."

Even though the whole story sounded rather like a bad soap opera, I couldn't help but feel a little bit sorry for Mendoza. "Well, obviously, Sam didn't marry the girl, and neither did you. So what happened?"

" I sat around for the rest of the night drinking my dad's beer and feeling really sorry for myself. I finally went to bed, and at about 2 o'clock in the morning, someone woke me by throwing pebbles at my window. I went to the window and saw Kimberly on my lawn. I didn't waste time and left the house to see what she wanted."

"Wow, I would have thought she'd have been snuggled up with Sam by then—with a diamond on her finger and a smile on her face."

"I had, too," Mendoza shrugged at the thought, "but that wasn't the case. She was on my lawn waiting to deliver the deathblow to my friendship with Sam. Actually, she had already delivered it, I just wasn't aware of it at the time."

Seeing my puzzled expression, Mendoza went on with his sorry tale.

"It turns out that the evening had gone pretty much the way Sam had planned—an elegant dinner, a few slow dances at the prom and then a trip to what we used to call Swan Lake. It was actually just a pretty little pond with some ducks hanging out on it, but it was about the only romantic setting to be found in the area. At the lake, he had spread out a blanket and put out a late-night picnic—complete with strawberries and champagne—that his parents had helped him put together"

"Wow, how romantic!" I sighed.

Mendoza snorted. "Yep, romantic all right, but it was mostly Sam's stepmother's idea. She even helped him pick out the ring."

"Party pooper." I accused Mendoza

Mendoza ignored me. " Sam popped the question and Kimberly said no."

"No?!" I hadn't expected that.

"No," Mendoza repeated. "Then, apparently she had gone on to tell Sam that she and I were involved and that she was carrying my baby."

"No!" I was in shock, then, after a moment's thought, I asked, "Were you? I mean, was she?"

"No!" Mendoza snapped. Apparently, I'd hit a soft spot. "Despite all the pent-up feelings I'd been carrying around, I never once lifted a finger to try to steal her from Sam," he continued. "As far as I was concerned, Sam was my brother. I couldn't hurt him!"

I held up my hand in a gesture of surrender. "Okay, okay! Down boy!"

Mendoza narrowed his eyes at me. "Are you making fun of me?"

Those narrowed eyes sent a jolt of electricity down my spine, and I knew better than to look anything other than sincere. "Absolutely not! You have my deepest and most sincere sympathy. But why would Kimberly tell Sam something like that? I mean, you'd think she'd know that the truth would have to come out. They had paternity tests back then, didn't they?"

"Yes they had paternity tests. I mean, it was only eight years ago. But no, the truth never did come out."

"Why? And why did she show up on your lawn that night?" I was really enjoying this in a warped kind of way.

"I asked her what she was doing there," Mendoza replied, "and she explained that she and Sam had had a fight. She said that she was pregnant, but it wasn't Sam's baby, and she couldn't possibly marry him under those circumstances. I asked her who the father was and she told me that Sam thought it was me. Then she ran away. That's the last I saw of Kimberly. It's the last anyone saw of her. She disappeared that night."

"Wow." I sat back, stunned. "Wow! What do you think happened to her?" I asked.

"I don't know," Mendoza replied. "No one does. Oh, there was a lot of questioning when she came up missing the next day and there was a lot of speculation around town. Sam was supposedly the last person she was seen with. I knew that she'd been okay when she left Sam, though, because she had come to see me. What happened after that is a total mystery. I told the police she'd come to see me but that I didn't know any more than that. With nothing to go on—no actual body and nothing to indicate foul play—she was ruled a runaway, and that was the end of the investigation. Her mother and stepfather moved out of town shortly after that."

"And Sam still thinks you betrayed him with his girlfriend?" I asked.

Mendoza nodded. "I recently discovered that he's convinced that I had something to do with her disappearance as well."

"You're kidding, right?"

"No, I'm not." An emotion so swift that I couldn't identify it crossed Mendoza's face. "After all those years of friendship too. Anyway, we graduated shortly after that and went our separate ways. He obviously went on to medical school—following in daddy's footsteps—and I went into criminal justice, and here we are today."

"Wow, thanks for sharing that with me." Now that I thought about it, I wondered why he did.

Mendoza answered my question before I could voice it. "Now that you know the history, maybe you'll tread a little more lightly where Sam is concerned. From what I understand, he's never gotten over the Kimberly thing and her rejection of him...well, perhaps *he* was somehow involved in her disappearance."

"What's *that* supposed to mean? That I shouldn't get pregnant and tell him the baby's yours? Or that I shouldn't fall too hard for a guy who may have made his girlfriend go bye-bye?" I was irrationally insulted that Mendoza was questioning my choice in men.

Mendoza had just finished shrugging back into his jacket, and he rocked back on his heels with a smirk on his face. "I like that first option. I mean, it could happen."

I threw one of my decorative sofa pillows at him. "In your dreams, buddy,"

"And maybe yours." His retort was just as quick. He was out the door, and it closed behind him before I could say another word. I picked up his card again and looked at the name: Roman Mendoza. He sure had some nerve and I decided that I liked it.

I checked my watch. It was just after 1 p.m. It felt like a year had passed since I'd woken with a thumping head in Haley's apartment. I went to my purse and took out my cell phone. It had been oddly quiet today, so I checked to make sure the battery was charged and the phone was on.

Sure enough, the battery was dead. I put the phone on the charger and took the empty latte cups to the kitchen. I then used the kitchen phone to call for my cell messages. The pleasant feminine voice programmed into the message center informed me that I had three new messages.

Whenever I would listen to my messages I'd have this image of a tiny lady sitting inside my phone, with a message pad in one hand and a pencil in the other, taking notes. I had had the same image of tiny people living inside my mother's kitchen radio when I was growing up as well. Although I now know the technicalities involved in radio waves and voice transmission, I still hadn't been able to completely lose the images of tiny people that I had carried around since my youth—they would probably live inside my electronics until the day I died.

I chose the new message option and listened. The first message was from my mother, who sounded hurt that I hadn't returned her phone call from the other day. I felt a surge of guilt and made a mental note to call her as soon as I finished listening to my messages. The second message was tagged as being from an unidentified caller. The call was from the hospital, telling me that someone named Horace was wondering about his fingers and had already called several times asking for me. I decided to deal with that issue tomorrow at work. The third message was from Sam, wondering if I'd made it home okay and if I was all right. I jotted down his phone number on my phone pad.

I called my mother. She answered on the second ring. "Meadows residence. May I help you?" When she answered this way it always irritated me. I knew my mother had caller I.D., and that she knew who was calling. I was getting the generic caller treatment because she was mad at me.

"Hi, Mom," I answered. "How are you?"

"Who is *this*? Do I know you?" came her sarcastic reply.

"Mom, you know very well who this is."

"I vaguely recognize the voice. Oh, you know what? You kind of sound like that girl I gave birth to—the one I gave my whole body and soul to, trying to raise her to be a good person, the type of person who might let her mother know that she's still alive now and then."

"Mom, " I tried to interrupt her.

"Where did I go wrong? Did I not give her enough hugs? Maybe I should have spanked her more."

I cut her off. "Mom, cut it out. I get the point! I'm sorry I haven't called, but it's been a little, err well, crazy lately with the new job and all." That certainly was the understatement of the year, I thought.

"Ahh, the new job. I'm so proud of you, sweetie—following in your mother's footsteps."

"Huh?" I asked. The only thing I'd told my mother about my job was that I'd be working at a desk job. "What do you mean?"

"Well, working in health care sweetie. That nice man who called last week said you'd be working in the Emergency Room, not at a desk like you told me. I guess you wanted to surprise me."

"What nice man, Mother? What did he want?" I was shocked that anyone had contacted my mother. I hadn't listed any information about my family on my application, and what possible reason could they have for wanting to speak with my mother in the first place?

"Oh, you know how I am with names. I can't remember who he said he was, but he had all kinds of questions about you."

"What kind of questions, Mom?" My stomach was doing flip-flops. This was so not right.

"He wanted to verify your birth date and information about your education. Oh yeah, and he asked questions about your social life and whether you'd been in any significant relationships lately."

"And this didn't seem odd to you?" I asked her, "'cause it sure seems odd to me, Mom. I mean, employers just don't go around calling applicants' mothers, and they sure don't ask about an applicant's social life."

"Well, sweetie, I just thought they were making sure you'd be a dedicated employee. I mean what better way to find out about someone then to ask their mother."

"Good God, Mom! You didn't answer his questions did you?"

"Well, of course I did, he was so sweet on the phone and...."

"Never mind, are you sure you can't remember his name?"

"Well, no. I just can't put my finger on it. Anyway, tell me, have you seen any good stuff in the E.R. yet?"

"Good stuff?"

"You know, blood and gore, mangled limbs, dead bodies?"

"Mom!"

"What? I don't get to hear about the fun stuff?"

"Mom, you worry me sometimes." I smiled wryly into the phone.

"Yeah, well you worry me all the time. How about doctors? Have you met any handsome eligible doctors?"

I smiled to myself. "Maybe," I said slyly.

"Maybe? Maybe, Shmaybe! You have to give me a little more information than that."

"When there's something more to tell, you'll be the first to know."

"Well, just don't screw up any opportunities like you did with that nice boy you dated in college. You know, what's his name? The Senator's boy.... Yeesh, you could be living the high life now, giving me little grandbabies...."

"Mom, you know why that didn't work out."

"Yeah I do, but I'm not sure I believe it. I mean you caught him kissing his golf caddie? His father's a senator, Charlie, it just wouldn't look good."

"It wasn't as though they were kissing in public, Mom. I'm sure he's more careful these days. Anyway, I gotta go, Mom."

"What, already? I finally hear from you and you have to go? What's so important that you can't give your mother a few minutes of your time? Your father would roll in his grave if he knew how little time you give me. I went through terrible pain to bring you into this world, and all I get is 10 minutes a week? Where's the gratitude? I should have been stricter with you, I should have...."

"Love you, Mom," I cut her off and hung up before she could say another word. I adored my mother, but once she got on a tirade, it could go on for hours.

I wondered who had called her and asked such personal questions about me. It should have shocked me but, after the last few days, it seemed not much could do that anymore.

I picked up the phone and dialed Sam's number. I got his voice mail and left a quick message, telling him that I was fine and that I'd see him tomorrow. I was feeling guilty about prodding Mendoza for the information Sam hadn't been willing to share, and I wasn't sure how to approach him with what I had found out—or if I should even tell him I knew. After all, in the scheme of things I really didn't know Sam any more than I knew Mendoza, and I decided to be very careful around both of them.

I felt for the skeleton key that I had slipped into my front pocket and felt a surge of satisfaction when my hand closed around it. I was anxious to start digging for answers.

I flopped back onto my living room couch and picked up Alfred's article that Mendoza had left behind and began reading it. The introduction was very dry, and reading it was tedious. I decided that food might help. Back in the kitchen, the fridge was ridiculously bare: a jar of olives, a jar of fingers, a tub of butter, and an ancient takeout container from Lulu's Italian eatery. I couldn't remember the last time I'd been to Lulu's and I certainly couldn't remember what was in the container, but I was sure it was probably alive by now. I was quite honestly afraid to look inside and afraid to throw it in the trash in case it somehow found a way to crawl out and slither across the floor to find me.

I sighed and checked the cupboard and found a box of Frosted Flakes, a container of dry pasta and a can of mushroom soup. I had been a nomad with NERT so long that I hadn't really gotten used to the idea of actually living in my apartment yet. I made a mental note to get some groceries and took the box of Frosted Flakes back to the living room with me. I crunched the dry cereal and picked up Alfred's article again, determined to make my way through it.

As it turned out the article got more interesting the further I read. Apparently, the Trufalics were a very sensual bunch of people. Just about everything they did had a sexual undertone to it.

No wonder Alfred had been so drawn to that culture, I thought with a shudder.

The Trufalics believed that the healers in their society received their extraordinary gifts through a ritual that was performed every nine years if there was a suitable candidate that year. The person selected to perform the ritual was usually an elder in the society and had to exhibit certain traits to be selected for the ritual—among them, extraordinary intelligence, an age not under 60 –(rare for those times) and a certain moral attitude. Apparently, it was felt that the "healing gift" could be used not only for good but also for evil, and the Trufalics wanted to make sure that the recipient of the gift would do no harm with it. I wondered about that: if it was a healing gift, how does one turn something like that into evil?

The article then went on to describe the ritual. It was held, as most rituals are, during the full moon—in this case, during the winter solstice. All three coins had to be present at the ceremony as well as a potion made from various nefarious ingredients, but Alfred's article did not list the contents of the potion. The final element in the ritual was the presence of a virgin. It did not matter if the virgin was male or female. However, the virgin did have to bear the mark of the healer, which, according to Alfred, was usually what he called the fourth coin. Each coin had a symbol etched in its center that, when joined with the other coins, held the words to the chant. The fourth coin—the mark on the virgin—was the key to the entire ritual, because it held the final words used in the chant during the ritual.

I thought about what I had read so far as I crunched on more Frosted Flakes. I was beginning to see what Mendoza was drawing his conclusions from. If Alfred believed in the Trufalic ritual and was indeed interested in obtaining the coins, then why not get the virgin too? If you think you've got a virgin living next door, why not scope her out a bit and try to discover if she has a symbolic marking somewhere by setting up some video equipment in the places where she might take off her clothes? My question was: Why would Alfred think I was a virgin? Sure, in the time I'd lived there I hadn't been in any significant relationships, but that didn't mean that I wouldn't have been previously. It just didn't make sense.

I tossed back another handful of Frosted Flakes and went back to the article. In addition to the elder and the virgin, other members of the Trufalic clan would be present at the ritual. Each had a specific role to play, and the article outlined the individual steps performed during the ceremony, with the culmination being the elder deflowering the virgin. (Of course, I thought wryly.)

The only illustrations in the article were sketches of the coins, and I studied them closely. I still had a nagging feeling that I'd seen them somewhere before. No matter how hard I tried, though, I just couldn't remember where.

There was a sudden rapping at my door and I sighed. I had been enjoying my quiet moment with my Frosted Flakes.

## Chapter 20

Dismayed at the interruption, I asked who was at the door.

"It's Haley, sweetie. Can I talk to you please?"

I took a few deep breaths. I wasn't sure that I wanted to face Haley yet. I wanted to know more about the vial first, but another part of me thought that maybe I could find something out if I did speak with her. I took another deep breath and heaved myself off the couch.

When I opened the door, I lost any sense of the anxiety I'd been feeling and burst out laughing. Haley's skin was completely orange, except around her eyes, which made her look like a raccoon. "What happened to your skin?" I asked her.

Haley sighed. "Oh, this. I let those nincompoops at the spa try their new spray tan machine out on me. I'm supposed to be a sun babe bronzed." She looked down at her arms and grimaced. "I guess I should have let them try it out on someone else first. That way maybe they could have gotten the bugs out first."

I tried to stifle another giggle. "Yeah, they need to get the bugs out," I managed to say and sounded semiserious.

"Well, are you going to invite me in?" Haley asked.

"That depends. Does that stuff rub off? I mean, do I have to put a towel down on the sofa or anything?" I couldn't help but start laughing again.

"Go ahead and laugh all you want, but no, unfortunately, this stuff is supposed to stay put for at least two weeks." Haley marched past me and trounced down on my sofa and wiggled in for extra emphasis. "They say the color fades gradually."

"Just as long as it doesn't fade off on my sofa," I replied and settled down next to her. "So what do you want to talk to me about?"

Haley studied her newly tinted arms for a moment, then chewed on one of her manicured fingernails. What ever she wanted to talk about was making her nervous. Haley treasured her nails, I had never seen her even bite one before—let alone chew on one.

She finally pulled her finger out of her mouth. "I was wondering if perhaps you might have found something and maybe borrowed it while you were in my apartment this morning," she managed to say.

I raised an eyebrow. "Does this something have a name?"

Haley stuck her fingernail back in her mouth and chewed on it reflectively. "I'd rather not say."

I thought I knew what she was asking about but decided to play dumb. "Well, how can I tell you if I borrowed it or not if I don't know what you're talking about?"

Haley shrugged. "Well did you borrow *anything*?"

"Nope," I answered. After all, I *hadn't* borrowed anything. I'd just sort of unintentionally ended up with a vial of some sort of woo woo drug that had just sort of happened to find its way into my body.

"Humph," came Haley's reply.

"Humph, yourself," I answered. "What's missing?"

Haley looked me squarely in the eye. "If I wanted you to know, I would have told you what was missing, now wouldn't I?"

I thought for a moment. "Why don't you just look into you crystal ball if you've lost something?"

Haley frowned and wiped at the orange on her arms as if trying to get the stuff off. "You know it doesn't work that way. I get what I get, usually with no rhyme or reason to it."

I debated sharing a little of my morning with her to see if I could rattle her. I decided it wouldn't hurt.

"Funny. Remember you telling me that I was in danger the other day?" I asked.

Haley stopped rubbing her arms and looked at me. "Yes, did anything happen?"

"Well, as a matter of fact, after I left your apartment, I realized mine had been broken into again."

"Really?" Haley asked. "Was anything missing?"

"No, but the fingers that I had lost yesterday were back in my apartment."

Haley didn't blink. "Oh well, that's good, I guess."

"And," I paused for emphasis.

"And?" Haley repeated.

"And ... I got arrested for suspected possession of drugs."

Haley's raccoon eyes grew three times the size they already appeared to be. "What? Why?"

"Because, as Detective Mendoza put it, 'I was acting in a somewhat erratic fashion and my pupils were enlarged.'"

Haley turned white beneath her orange skin. "So I'm afraid to ask what happened."

"Well," I went on, "I was so sure I wasn't on drugs, because I never ever do anything harder than cold medicine, that I let Mendoza take me in for a drug test."

"Oh my God!" Haley's face turned even whiter. It was at that moment that I knew she had been the one who gave me the drug.

"No big deal, right? I knew I was innocent. So I went in for the test, and guess what?"

Haley didn't answer. She was chewing on just about all 10 of her fingernails now.

"I did have drugs in my system. Something called benzodiazepine. Do you know what that is, Haley?" At this point, I was getting kind of worried that she was going to choke or something. "Haley, your fingernails!"

She stopped chewing and slowly extracted her fingers from her mouth, wiping them on her skirt. "Oh my goodness!" she said. "That must have been horrible for you."

I nodded. "Do you know what benzodiazepine is?" I asked again.

She shook her head up and down, saying, "Hmm, can't say I do. Not me, I don't do drugs." She stood up abruptly and looked at her wrist, which was bare of a watch. "My, my, would you look at the time? I've got to get myself presentable for the opera tonight."

"Opera?" I repeated.

"Yes," she said and quickly walked to the door. "I have a date, a very important date. And I'm orange of all things." She disappeared through the door, slamming it shut behind her.

I sat on the couch feeling a little like Alice down the rabbit hole. All my instincts told me that, beyond a shadow of a doubt, Haley was behind the drug found in my system, but I had no idea how to prove it unless I could find something in her apartment. She'd said she had a date for the opera. There was only one place in town to see an opera. I decided to check the Internet to see what time the show would start and wondered if she would be going out to dinner beforehand.

It was almost 4:30 p.m. now. If the opera started at 8 p.m., she'd have plenty of time for a dinner date—unless it took her that long to cover up her orange skin, that is.

I went to the little desk in the corner of my living room and pulled my laptop out of the top drawer. I plugged it in and did my homework. The opera did start at 8 o'clock. It was the rock opera,

"Evita." That meant I had at least three hours to tackle Haley's apartment in her absence.

I checked my e-mail while I had my laptop out, downloaded 52 messages, of which 47 were spam. There was an e-mail from Sherrie that depicted hot guys whipping up favorite recipes in the kitchen, each guy in various stages of undress. I liked the guy wearing nothing but an apron and did a mental head slap when I realized he resembled Mendoza.

There were two messages from my mother, both wondering why I hadn't called, and one from the power company, stating that my bill was overdue and my power would be cut off at the end of the month. I really had to balance my checkbook. The last message was from Alfred Tenny and I deliberately saved it for last. I remembered his last phone call, and goose bumps rose on my arm as I realized that I had received yet another missive from a dead man.

I opened Alfred's e-mail and read the lines in front of me.

"Dear Tenant:

Your rent is past due. Please remit the sum of $650, plus a late fee of $100 immediately. If said amount is not received within one week of this notice, eviction proceedings will follow.

Sincerely,

Alfred C. Tenny

I felt my face burn. $100 late fee! That slimy, little penis-wielding extortionist! How dare he? Who ever heard of a $100 dollar late fee? For that matter, who sent rent notices via e-mail? I was so angry, I had a wild urge to call Haley and tell her that Alfred had a little wee wee. Then I remembered that Alfred was dead, and I didn't even know who to send my rent to. The notice was dated three days ago, giving me four more days to come up with the rent if he were still around. I hoped that it wasn't a sin to be relieved that I didn't have to pay rent, because Alfred was dead. Although I hadn't inherited my family's love of organized religion, I still had a sense that my bible-toting father would be rolling in his grave if he knew half the things that went through my head.

Resisting the urge to check out my horoscope and Youtube, I closed my laptop and put it back in the drawer. I sat for a moment and considered my next move, which ended up being going back to the sofa, where I stretched out so that I could think better—and immediately fell asleep.

I must have been extremely tired because the next thing I knew I was awakened by a pounding on my apartment door. The room was pitch-dark, and I had to feel my way to the wall where the light switch was. I flipped the switch and squinted when the room was bathed in light from the overhead fixture.

I checked my watch and noted that it was already 7: 30 p.m. I went to the door and opened it, fully expecting to see Sherrie there—arriving early for sentry duty. I should have known better, though, because Sherrie was never on time for anything, much less early. When I opened the door, I found Sam on the other side, flowers in one hand and a brown paper bag that was emitting an intoxicating odor in the other.

My heart sank. This certainly threw a monkey wrench into my plans, now didn't it?

## Chapter 21

Sam must have read the look on my face. "Um, you were expecting someone else? Or is this just a bad time?"

I managed a smile and avoided the question. "With your hands all full of stuff like that, how'd you manage to knock?"

Sam relaxed a little at my joking tone and smiled back. "I knocked with my foot."

I did a mock survey of the door and shook my head in disbelief. "Would you look at those boot prints on my door? Those are going to cost you, Mister."

Sam leaned in a little closer. "Dare I hope that my punishment will be a spanking?"

I put my hands on my hips in mock indignation. "Dr. Macgregor, you are a naughty little boy!"

"Oh good," he replied, lightly brushing my lips with his as he stepped around me and into my apartment. "I am going to get a spanking, aren't I?"

I followed him, his kiss still tingling on my lips. I was desperately trying to figure out how to get out of my impromptu dinner date. He went directly to the kitchen and started unloading the bag. I followed behind, and he paused long enough to hand me the flowers. "I couldn't resist. It's been a long time since I felt like buying anyone flowers."

I absentmindedly set the flowers on the counter, rehearsing a "you have to go" speech and saw the dismay in his eyes at my lack of response. I immediately picked the flowers back up, and he smiled as I buried my nose in them. Too late, I realized that carnations were among them. I was intensely allergic to carnations. My eyes immediately started watering, and I started to sneeze uncontrollably.

Sam paused and stared. He had a container of what looked like wonton soup in one hand and another less obvious container of Chinese food in the other.

I was helpless, caught in my riot of sneezing, hacking allergic reaction to what are usually quite innocent flowers. I felt my lips start to swell. They must have brushed one of the carnations. Tears poured down my face, and I felt hives welling down my neck.

Sam continued to stare at me in unabashed horror.

I finally caught a breath in between sneezes and grabbed a fistful of paper towels in the hope of wiping my runny face. Both my nose and my eyes were running now, and my lips felt like they would touch my nose at any moment.

At my desperate swipe for paper towels, Sam finally broke into action. He dropped the containers of Chinese food on the counter and ran to the bathroom. I stood helplessly sneezing and wheezing until he returned with a bottle of cold medicine. "Take a swig of this," he ordered and held the bottle out to me.

I took the bottle and brought it to my bloated lips. I managed to get some of the cough medicine into my mouth while the bulk of it ran down my neck and into my sweater.

Within minutes the sneezing abated.

"Wow!" Sam said. "You scared me for a moment."

I sagged against the counter, still wheezing a little, and mopped at my nose and neck. "Carnations!" I gasped. "Awergic."

Sam nodded, "So I gather. The benadryl in that medicine helped some, but I think we should get you to the E.R."

"Doh!" I screeched.

"Doh?" He echoed.

"Doh," I stated. "Dare's doh way I'm going to da E.R. wike dis."

"Wike dis?" He echoed.

I crossed my arms and shook my head. "Doh way!" I answered. "My wips feel funny," I added, trying to explain my inability to speak correctly.

"That's because they look like you have a mega dose of cortisone in them," he answered.

I ran to the bathroom and looked in the mirror. I looked like I'd just stepped out of a horror flick. I had reddish, purplish hives all over my face and neck. My eyes were bloodshot and still watering, and my lips looked like Mick Jagger's on steroids. Huh, I thought, no wonder I can't talk right.

I returned to find Sam setting the table in the dining room. The flowers were nowhere to be seen.

"Where's da fowers?" I asked.

"I gave them to your neighbor. You know, Haley. Did you notice that she looks kind of orange today?"

"Ib's supposed da be sun babe bronzbed," I affirmed.

Sam nodded, as though he had really understood what I had just said, and went on, "I just wish I'd known about your allergy. Since you won't go to the E.R., I guess I'll just have to stay around and keep an eye on you."

"Doh!" I exclaimed.

"Doh?" He repeated. He finished setting the table and held a chair out for me.

I sat down, because I was feeling a little dizzy. "I hab plans."

His eye's flashed. "What sort of plans?"

"A fwend is combing ober," I answered and stuck my spoon into the wonton soup. I tried to take it to my lips but misjudged their size and ended up pouring the soup down my neck. I grabbed my napkin and tried to mop my shirt again.

"Oh?" Sam's eyes narrowed. "What fwe… I mean, friend?"

"Sherrie," I answered. I was proud of myself for getting her name past my lips properly.

Sam's eye's lost their glint, and he relaxed a bit. "I guess I should have called before marching over here."

I reached out and squeezed his hand. "It was weally sweeb ob you," I said.

"Yeah, you probably say that to everyone who nearly kills you with flowers." He smiled wryly. Unbelievably, given my current condition, that smile sent liquid heat strait to my crotch.

"Doh, onby da sexy ones." I looked at my watch. It was exactly 8:00 p.m.

Sam noticed the gesture. "When is Sherrie supposed to get here?

I shrugged. "Any timb now." I looked longingly at the soup and assorted other Chinese dishes spread out on the table. My stomach rumbled in response.

Sam was busily helping himself to everything, including steaming spring rolls—my personal favorite. I speared one with my fork and tried to take a bite. I ended up biting my lip so hard that my eyes teared up again.

Sam had watched the whole thing. "Maybe you should wait until you lips are a little less, um, fat, I mean big, to try to eat," he suggested. "As it is, you're bleeding, and if you chew up your lips, they'll only stay swollen a lot longer."

I glowered at him.

He hesitated a moment, weighing his options under my glare, and came to a conclusion. "Um, I'm going to get you some ice for your lips and put supper away for later." He didn't wait for an answer and disappeared into the kitchen.

My stomach rumbled again, and I wondered if Sam knew how close I'd come to sticking a fork in him. Fat lips, huh? I dabbed at my lips with a napkin, trying to squelch the trickle of blood where I'd bitten them, and breathed a sigh of relief when I heard what I hoped was Sherrie's knock on my door.

I went to living room and swung the door open. I was wrong again. This time it was Mendoza and he was carrying a La Carreta bag. Mendoza glanced at me through his long dark lashes and did a quick double take. "Holy shit! Who beat the crap out of you and where can I find him?"

The scent of the city's best Mexican food found its way under my nose and my mouth watered while my stomach rumbled again.

"Wab are you doing herbe?"

"Wab, what?" Mendoza asked.

"WAB ARE YOU DOING HERBE?" I repeated.

"Oh." Mendoza got it that time. "I thought we could talk about my thoughts on the article I gave you and eat at the same time." He waved the bag full of Mexican food under my nose.

"I'be alreaby got combany," I responded.

Mendoza took a few seconds to decipher what I had said. "I know," he answered and grinned mischievously.

Sam came around the corner and stopped dead in his tracks upon seeing Mendoza. Sam's easygoing demeanor disappeared, and his eyes turned a dark cold emerald. "What are you doing here Mendoza?" he asked through gritted teeth.

"Just taking care of my witness, criminal—whatever," Mendoza replied breezily. "Did you do that to her face?"

Sam clenched his fist, and his face reddened. I had a feeling that Sam was already blaming himself for my allergic reaction, and Mendoza's presence was just adding fuel to the fire.

"Hobe on herbe you du." I put my hands up.

"What did she say?" Mendoza asked Sam.

"I think she said you have herpes," Sam answered very solemnly.

I gasped. "I dib not!" I yelled.

Mendoza took a menacing step toward Sam. Sam took a step toward Mendoza with his fists still clenched. I stepped in between the two men and stuck a hand on each one's chest in an attempt to keep them apart.

"You tube are nob gonna fibe in my hoube." I gritted through clenched teeth.

Both men stopped in their tracks and stared at me. Mendoza was the first to step back. He looked at me for a moment and asked Sam, "Is she gonna stay that way or is she ever going to be able to talk right again?"

Sam sighed. "The swelling should go down soon."

Mendoza looked relieved and looked back at me. "You're a mess! What happened to your sweater?"

I looked down and surveyed the spilled cold medicine and soup. "I tribe to eat, but my wips dept getting in da wabe."

Mendoza laughed and Sam took the opportunity to relax his fists and step back. "Yeah, your lips are kind of big. It's an interesting look for you," Mendoza replied. "And how did all this happen?"

"Fowers."

"Fowers?" Mendoza repeated, obviously confused.

"Yeb, Samb bwought fowers," I tried to explain.

Mendoza looked over my head at Sam. "What'd you do, beat her over the head with them?"

Sam tried to lunge for Mendoza again, and Mendoza went back into his fight stance.

I'd had it. I was starving. For the first time in ages, I had a variety of food in my apartment and couldn't touch it. I had plans to break into my neighbor's apartment with my sidekick, who was due to arrive at any moment. I had two handsome, virile men within touching distance and I was a swollen, oozing, spilled-upon mess. Plus I had to get rid of the two men double-quick for two reasons. First, if Sherrie got here before they left, I was positive she'd completely forget about our plans and keep the two of them here as long as possible. Sherrie lost what was left of her brain whenever a handsome man was in sight. Second, I was pretty sure Sam and Mendoza would come to blows if I didn't get rid of them quickly.

"Otay, boybs." I was still holding Sam away from Mendoza with one arm and I was poised to do the same to Mendoza with the other. "Tabe it outswide, pwease."

They stopped staring each other down and looked at me incredulously.

"What?" they asked in unison.

"Du heard be. WEAVE!" I grabbed Sam by the lapel of his blazer and Mendoza by his belt and led them to the door. "Oub!" I pointed to the door and let go of Mendoza's belt to open it.

I pointed to the empty hall. "Oub! Nowb!"

Mendoza and Sam looked at me, then at each other, and then back at me. I stomped my foot. "GO HOMB!" I yelled.

Mendoza was the first to move and he walked into the hall. "Now look what you've done!" he accused Sam.

Sam followed into the hall and answered, "It's your fault! What right do you have to just show up here any time you choose?"

Mendoza sneered at Sam. "At least I didn't try to maim her with flowers."

That was the straw that broke the camel's back. Sam threw the first punch, and the next thing I knew the two men were rolling around in the hall, trying to beat each other to a pulp.

I watched for a moment, then went into the apartment and filled a bucket with cold water. I went back into the hall and threw the water on the two men. It had the intended effect, and they stopped grappling for what I hoped would be long enough to come to their senses. I started to go back into the apartment, reconsidered and stepped back into the hall long enough to retrieve the abandoned La Caretta bag. Mendoza noticed and yelled, "Hey, that's my dinner!" I slammed the door shut and locked it. I leaned against the door and smiled. Slamming the door and locking it had felt really, really good.

## Chapter 22

Sherrie finally showed up about 15 minutes later. When I opened the door, I surreptitiously glanced over her shoulder into the hall and saw no evidence of the two men. All I saw was a big wet spot on the floor. I breathed a sigh of relief.

"Good God, Hoochie girl! What happened to your face?" Sherrie asked with real concern. I had changed my sweater and iced my lips but, even though I could speak more clearly now, the hives and some swelling remained.

"Carnabtions," I stated.

"Oh Jeez, too bad for you!" Sherrie was well aware of my allergy to carnations, because she had given me a carnation-scented sachet for Christmas three years ago. "How did you get into carnations?" she asked.

"Sbecial delibery," I replied. Sherrie had just taken her coat off, and I blurted, "Whab the heck are you wearbing?" Sherrie was dressed from head to toe in black spandex and, if I guessed correctly, she was holding a black stocking cap in her hand.

Sherrie grinned and pulled the cap over her riotous red curls. "We're breaking and entering right? So I thought I'd dress the part. Here," she said, tossing me a matching cap. "I brought one for you too."

I sighed. "Sherrie, you're the loobout. You're supposed to blend and loob innocent. Nob like a sexy, hob, cat burglar!"

Sherrie shrugged, still grinning. "I guess I was kind of hoping that yummy Mendoza might show up and arrest me!"

I slapped my forehead. "Sherbie, I've been arrested by Mendoza and. believe me. it's not nearly as exciting as you might think it is."

"That's because you're a fuddy-duddy. I bet you he's a whole lot of fun with the right encouragement."

I glanced at my watch and gave up trying to reason with her. "We'd better geb moving. Haley's opera is over at 10:30 and ib's almost 9:00 already."

"Alrighty then. What do you want me to do?" Sherrie asked.

"I was going to hab you stay in the hall by the outside exit so you could see anyone coming in, but dressed like that, maybe you ought to stay just inside my door and call me on my cell ib you see anyone coming."

"I'd rather be by the exit," Sherrie pouted. "No one will see me in my outfit if I'm stuck in here."

"My point exably," I stated dryly.

Sherrie gave up, knowing that I wouldn't change my mind. "Alright then, do you have anything good to eat?"

At my incredulous stare, she said, "What? I can't eat and peak out the door at the same time?"

I shook my head, went to the kitchen and grabbed chips and salsa from Mendoza's contribution to my newly acquired stash in the fridge. When I handed the snacks to Sherrie she grinned. "Got any beer? You can't eat salsa and chips without beer, you know."

"No beer," I stated firmly. "Okab, I'm going now. Are you all set?"

Sherrie shrugged. "Except for the beer, sure." She settled into a chair near the door and started munching.

I stepped out of my apartment and crossed the hall to Haley's door. I looked up and down the hall, which showed no signs of life. I pulled the skeleton key from my pocket and, after one more glance up and down the hall, inserted it into the lock. The lock turned easily, and within seconds I was in Haley's apartment with the door closed behind me. Fortunately for me, Haley had left a small alcove light burning in her living room. I paused for a moment and tried to figure what to do next. I was new to breaking and entering and really hadn't formulated a plan.

I jerked in fear when my cell phone started ringing. I glanced at the number and felt even colder fear when I saw Sherrie's phone number displayed. I grabbed the door handle and flung myself out the door, ran back to my door and hurtled through it.

I must have startled Sherrie, who still had her phone to her ear and a handful of chips in her other hand. She dropped the phone in surprise and started choking on the chips.

"Whab?!" I cried. "Dib you see someone?"

Sherrie finished choking and looked at me like I was crazy. "No, but you forgot your cap." She held it out to me. "Don't scare me like that. I could have died choking on those chips with no beer to wash them down!"

"Don't scarb you?! Listen here, miss seby cat burglar with the chibs, DON"T call me unleb you see someone approaching Haley's abartmenb. You scarbed me to death!"

Sherrie pouted. "I just thought you might want your cap. I mean I, brought it all the way over here for you and everything."

I grabbed the cap out of her hand and pulled it over my head. "There! Satisfied?" I asked.

Sherrie grinned and nodded.

I left again and made my way back into Haley's apartment. My legs were shaking, and I noticed a tremor in my hand when I turned the key. I was quickly losing my nerve. I surveyed Haley's cozy living room, trying to decide where to start. I decided that there was nothing left to do but check everywhere as quickly as possible.

I looked under couch cushions, rifled through magazines, pulled books out of the bookshelves and flipped through the pages. After exhausting the possibilities in the living room, I went to her bedroom, but I had to talk myself into entering. There's something sacred about a person's bedroom, and it felt plain wrong to invade Haley's. Then I thought about the benzodiazepine and got angry enough to not care. I flicked on the wall switch and went straight for her dresser drawers.

Thirty minutes, later I knew exactly what kind of unmentionables Haley preferred, and I discovered that she had a fondness for brightly colored vibrators and beanie babies, but still hadn't found anything to connect her to the drugs. I looked under her bed, but found only dust bunnies and a baseball bat. I made a mental note to myself to never startle Haley when she was in bed. I looked between the mattress and box spring, which yielded nothing, and headed for the closet.

Haley's closet put mine to shame. Everything was neat and orderly—right down to the shoes. Each shoe was paired with its mate and in its own lidless cardboard box. She had some really cool shoes too. I bent down to touch a pair of what I could have sworn were Prada sandals, when I noticed one cardboard box that had a lid. I would have never seen it had it not been for the sandals, because the box was mostly hidden by a long evening gown that reached the floor. I forgot about the sandals and pulled out the shoebox.

Although my heart was already beating pretty quickly, it sped up a bit as I anticipated what the box might contain. I took it to the bed and quickly removed the lid. The box held a micro-mini-tape recorder and assorted tapes. I checked my watch—it was

10:05. Boy, time went quickly when you were snooping through other people's stuff.

I picked up a tape and looked for a label. The only identifier on the tape appeared to be initials. This one was labeled K.H. I checked another tape—that was K.H. II. I found one with C.M. on it and had a sinking suspicion that the initials stood for Charlene Meadows.

I popped the tape into the recorder and hit the play button. I heard a rustling sound and a male voice saying, "Do you think she's ready?"

A voice I recognized as Haley's said, "I told you 20 minutes, didn't I? Well, it's been 30."

There was a pause and then the male voice said, "How do we do this?"

"You're the doctor, you tell me."

Another pause. "Okay, I guess we just start."

"So start." It was Haley's voice again. She sounded halfway put out.

"Okay then. Um, Charlie, are you with us?"

There was silence for a moment. The male voice asked another question: "Charlie, can you hear me?"

I felt the hair rise on my arms and the back of my neck. This was just too weird! I just about fell over when I heard myself laughing on the tape. "My, aren't you the handsome one?" I heard myself say.

I heard a low masculine chuckle at my compliment. "Why thank you, Charlie. How are you feeling?"

There was a pause and then I heard myself speak again. "A-OK, fit as a fiddle. Couldn't be better, Doc!"

I was getting the willies. This was way too weird. I had no recollection of this conversation at all.

"That's wonderful, Charlie," the male voice was speaking again. It was a smooth voice, and I felt a twinge of recognition but couldn't quite put my finger on it. "I need to ask you some, um, rather personal questions. Is that okay with you?"

I heard myself answer, drawing my words out slowly. "Depends on how personal, Doc." There was a purr in my recorded voice and I was startled when I realized that I was apparently flirting with the mysterious doctor whose voice was on the tape.

"Well then, I guess I'll get right to it and we'll see how it goes," came the unknown doctor's reply.

"Shoot." I heard myself say. It seemed that I had been in a playful mood. I shook my head in exasperation, still desperately trying to come up with some sort of recollection of this conversation.

"I'll get right to the point," the doctor replied. "How's you sex life been lately?"

I heard myself giggle. "You're kidding, right?"

"No, I want to hear all about your, err, sexual escapades of late."

I heard myself fall into a fit of laughter. I had obviously found this question amusing. At the moment, though, I didn't find it amusing at all.

"Sorry, Doc. It's just soooo funny, because apparently I've been cursed."

"Cursed?" he asked solemnly.

"Yes, cursed. You see, no one seems to find me the least bit attractive that way. I mean, God knows, I've tried to have sex in the past, but no one ever seemed willing—at least, not the *men* I've been involved with." There was a pause on the tape, and I think I heard myself sniffle. "I almost had sex tonight, though. But she ruined it." I assume I had been somehow gesturing at Haley when I said that.

Haley broke in. "You barely knew that man. You should thank me."

"See ... I'm cursed. The first chance to get some that I've had in ages, and my nosey neighbor thinks she knows what's best."

"Hey," I heard myself continue. "You're a man. Look at me... look at these legs. Would you like to have sex with me?"

"Charlie," answered the doctor, "I hardly think that's appropriate.

I heard sobbing and assumed I had started to cry. "See, even you don't want to. What? Do I have bad breath, for God's sake?"

There was another pause and I heard more sobbing. I couldn't believe what I was hearing.

"Charlie," came Haley's voice, "get out of his lap. He said no, for God's sake."

"Umm." I was purring again.

"Doctor!" I heard Haley admonish him. "It would help if you'd take your hands off her. Caressing her like that is only giving her ideas."

I was being caressed? Yikes! I felt nauseous and violated, even though, according to the tape, I appeared to be asking for it.

I glanced at my watch and realized I was out of time. I clicked off the recorder, somewhat relieved that I didn't have to listen to any more of the weird conversation. I hesitated for a moment, wondering what to do with the tape and decided to take it with me along, with the shoebox and its contents. After all it was *my* voice on the tape.

I did a quick survey of the bedroom and felt almost sure that everything except the box was back in its place. I shut the light off and went back to the living room. Everything appeared okay, and I quickly stepped out the door and into the hall, closing the door quietly behind me. I looked up and down the hall with a sigh of relief and opened the door to my apartment. Sherrie's chair was empty but the couch was not. Mendoza sat there with a very amused expression on his face, which was also sporting the start of what looked like a shiner—compliments of Sam, no doubt.

"What are you doing here, where's Sherrie, and whab's so funny?" I asked. My heart was doing a rat-a-tat-tat in my chest. I had almost been caught breaking and entering.

## Chapter 23

Mendoza stretched lazily. "Sherrie went to the ladies' room. I'm hungry and you have my dinner. As for what's so amusing, I'm wondering why you're wearing a black cap and why Sherrie was posted as a sentry at your door and wearing what, I might add, is a slightly ridiculous outfit and a cap that matches yours."

"You didn't like her outfit?" I asked, yanking the cap off my head. I had honestly forgotten that it was there. I was also relieved to find that I could speak almost coherently again.

"I didn't say that. I said that it seemed a bit ridiculous, unless, let's say you were intending to break in somewhere—somewhere sexy, that is."

My cell phone rang and I jumped. It was Sherrie. I assumed she was calling me from the bathroom to warn me about Mendoza, so I ignored the call. "So you *did* libe the outfit?" I teased Mendoza.

Mendoza grinned wider. "What's not to like?" He gestured to the phone. "Are you gonna answer that?"

"Nope." I turned the phone off and tossed it onto the end table along with my cap. I knew how difficult Sherrie could be on the phone and I didn't want to even attempt to try to explain to her that I was already back in my apartment.

"So?" Mendoza asked.

"So whab?" I asked rather absentmindedly. I was wondering if Sherrie was ever going to come out of the bathroom or if she was going to stay in there trying to call me all night.

"So what's up with the outfit?" he asked, somewhat exasperated.

"Why don't you ask Sherrie?" I was stalling for time.

"Because I'm asking you. And, since your cap matches hers, I'm relying on my excellent investigative skills that tell me you two are in on something together—something that has to do with that box you just brought in."

"The box?" I asked innocently.

"The box," he repeated.

I followed his gaze to the shoebox that I'd left on Sherrie's abandoned chair and thought fast. "What could my new shoes possibly have to do with what Sherrie's wearing tonight?"

Mendoza shrugged. "Let's just say I have a gut feeling. That and the state of your face and lips make me doubt that you were just out shoe shopping a minute ago."

I was saved from answering him because, at that moment, Sherrie came out of the bathroom. She stopped dead in her tracks when she saw me. "Oh good, you're back."

I nodded. "Yes. I was just telling Detective Mendoza here about my newb shoes."

"Shoes?" she asked with a confused look on her face.

"Yes, the ones you said you just had to see right now. The ones I left in my car."

Sherrie recovered her composure. "Oh, yeah, those shoes."

Mendoza broke in. "So let's see them." He knew something was up, and I could tell he wasn't going to take no for an answer.

I decided to try to change the subject. "So, Sherrie, Detective Mendoza wants to know what's up with the outfit. He really likes it."

Sherrie looked down at her spandex-clad body. "Do you really like it?" she asked Mendoza. She walked over to where he was seated on the couch, sat down next to him and draped her arms over the back of the couch, displaying a tightly clad bosom. I had to hand it to Sherrie. She knew all about distracting men.

Mendoza's eyes were drawn immediately to the area Sherrie had intended him to focus on. "Um, you could say that."

Sherrie leaned in close to him and whispered something in his ear. Mendoza's eyes bulged a bit, and I could have sworn that a fine sheen of perspiration appeared on his forehead. Sherrie sat back again and grinned.

I wasn't quite sure what to make of all this but I was relieved that his attention was off the shoebox for a moment. Mendoza was still staring at Sherrie in shock, or something akin to that, when her phone started ringing. She looked at the display.

"Oh damn! It's Eddie. I was supposed to be at his house a half-hour ago."

She answered the phone. "Hi, sweetie. I'm not sure I'm going to make it tonight." There was a pause, and Sherrie grinned into the phone. "A surprise? For me? This doesn't have anything to do with Big Man Eduardo, does it?" There was another pause, and then Sherrie squealed. "Oh Eddie, I'll be right over!"

Sherrie hung up and put her coat on to go while Mendoza stared at her—his mouth wide-open. "Gotta fly, guys. Eddie has a surprise for me, and he says it's packaged in a little box instead of in his trousers this time." She started to go through the door, then stopped, turned back and looked at Mendoza. "Would you be a sweetheart and walk me to my car? There's been a lot of scary weird stuff going on around here lately, you know."

Mendoza shook his head as though to clear it and stood up. "Sure," he uttered and followed her through the door. I knew he'd be back in a minute, because he didn't take his coat, which was thrown over a living room chair. I quickly grabbed the shoebox, took it into my room and slid it under the bed. Out of sight, out of mind I hoped.

I went into the kitchen and started pulling out the Mexican food—not because Mendoza said he wanted his dinner, I knew that wasn't the only reason he was back, but because I was starving. My lips felt like they were almost back to their normal size, and I was sure I could get some food past them. At that point, I was too hungry to care if I chewed them off anyway.

I had the makings of fajitas warming in a pan when Mendoza came back in. It appeared that he had regained his composure. "Wow! Who *was* that oddly clad woman I just escorted out of here?"

I smiled thinly. In retrospect, I wasn't all that happy about Mendoza's reaction to Sherrie. Once again, I felt that odd sensation of jealousy and I was uncomfortable with it. "That, Detective Mendoza, was Sherrie in her finest Sherrie form. She has a history of being a bit man-crazy."

Mendoza smiled. "I don't know whether to be flattered by the suggestion she whispered in my ear or insulted that she threw me over so quickly for a little package." He looked at the food on the stove. "You know, I didn't really came back for the food."

"I know," I answered. "But what I don't know is what would have brought you back so late in the evening."

"Well, it's odd," he replied. "I got back to the station earlier today and there was a message on my desk stating that the results of your blood test were in error."

"Huh?" I stopped stirring the mixture in the pan and looked at him in confusion.

"Yes, apparently the head of pathology sent down an order resending the original results, saying that they were in error and that no drugs were present in your system."

I stared at him, dumbfounded. After all, I had a tape in my possession of a conversation I couldn't remember—a conversation that, for all intents and purposes, suggested that I had indeed been on drugs of some kind.

"I don't understand."

"Neither do I. We did a chain of custody draw. It's unheard of for that type of lab result to be in error. So, what I want to know is what sort of relationship do you have with Adam Petrovich in the pathology lab?"

I stared at Mendoza in shock. If I understood him correctly he was alleging that I had somehow gotten Adam to change the lab results on my behalf.

"I only know Adam from work. I just met him yesterday, when he handed Horace Schmidt's fingers off to me." I pulled the pans off the stove and transferred the food to plates.

Mendoza studied me through a brilliant blue eye (the other was half-closed because of the shiner), then nodded. "I believe you."

"I didn't ask you if you believed me. Actually, it seems that since the moment we met you've been trying to believe the worst about me and, quite frankly, I don't give a shit." I realized that I was getting extremely angry. For this preacher's daughter to swear, I had to be getting pretty close to the end of my rope.

Mendoza was silent for a moment and then picked up the plates. "Come on, let's eat this before it gets cold, then we'll see if we can figure any of this out."

I grabbed the two beers that had come in one of the Mexican bags and followed him to the dining room. I honestly hadn't known the beer was in there when Sherrie had asked for one.

We sat down and ate silently for a few minutes.

Mendoza downed his food with the ferocity of someone who hadn't eaten in days. When the last bite was gone, he turned his attention back to me. "You're right. I haven't been all that fair to you and I apologize."

I looked at him warily. Was this Mendoza calling a truce or was this Mendoza trying another tactic in an effort to soften me up for the kill? It really didn't help much that he was so insanely sexy in his perfectly molded faded jeans. His sheer sexiness seemed to befuddle my brain.

"I really am sorry and, even though you seem to be cleared drug-wise, I can still get you on possession of an illicit drug or the fact that you told Officers Gorman and Stefansky that you would have liked to kill Alfred Tenny. That makes you a suspect in his murder, so you're not really off the hook. But if you cooperate, I'm willing to let it go for now."

So, that was it. I studied his face. He looked sincere enough.

"Why would I want to?" I finally asked flatly.

Mendoza finished his beer. "Because, whether you like it or not, I think you're involved up to your eyeballs in the Alfred Tenny murder."

I raised my eyebrows. "So now I'm a murderer?" I asked in shock.

Mendoza shook his head. "I'm thinking no, but if what I've found out has any basis in fact, your life is in just as much danger as his was."

"That sounds pretty ominous." I was being flip.

"How about you hear me out and then decide whether or not I have anything here?"

I shrugged. "What have I got to lose except sleep?" It was already past 11 p.m. and I was feeling the effects of the long weird day and the beer. My eyes were heavy and I was tired.

Mendoza looked hard at me over the empty plates. "You're exhausted," he stated. "I want you to have a clear head and be well-rested when we discuss this, so I'm going to do your dishes for you and you're going to go to bed."

I looked at him in amazement. "You're ordering me to bed?"

He crossed his arms and nodded. "And I'm going to clean up your dishes for you. Are you working tomorrow?"

I nodded. I didn't want to miss any more time at work, especially now that I was cleared of the drug charge. After all, I had a reputation to restore.

"Do you get a lunch break?" I nodded yes, and Mendoza said, "I'll meet you for lunch at the hospital then."

I wanted to argue because, for some reason, I liked to argue with Mendoza, but I didn't have the energy. Besides, I really didn't feel like doing the dishes.

"Okay, say 12:00 noon tomorrow, and you'll lock up when you leave?" I asked.

"Of course," he answered. "I hope you'll tell me about the shoebox at lunch too."

Damn. I was hoping that he had forgotten about the box. I should have known he was too sharp to be diverted completely by Sherrie's antics. I tried to think of a good answer; instead, I just said, "I'm going to bed then." I stood up and turned toward the bedroom.

"Nighty night," he said.

I stopped and turned back. "Detective Mendoza?"

"Yes?"

"I hope you got a good punch in too."

Mendoza grinned and winked with his good eye.

I went to my room and slipped into a nightgown. As I climbed under the covers, I couldn't help thinking how *nice* it felt to have him cleaning up in my kitchen while I went to bed. I tried to label the feeling and, as I dozed off, all I could think of was that I felt warm and tingly and cozy and safe.

Not much later, I woke up to the sound of my bedroom door opening. I could see Mendoza silhouetted in the doorway as he stood gazing at me. I held my breath for what seemed like eons, wondering what he was doing and what he was thinking—almost wishing that he would come into my room. Then the door clicked shut and he was gone. I sighed and buried my head in my pillow. I really had to get the virginity thing taken care of.

**Chapter 24**

The next morning came all too soon, and I struggled through my morning routine with little enthusiasm. At least my face had returned to normal. My lip was swollen just a tad where I'd bitten it. I wasn't looking forward to walking into Cedars—a.k.a. Gossip Memorial Hospital—as the druggie returning to work. Nonetheless, I got dressed and drove to work. I took a deep breath and pushed my way through the doors of the hospital with one arm, holding Horace Schmidt's fingers securely in the other.

I immediately went to the employees' lounge and stowed my gear and Horace's fingers in my locker. Then I picked up my phone and headed to what I hoped would be my desk for the day. Katy Dee was in the triage office, and, thankfully, I didn't encounter Joyce on the way. My desk was vacant of bossy volunteers, and I'd just settled in when my little phone started buzzing. I answered and heard Horace Schmidt's voice on the other end of the line.

"Is this Miss Charlie?" he asked gruffly.

"Yes, it is." I answered pleasantly. I was very anxious to get the finger handoff over with and was happy to hear from the guy for once.

"Where the heck have you been, lady? I've been calling and calling and they kept telling me you was out. I was starting to get the idea that you've been avoiding me."

"I was out, Mr. Schmidt. You'll be glad to know that you can come pick up your fingers anytime today before 4 o'clock"

"Well ain't that somethin'," he replied. "I'll be there before noon." He hung up before I could say another word.

I clicked the phone off and surveyed the waiting room. It was relatively empty, except for a young man with a bloody bandage wrapped around his head and an elderly woman reading a magazine. I checked in with Katy Dee, who had her feet up on the desk and her face buried in another romance novel.

"Good morning, Katy Dee," I greeted her.

She glanced up from her book. "What, no handcuffs today?"

"Oh, you heard about that, huh?" I tried to play it cool.

"Me and everyone else at Cedars. They said you must have been crazy on drugs 'cause Mendoza had to drag you in here in cuffs." She arched her brows at me, waiting for the inside scoop.

"Jeez, doesn't anyone around here have a life?" I asked.

"Yours just seems so much more exciting," she quipped.

"Well," I answered smugly, "it turns out that the results of my blood test were clean, and the handcuff thing? Well, I accidentally ticked Mendoza off a little."

"Yeah, well it takes a lot to rattle Mendoza. He's known for being a pretty cool customer. On the other hand, if anyone was going to cuff me ... well, let's just say he'd be the one I'd let do it."

"Anyway..." I said, trying to change the subject, largely because of the heat I felt creeping up my neck at the thought of Mendoza and handcuffs in other circumstances. "Is there anything I should know about today with regard to work?"

Katy Dee shrugged. "It's slow this morning. The nail gun guy should be going to an exam room in a few minutes, and the little old lady with the pooper problem has been waiting to poop for two weeks—another half-hour shouldn't matter much."

"Nail gun guy?" I couldn't help asking.

"Yeah. The guy decided to scratch his head with a nail gun in his hand and put a nail in his skull. He must have a hard head though, because it's not in too deep." Katy Dee picked up her book—a sure sign that I was dismissed.

"Oh, by the way," she said, nose still in her book, as I turned to leave. "Dr. Caudill asked me to send you to him when you came in."

"Oh boy," I muttered under my breath and headed to Dr. Caudill's office.

His door was open, and he waved me in absentmindedly while he finished a phone conversation.

I stood in front of his desk nervously, feeling like a delinquent kid in the principal's office.

He finished his phone conversation and said, "Sit, sit! We need to talk."

I sat down and waited while he riffled through the papers on his desk. He finally found what he was looking for and handed it to me. It was a copy of the results of my blood test.

"Okay," he began, "first, I'd like to apologize for the mix-up in lab results yesterday. It seems that you missed a whole day of work because of our error, so we're going to pay you for yesterday. Second, I'm not sure what you did that Mendoza felt he had to bring you here in handcuffs, but I spoke with him and he assured me that you had been cleared of any offenses and that I didn't have to worry about letting you continue to work here. He said it was essentially a personal misunderstanding?"

I almost laughed out loud. Personal misunderstanding was an interesting alternative description for getting kneed in the groin. "You could say that," I answered.

"Well," Dr. Caudill said. "You certainly aren't a dull person to have on staff are you?" He didn't wait for me to answer. "I lost another C-note, but I think I'll start putting the odds in your favor from now on."

I grinned, and then my phone started ringing. I answered in my best professional voice, considering that I was seated in front of my boss. "Charlene Meadows, Cedars Memorial Hospital Emergency Room. May I help you?"

"Hey, Charlie, it's Katy Dee. There's some guy here in the E.R. looking for you. He says you have his, um, fingers?"

"Oh good," I answered. "Tell him I'll be there in a few minutes."

"No problemo." Katy Dee replied and hung up.

I stood to leave. "Thanks, Dr. Caudill. I have to go."

He dismissed me with a wave of his hand, and I headed to the employees' lounge to get Horace's fingers. I was smiling to myself in anticipation of getting rid of the dreaded digits when I ran smack dab into Sam. He was sporting a split lip and looked like he had a few stitches that had closed a laceration on his cheekbone.

"Wow!" I said before I could stop myself. "Did you get the license tag on that bus?"

He wasn't very happy today and didn't crack so much as half a smile when he said. "Yeah, it's registered to your *friend*, Detective Mendoza."

"My friend?" I snorted. "Hardly."

"Oh, so your non-friends bring you dinner?" His eyes were positively stony, but the stitches on his cheek gave him a rakish air and I felt tingles trying to start up my body.

"What are you saying?" I asked.

"That you obviously were not all that happy to see me last night. Then you said you had plans with Sherrie. Then, low and behold, Mendoza shows up with dinner—no Sherrie in sight. Just seems a bit odd is all." The fierceness of his gaze was astounding—and sexy.

I narrowed my eyes at him, trying to be mad instead of turned on. "So you think my plans with Sherrie were really plans with Mendoza?"

"Are you denying it?" he asked.

His response put a damper on my libido. How dare he question my integrity? "First of all," I answered, "I don't report to you. Secondly, I'm a born-and-bred preacher's daughter and I do not lie. How dare you accuse me of trying to put one over on you? I'm not like that."

His face remained immobile. "Then why was Mendoza's car in your parking lot past 11 o'clock last night?"

I drew in a deep breath. "You were spying on me?"

He shrugged. "I was worried about you."

"Then why didn't you call or knock on my door? Why did you wait till 11 o'clock to check on me?"

"Maybe because I was busy getting a few stitches before then?"

I felt my anger turn to mush, but his mistrust kept me still. Finally, without another word, I turned on my heels and walked away. I didn't owe him or anyone else explanations, plus I had fingers to deliver.

## Chapter 25

I retrieved the jar from the lounge and headed for the E.R. When I entered the waiting room, I picked out Horace immediately and not because he was missing most of the fingers on his very large right hand.

He was a very tall, very large man in general, garbed in bib overalls over a flannel shirt. His dark hair was longish and pulled back into a ponytail with an ordinary rubber band and he probably hadn't shaved for a few days. His eyes were an intense gray and were made all the more intense by the midnight shadow on his face. He honed in on the jar and me when I walked into the room, and he immediately made his way toward me. All in all, Horace Schmidt was a scary looking man.

For such a large man, he moved fairly gracefully and was in front of me in no time. "Are you Miss Charlie?" he drawled.

"Yes, Mr. Schmidt," I answered in a small voice. His sheer size up close was alarming, to say the least, and I was suddenly very nervous.

"I see you got my fingers there." He made an attempt to take them from me, but I quickly moved the fingers and myself away from him.

"You see correctly, sir, but I need you to sign for them before I can release them to you. So, if you don't mind following me to my desk?" I turned to head there without waiting for an answer, and he followed just a step behind.

I sat down, set the jar on the desk and retrieved the paperwork Adam had given me from a folder in the desk drawer.

"Okay," I said, sliding the paper over to him. "I just need you to sign next to where your name is printed."

Horace didn't move. He stood staring down at the jar on the desk, seemingly transfixed by what was floating in the jar.

"Horace?" I asked.

He pulled his attention away from the jar and looked at me with a hard glare. "Where's the other one?" he asked.

My mouth dropped open. "What other one?"

Horace held up his right hand. "Count 'em."

"Excuse me?" I asked.

"You heard me," he gritted. "Count how many fingers I have on this hand."

"Okay. One," I answered.

"What's one minus five?"

"Um, four?" I answered.

"Yep. Four. How come there are only three fingers in that jar?"

I stared at the jar and counted... one, two, three. He was absolutely right. There were only three fingers in the jar. I tried to remember the last time I'd actually counted the fingers. I knew I'd counted four when Adam delivered them. Beyond that, I couldn't think of any time I'd actually spent counting the fingers inside it.

I looked at Horace's angry visage, realized that my mouth was still hanging open and willed myself to shut it.

"I ... I just don't know what to say."

"Miss Charlie, I can tell by the look on your face that you don't know a rat's ass about where the other finger might be. Do you?"

I shook my head no—still fairly speechless. I looked up at Horace and discovered to my dismay that he looked like he was going to cry. Sure enough, a tear escaped from one eye and trickled down his cheek.

"Oh, Mr. Schmidt!" I finally found my voice. "I'm so sorry! Is there anything I can do to help?"

More tears escaped, and he rubbed his eyes with a balled fist. He stood in front of my desk with his shoulders heaving, crying like a baby.

"Can I get you a glass of water or anything?"

He shook his head vehemently from side to side, rubbed his eyes again and, with a great hiccupping sigh, tried to pull himself together. "Them fingers, Miss Charlie, they're mine. And, well, it's just been so hard."

I came around to the side of the desk and gave him an awkward hug. "I know it can't be easy, Mr. Schmidt."

He stiffened at the hug, which I realized was a huge mistake on my part, then he pulled me in closer and sobbed a little more. I hadn't expected *that* and I certainly didn't expect it when he grabbed one of my buttocks with his good hand and gave it a hard squeeze.

"You sure are a nice looking thang," he whispered in my ear.

I pulled myself away and looked up at him in total shock. "Mr. Schmidt!"

He grinned, all signs of grief completely gone. "How about you and me get together for dinner sometime?"

"I don't think that's a very good idea, Mr. Schmidt." I tried to assume a professional demeanor.

Horace gave me a thorough up-and-down assessment. "I think it's a great idea. As a matter of fact, let's call it a trade. One dinner date for one finger."

"Are you off your rocker?" I asked before I could help myself.

"Are you calling me crazy?" Horace asked. A look flashed into his eyes that immediately backed up the idea that he may not be operating on all four cylinders. "I had enough people telling me I was crazy up at that Happy Acres place, so I don't let no one call me crazy."

"Mr. Schmidt," I replied with as much authority as I could muster, "I by no means said anything about you being crazy. I asked you if you were off your rocker. There's a difference."

"There is?" he asked with a childlike confusion.

"There is." I picked up the paper he was supposed to sign and handed it to him with a pen. "Will you sign for the three fingers?"

He looked at the paper, wrote on it with his left hand and handed the form back to me. "I want my other finger or a date. I marked out where it says four fingers and put three, so no one can say I signed for four fingers."

I sighed. How could someone go back and forth from not so smart-to-smart so quickly? "I'll find the other finger and get it to you," I stated with more conviction than I actually felt.

Horace nodded his big head. "You have three days, Miss Charlie, and then you'd better think about putting on a sexy little dress and stepping out with me." He turned and strode out of the waiting room.

I sat back down behind my desk and once again felt like banging my head on it. I was fairly sure the fourth finger had disappeared when the jar went missing for a while before it ended up back in my refrigerator. I had no idea who'd taken them. But, then again, maybe the finger was laying in the hospital parking lot, where I had dropped the jar when Mendoza was taking me in for a blood test. I didn't think so, though. I had been present when Mendoza retrieved the fingers, and I was positive we hadn't left one lying on the pavement. So I had no idea how I was going to find out where Horace's finger was or who had it now.

The thought of the dinner date was enough to make me lose my appetite for a week. There was something very amiss about Horace Schmidt, and I decided to find out what sort of place Happy Acres was at my first opportunity.

The E.R. was getting very busy, and I spent the next few hours signing in patients and delivering ice packs and pink tubs to those who needed them in the waiting room. Sandy was back again—this time simply to get out of the cold. I took her some crackers and juice, and each time I glanced her way, she seemed calm and she wasn't speaking to invisible people. I was beginning to think that, other than the visit with Horace, the day might turn out to be pretty normal, until Mrs. Lancaster came in.

## Chapter 26

During a lull in patient arrivals, I was sitting at my desk, trying to read an article on doctor-patient confidentiality protocols but really dwelling on the problem of Horace and his missing finger, when I heard a feminine voice say, "Excuse me, miss?" I glanced up and found an attractive, elderly woman standing at my desk. She was stylishly dressed in a tan skirt and a cream cowl-necked sweater and wore perfectly matched accessories. Her hair was completely silver and cut into a bob that almost reached her shoulders.

"May I help you?" I asked, trying to pull my thoughts back from Horace.

Her hair swung as she nodded her head in the affirmative. "Well, um, you see..." She didn't seem to know where to start.

"Do you need to be seen by a doctor?" I asked, trying to be helpful.

"Oh no, not me." She answered. "It's my son. Mark. He was brought in last night, and, well, they said he died."

"Oh my," I responded, "I'm so sorry to hear that Mrs.?"

"Lancaster," She nodded again. "They said I could visit him here before they take him to the funeral home. I don't know whom to see about that."

Neither did I, but I wasn't about to tell her that. I came around the desk and gently took her hand and led her to a seat. "Why don't you sit here while I call my supervisor?" I suggested.

She sat down, and I went back to my desk and clicked on my little phone. I checked the extension list that had been provided for my use, called Dr. Caudill and explained the situation, then I asked him if we actually allowed family to see their dead loved ones before they were moved to a funeral home.

"Oh yes, it's a given," he answered. "Most people, especially mothers and fathers, won't believe that they've lost a loved one until they see them with their own eyes. We're proud of our open-door policy in the morgue. I'll send Adam down and he'll show you the ropes."

"Ropes?" I squeaked.

"Oh yes, that's one of the duties we're handing off to you. Do you have a problem with that?"

"Oh, oh, no," I answered, lying through my teeth. I did not want to go to the morgue today—or ever.

"Good, good," Dr. Caudill answered brightly. "After all, you said bodies weren't a problem for you."

I did. I remembered that conversation. I just didn't think it meant that I was expected to go to the morgue or to hold onto and lose fingers or to discover that Alfred Tenny had a little wee wee.

"I'm fine, Dr. Caudill." I managed to squeak. "Tell Adam I'm in the E.R. waiting room with Mrs. Lancaster."

"Sure thing. He should be there shortly." I hung up and went to sit with Mrs. Lancaster until Adam arrived.

I offered her coffee or water, which she politely declined. She looked the picture of calm as she occasionally rubbed her hands together. "You know," she said, "I've always thought that if something dire happened to one of my children I would know it—like I would feel it in my heart."

I nodded and she went on.

"Well, I just don't feel like anything happened. I feel like I'll get a phone call from my son at any moment, and he'll tell me he's been busy but wanted to call."

I didn't know quite what to say, but luckily Adam arrived and I didn't have to answer. He walked straight to where we were sitting and extended his hand to Mrs. Lancaster. "Hello, Mrs. Lancaster. I'm Adam Petrovich. I've been told you'd like to see your son?"

Mrs. Lancaster stood up and shook Adam's hand. "Yes, that's right."

"Is any other family member here with you?" Adam asked.

"No, no." She shook her head and her hair bobbed. "It's just me. His father passed away last year and his brothers live out of state." Her eyes welled up, and she dug in her stylish handbag until she found a tissue.

"I'm so sorry, Mrs. Lancaster. This can't be easy for you." Adam looked and acted like a well-rehearsed actor. I wondered how many times he had morgue duty. Actually, I was really wondering how often I would have morgue duty.

I stood there awkwardly, unsure about what to do.

"Did Ms. Meadows explain to you our procedure here?"

Mrs. Lancaster shook her head no.

Adam gave me a stern look, and I felt chastised. But how was I supposed to know the procedure when I'd never done this before? I tried really hard to keep my mouth shut and did an excellent job of it.

"Well, what we are going to do is escort you down to the morgue. You'll wait a few minutes outside the door there while we go in and prepare your son for you to see. Then we'll bring you into the room. Does that sound alright to you?"

Mrs. Lancaster was still amazingly calm, except for a little tremor in her chin. She nodded and off we went.

It turned out that the morgue was located in the basement of the hospital. I'd never been there before. We walked down a corridor, took a flight of steps down, and walked along another corridor. When we reached the morgue, I noted that it was very close to the freight elevators and the loading dock. A stuffed chair and a table with a lamp on it sat to the side of the morgue door. They looked ridiculous sitting in the stark corridor, but I realized our guests needed to have somewhere to sit.

"Just have a seat, Mrs. Lancaster, and we'll be back for you in a moment." Adam spoke with almost overdone solicitude.

"Would you like me to wait with Mrs. Lancaster?" I asked, hoping he would say yes. I still wanted no part of the morgue, especially the "getting the body ready for viewing" part.

"No, no, Charlie. I think it's important for you to come with me."

I sighed and followed Adam through the door into the dim room beyond. We were in a small antechamber furnished with yet another overstuffed chair, table and lamp. Adam gestured toward the chair. "This room is where the body will actually be viewed. We find that a lot of people need to sit down, hence the chair."

Okay. So far so good, I thought. There wasn't much that was scary about this room.

Adam took out a key and unlocked another door, and I reluctantly followed him through it. This was the actual morgue—a large dimly lit room with a bank of rectangular doors on one side. In the center of the room were several empty stretchers with huge dome lights above them. Sinks and a litany of equipment and cupboards were lined up along the other wall. I assumed the autopsies were conducted here as well. This room was chilly and carried a chemical odor that wasn't very pleasant. This room was definitely *very* creepy and I swallowed hard.

Adam went to the bank of doors. He started looking at each door and explained what he was doing as he went along. "Each body is placed in one of these drawers. The deceased's name and birth date are placed on the door for identification. When you find the correct drawer, you use this universal key to unlock it." Adam must have found Mark Lancaster, because he used the key to unlock the drawer. After unlocking the drawer, he swung it open and started pulling it out. It consisted of a steel slat, about two feet wide and 7 feet long. I drew in a deep breath, not sure what I was going to see. As he finished pulling out the drawer, I exhaled in relief. The body was encased in a white bag.

Adam walked over to me and dropped a set of keys in my hand. "The big one is for the morgue door, the smaller opens the drawers. Oh, that is, except for drawer number nine."

"Why not nine?" I asked.

"Nine's refrigeration system hasn't worked in years, so we don't use that one," he answered.

"Oh, I see," I said. "So why don't they fix it?"

"Because it's an unnecessary expense. We've got 20 drawers here and have never had to use more than 15 of them at a time. The hospital administration has decided that the repair would be an unnecessary expenditure."

"Aren't you part of the administration?" I asked glibly.

Adam smiled, but he looked annoyed. "I'm just one of several administrators." He walked to a gurney, rolled it over to the drawer and slid it underneath the slat. "There's a hinge on either side of the slat. Just hit the release on each of them and your body is ready to roll." I watched as he released the levers and pulled the stretcher away from the wall. The body lay neatly on the stretcher.

"Now for the fun part," Adam went on. "First, we unzip the bag. Please do the honors." He'd lost his annoyed look, and his eyes were warm and appreciative as he placed his hand on the small of my back and caressed my spine.

I looked up at him, trying to hide my shock. "What are you doing?" I asked.

"What do you mean?" Adam feigned innocence.

"You're not trying to come on to me next to a dead man's body, are you?"

Adam didn't miss a beat and he continued caressing my back. "Would you like that?" he asked.

I looked directly into his eyes and said flatly, "No."

He smiled. "It's okay to admit it, Charlie. A lot of people are turned on by death. It's nature's way of restoring balance."

My mouth opened in astonishment and I was speechless.

Adam went on, "When one life is lost, the human response is to restore it, and the only way to create a new life is to have sex. That's why some people get turned on by death."

I stepped away from Adam's roving hand and nearness and looked directly into his eyes. "I am in no way turned on Dr. Petrovich."

"Okay, okay, I get it." he said and winked, looking anything but convinced. "Now, how about unzipping that bag."

I stared at the bag in trepidation and took several deep breaths. "I've never done this before," I said turning back to him.

"That's what I understand," he replied. "I'm so pleased to be the one leading you through your first." He grinned his Cheshire cat smile and winked. "Oh, by the way, you can get some gloves over there on the counter. You never know what you're going to find in one of these bags or what might have soaked into the zipper."

"Great." I managed a half-smile and got some gloves while I tried to suppress the nausea that was threatening to overwhelm me. I wasn't sure if my upset stomach was caused by the conversation I'd just had with Adam or by my fear of what the bag contained.

After pulling on the gloves, I walked back to the gurney and looked at Adam. "Here we go," I said with more enthusiasm than I felt and grabbed the zipper at the bottom of the bag with trembling hands. As I pulled the zipper up, the bag opened and revealed booted feet and a pair of legs in denim jeans. I stopped unzipping and gave Adam a questioning look.

"Mark came in dead on arrival, the result of a motor vehicle accident. We rarely undress them if they're D.O.A. and the cause of death is obvious. We let the funeral home do that."

"Oh," I replied and continued to unzip the bag. I was a little more confident now that I knew I wasn't going to run into a little wee wee. I slowed down a bit when I reached the head area, though. There was a lot of blood on his checked shirt and I was afraid of what I'd find.

"Go on" Adam said in a teasing voice. "He won't bite you."

I finished unzipping the bag in a hurried flourish. As the bag came away from Mark Lancaster's face, the cause of death became very evident.

Oddly enough, I didn't feel like throwing up or fainting. What I saw was a young man with a huge dent in his forehead. His eyes were closed as though he were sleeping. The blood had poured from his ears into his shirt. The dent in his forehead looked suspiciously like the imprint of a steering wheel.

"Seatbelts!" Adam exclaimed. "If only everyone would wear seatbelts! I hope you wear yours, Charlie."

"Of course," I replied. I mean, I sure would start wearing them after seeing Mark Lancaster.

"Okay," Adam continued, "now that the bag's unzipped, we take a sheet and cover him and wheel him into the next room. Could you hold the door open please, sweetheart?"

Sweetheart? I was starting to wonder if Adam was on drugs. I held back a sharp retort and went to the antechamber door. I yanked it open and watched as Adam wheeled the stretcher through.

We arranged the stretcher neatly in the corner, and Adam gave me a quick summary on viewing how-to's, all the while studying me in a way that made me feel completely naked, or that he was imagining me that way. "First, you want to make sure that the relatives really and truly want to see the body," he instructed. "Then, explain about any trauma or oddities they'll be seeing—in this case, the imprint of the steering wheel in our guy's forehead. Next, ask again if they're okay with seeing the body. Then it's show time."

For the life of me, I couldn't imagine ever sharing Adam's enthusiasm for this job. I decided that he was just a bit nuts. I walked back into the corridor and followed Adam's instructions. Upon hearing about her son's forehead, Mrs. Lancaster's face paled a bit, but she insisted on seeing his body.

I nodded and asked Mrs. Lancaster to follow me into the antechamber, where Adam was waiting for us. He immediately put an arm around Mrs. Lancaster and walked her over to the stretcher. He mumbled a few words to her that I couldn't make out and, when she nodded her head, he pulled the sheet back.

She stood staring at her son for a minute or two, when, out of nowhere, her knees buckled and she was on her way down. Adam and I grabbed her before she hit the floor and half-dragged, half-walked her to the overstuffed chair a few feet away.

She sagged into the chair and buried her face in her hands, her shoulders shaking. A shrill keening sound escaped from the hands that she had placed over her mouth.

I knelt in front of the chair and asked, "Are you okay, Mrs. Lancaster? Can I do anything for you?" I felt totally helpless and so sorry for the grieving woman until she removed her hands from her face and I realized that the sound coming from her was laughter. She was absolutely hysterical with laughter. I was afraid she'd lost her mind.

"Mrs. Lancaster?" I said.

She bit the palm of her perfectly manicured hand in an effort to stop the laughter. When that didn't work, she quit biting her hand and buried her face in her hands again. Great gales of laughter intermingled with very unladylike snorts erupted from behind her hands. I stood back and waited. I mean, she had to quit sometime. Didn't she? I glanced at Adam, who was studying *me* just a bit too closely. He shrugged and turned his attention back to Mrs. Lancaster, who was still laughing.

"Should we call someone?" I asked.

"What for?" Adam asked.

"Oh, I don't know. Maybe she needs someone to shoot her with a tranquilizer or something?"

"That's against protocol," Adam admonished.

"Too bad," I replied.

I leaned against the wall and crossed my arms, prepared to wait God knows how long. Mrs. Lancaster's laughter didn't seem to be winding down at all.

Adam and I waited a good 10 minutes until Mrs. Lancaster's laughter suddenly came to a complete stop. I moved away from the wall and uncrossed my arms in an effort to appear a little more respectful.

Mrs. Lancaster stood and smoothed her skirt, then turned and leveled her gaze on Adam and I. Speaking with the same calm she'd exhibited earlier, she said, "I'm sorry to have to inform you that the poor young man on the stretcher is definitely not my son. Can we go now?"

My mouth was hanging open in surprise, and I quickly told myself to close it. "Are you sure?"

Mrs. Lancaster nodded. "I told you I'd know if one of my children were in trouble. I knew it couldn't be him."

"Are you sure?" I asked again dumbly.

Mrs. Lancaster looked at Adam. "Is there something wrong with her? Why does she keep repeating herself like that?"

Adam shook his head. "She's new, you know."

"Ohh, " Mrs. Lancaster nodded, as though that explained everything.

"Charlie," Adam said, "I'm going to take Mrs. Lancaster upstairs and try to clear up this, err, misunderstanding." He took Mrs. Lancaster's elbow and started directing her to the outer door. I followed them.

Adam turned back and looked at me questioningly.

"What?" I asked.

"I need you to tidy up here." He looked pointedly at the now unidentified body lying on the stretcher.

"You can't be serious?" I stated flatly. I didn't care if Mrs. Lancaster heard every word. I was *not* going to be left alone in the morgue with the body of the day.

"Of course, I'm serious." The look that came into his eyes was positively cold and scary, and I felt a sudden chill. Adam obviously didn't like his authority being questioned. I decided to tidy up after all and walked over to where "we don't know who he is" was lying.

I heard the door close behind Adam and Mrs. Lancaster and decided to take a few minutes to compose myself. I plopped into the chair Mrs. Lancaster had just vacated and stared at the now unidentified man on the stretcher. I wondered if I should put him back in the drawer labeled "Mark Lancaster" or in a drawer without a name. If I were Mark Lancaster I wouldn't want some dead guy in a drawer with my name on it. I thought about stealing a finger from the body and wondered if Horace would notice that it wasn't his. I tossed aside that idea immediately. I was no finger thief and, besides, I was positive that Horace would notice.

I closed my eyes and tried to sort out my life. What was up with Adam and that whole turn-on thing earlier? I was sure that wasn't normal behavior for hospital administrators and thought I'd mention it to Sam, which led me to another question. Why, after only one almost dinner date, did Sam get so upset about Mendoza's presence in my apartment? The obvious reason was their old baggage. He still blamed Mendoza for his old girlfriend's untimely disappearance. I tried to place myself in Sam's shoes. If I were Sam and truly believed that Mendoza had had something to do with my high school sweetheart's disappearance and felt that the same guy was honing in on my new girlfriend on top of that, well then I'd have to admire his restraint. I probably would have killed Mendoza by now.

Then there was the matter of the tape I'd found in Haley's apartment. I really wanted to get to the box I purloined and see what else was in there and what else was on the tape. For all intents and purposes, that tape clearly showed that I had been drugged. So why did Adam have the results of my drug test changed? I felt like I was on some reality T.V. show and at any moment they'd say surprise! Had ya going, didn't we?

I sighed and heaved myself out of the chair. I decided that the guy in the bag wasn't going to get up and put himself away in the drawer. Pushing the clamor in my head aside, I decided to zip up the body bag first and did so as quickly as I could. I then pushed the lever on the door and discovered that it was locked. Apparently, this door locked automatically from the inside. I pushed the larger of the two keys Adam had given me into the lock and turned it.

I pushed the door open with the stretcher and congratulated myself on managing to get the guy through it without having to have anyone hold the door for me. I wheeled the stretcher to the wall of drawers and started searching for the one that had housed him. I noticed that one of the drawers was marked "Alfred Tenny" and wondered if he was still in there. The idea made me shiver, so I moved on quickly. I found the drawer labeled "Mark Lancaster" and took a pen from my pocket, scratched out the name and wrote

"John Doe" underneath. I hesitated and, feeling sorry for the guy, added "for the time being."

I went back to the stretcher and maneuvered it up to the drawer. I opened the door and, after much adjusting and going back and forth on the height of the stretcher, got it reattached to its hinges and slid the body inside. I closed the door and exhaled in triumph. "I am morgue girl, hear me roar!" I muttered under my breath as I stripped off the rubber gloves and tossed them in the trash.

I washed my hands in one of the sinks and went to open the door. Unfortunately, it appeared to be locked and I remembered too late that Adam had inserted the key from this side as well. My stomach dropped as I realized that I'd left my keys in the door on the other side. I tried the handle again, wiggling it back and forth, and tugged at the door, hoping it would open somehow. I tugged and tugged and tugged. Finally, I had to admit defeat and turned away from the door.

My eyes immediately went to Alfred's drawer. I was locked in the very creepy morgue with even creepier dead guys. My hand went to where I kept my little phone clipped to my belt. It wasn't there, and I remembered how easily it would slip off when I sat down. So, it was most likely that the phone was on the chair in the other room. I searched the morgue for a phone. There was one hanging near the work area, and I sighed in relief as I hurried over to use it. I picked it up and went to dial but I hadn't had a chance to memorize the phone number of anyone in the hospital yet. I tried 0 hoping for an operator and simply got a series of beeps—no operator's voice. I was stumped.

I slid down the wall and sat on the floor, staring at the drawers on the other side of the room. I'm not sure how long I sat there. I just kept staring at the drawers. I had a ridiculous notion that the moment I took my eyes off them one or two might swing open. Then I'd turn around and I'd see Alfred Tenny coming toward me saying, "Where's my rent. I waaaant my rent."

I got up and tried the door again. No luck. I sat on the floor again, then got back up and picked up the morgue phone and started dialing random numbers, hoping to hit a hospital extension. I realized that I was sweating in the overly cool room and continually kept one eye on the morgue drawers. I still had no luck with the phone. I slid back to the floor and studied the morgue drawers some more. I couldn't be sure, but I was almost sure that I saw one of them move the teensiest bit. I decided that I didn't want to stare at the drawers anymore and buried my head in my arms. With my eyes closed, I started counting slowly to try and calm myself. I heard someone laugh and I shrieked in terror, lifting my head to look around wildly, only to find Mendoza staring down at me.

## Chapter 27

I looked up at Mendoza, dumbfounded. He was dressed in nice-looking form-fitting slacks and a halfway decent-looking shirt. He was shaved for a change, and, if anything, his eyes looked even more impossibly blue than they did when his face was covered with the stubble I was used to. His shiner had gone down a bit, and the black-and-blue markings actually gave him a rugged, tough guy look.

"I assume these keys are yours?" he asked with a cocky grin and tossed them down to me. "What are you doing sitting on the floor?"

I ignored his question and fired back, "What are you doing here?"

"We have a lunch date. When I asked for you at the triage office, they told me that the last they knew you were headed to the morgue with Adam Petrovich. I waited a bit, then decided that we were going to miss our date if I kept waiting for you, so I decided to come get you myself."

"Oh," I replied.

"So?" he asked.

"So what?"

"So, did you lock yourself in here?"

I grimaced. It made no sense to deny the obvious. "Yep."

"So, I guess that means I'm a bona fide hero in your book, huh?" He grinned a lazy, self-satisfied grin.

"If I admit to that, are you going to hold it over my head for the rest of my life?"

"No, in some cultures it just means you're my slave until you return the favor."

I laughed. "I think that only applies when you save someone's life. I was hardly in a life-threatening position."

Mendoza raised his eyebrows and reached down to help me up. The contact of his warm fingers on my icy-cold hand felt good. "What if no one came down for days?" he asked. You could have starved to death, or seeing the way you were trembling with your hands over your eyes, you could have scared yourself to death long before then. Yep, I definitely saved your life. You're my slave girl for now."

I wobbled up to my feet with Mendoza's aid and tried to remove my hand from his, but he refused to let go of it. I looked at him startled, and knowing that he had my full attention, grinned and said the words again. "Slave girl." I shook his hand off, harrumphed, and walked out of the morgue with Mendoza close on my heels.

My hospital-issued phone was exactly where I thought it would be—on the chair in the small antechamber, where Ms.

Lancaster viewed the body that was not her son's. I grabbed the phone without missing a beat and headed toward the cafeteria. Mendoza wasn't finished ribbing me yet, though. He fell into step beside me and studied me in an amused fashion.

"What?" I asked in an annoyed tone.

"You were scared, huh?" He seemed to be thoroughly amused by my plight.

"Scared?" I repeated. "Uh-uh, not me!"

"Come on, admit it. You were afraid one of those drawers was going to slide open and a zombie like body was going to pop up and come after you."

"Zombie like body?" I played dumb. There was no way I was going to admit I'd been imagining just that.

"You've never seen 'Night of the Living Dead'?"

"Nope."

Mendoza did his famous head scratch. "Wow! I thought everyone had seen that movie."

"Not me."

Mendoza fell silent as we entered the cafeteria. He seemed truly disconcerted that I'd never seen the movie. He looked like a disappointed little boy. I wondered what he'd been like as a little boy and realized that I knew next to nothing about the man—that is, other than the fact that he was incredibly annoying and incredibly attractive at the same time.

I studied his back as he ordered food from the cafeteria matron and wondered if he'd ever been married or had kids. Did he live by himself, with roommates or with his mother? Then, I shook myself because, in all actuality, I really shouldn't care one way or another.

It was my turn to order and I got a chef's salad in an attempt to be good to myself, and an order of cheesecake for the same reason. The way things were going in my life; I figured I deserved comfort food.

Mendoza paid for both lunches, and we made our way to a table in the corner of the cafeteria. That was about as cozy a place as you could find in the utilitarian environment of the hospital's cafeteria.

"You look cute when you're asleep," Mendoza stated as he sat down.

If he'd been trying to shock me, he succeeded. I was in the process of trying to rip open a packet of blue-cheese dressing and I squeezed too hard, making the dressing shoot straight into Mendoza's good eye.

"Oh my gosh! I'm so sorry," I gasped and leaned over the table with my napkin to dab at his eye.

It was at that moment I heard Sam's voice behind me. "Well, if this isn't a cozy little scene."

I turned and attempted to explain. "I shot blue cheese dressing in his eye."

Sam raised an eyebrow. "The good one or the bad one?"

"The good one. Want to join us?"

Sam put a hand on my shoulder and leaned down to whisper in my ear. "I'd like to have you for lunch." Then he straightened and said, "As a matter of fact, I just ate. Maybe some other time." He squeezed my shoulder and walked away.

Now I knew what it felt like to need a cold shower. I had felt Sam's whisper all the way to my groin and back.

"Did you ever get the sense he doesn't like me?" Mendoza joked, as he finished wiping the dressing away from his eye.

"Why would he," I asked, "other than because you might be stealing his girlfriend again? He drove by last night and saw your car in my parking lot," I added.

Mendoza paused in mid-bite of his sandwich. "Oh, he thinks you and I . . . ?"

I nodded.

"It's not such a bad idea."

"You want more dressing?" I asked sweetly.

"Really! But it's too bad I never mix work with pleasure."

"Never?" I asked, feeling slightly disappointed for no good reason that I could think of.

"What, you considered the possibility?" he asked with an amused expression on his face.

"Of course not!" I replied a little too passionately.

"I see. Well, then, let's get down to business. The sooner we close this case, the sooner we can explore other options."

"Humph," I replied. I felt like an erotic Ping-Pong ball bouncing back and forth between Sam and Mendoza.

"Humph, yourself. You want me and you know it."

"Cheeky bastard, aren't you?"

Mendoza stopped eating and leveled his gaze at me with searing intensity. "No, just brutally honest."

I decided to change the subject. I had all kinds of fluttery feelings that I couldn't deal with at the moment and decided that the business at hand was a better subject. "So what did you want to talk to me about?"

Mendoza leaned back in his chair and studied me carefully. "Okay, I want you to hear me out before you call me crazy."

"I already know you're crazy, so shoot," I answered sarcastically.

"I think someone is trying to reenact the Trufalic clan ritual, and I think you've been targeted as the virgin they need."

My mouth dropped open. "You're crazy!"

"Think about it. Alfred's interest in the Trufalics, the surveillance he had you under and the very coin he wrote about, disappeared. Plus you bear the mark."

"The mark?" I was lost.

"When you showed me the bruise on your hip the other day, I noticed you have a birthmark a little lower that could be interpreted as the form of the fourth coin."

"Huh?" I rolled my eyes. I knew I had a birthmark back there but had never really given it a second thought.

"Seriously, I think you're in danger of becoming a clan sacrifice." Mendoza took a healthy bite of his club sandwich.

"Okay, let's say this is all true. How would these people know I was a virgin and, with Alfred dead, who else has an interest in this stuff?"

"Truth serum and the bruise on your hip. I think they injected you with the benzodiazepine and they asked you point blank. That's where your bruise came from. It looks a lot like some of the track marks I've seen on junkies."

I thought of the tapes under my bed and studied Mendoza as he chewed his sandwich. I had a desperate need to share my information, and it appeared that Mendoza would believe that at least I didn't take the drug willingly.

"Do I have food on my face or did I sprout a second nose or something?" Mendoza asked, startling me from my thoughts.

"What?" I asked.

"You were burning a hole through me with your stare. What are you thinking about?" he asked.

"You need to come to my place tonight," I stated directly.

Mendoza smirked. "I thought I just told you I don't mix business with pleasure."

"Not that way. I have some information I need to share."

"What kind of information?"

"Something I found last night."

"Does it happen to be contained in a shoebox?"

I flushed and nodded yes.

He looked triumphant. "I knew there was more to that box than shoes!"

"Whoo hoo! You get the sleuth of the day award," I replied dryly.

Mendoza shrugged. "I like being right."

I nodded. "I kind of got that impression."

He leaned back in his chair. "So what time do you want me to come over?"

It was my turn to shrug. "Anytime after 6 o'clock, provided it's not like close to midnight or something."

"Afraid Sam's going to come spying again?" he put in mischievously.

"No, I just want to get to bed at a decent hour for once."

"Did I tell you that you look cute when you're sleeping?" he asked.

"Do you want my fist in your good eye instead of blue cheese dressing?" I flushed again and he noticed.

"Are you blushing? You *are* blushing!" He stopped talking, and a bemused expression crossed his face.

"What?" I asked perturbed again.

Mendoza lost the bemused expression and focused his gaze on me again. He was all business now. "Okay, so who else would know that you're a virgin? I mean, where would Alfred have gotten that information initially?"

I took a bite of my salad and chewed thoughtfully. I truly couldn't think of anyone, and shook my head no. "I don't know of anyone. Not even my mother knows that."

Mendoza took a rather large bite of his sandwich, finishing it off. "Maybe it'll come to you later. It's important because whoever had that information shared it with Alfred and whoever else is involved in this. That person is probably the key to unraveling this whole thing."

"You're proceeding as though your assumption is correct. Maybe my virginity has nothing to do with Alfred. Maybe he was just a pervert getting his jollies. Did it ever occur to you that this whole Trufalic clan idea is just a teensy bit nuts?"

"Lady, just about everything that's happened since I laid eyes on you has been nuts—but you're real. Plus I have a hunch about this case, and I'm legendary in the hunch department."

I raised an eyebrow. "A real bona fide legend, huh?"

Mendoza stood up and gathered the remains of his lunch. "In the flesh," he countered. "See you tonight, slave girl." He winked and was gone.

I was left alone with my half-eaten cheesecake. I looked at it and suddenly had no appetite. If what Mendoza had said was true, my virginity could very well be in danger—not to mention my life. Although I had to admit that my virginity wasn't something that I felt a need to protect. After all, I was trying to get rid of it, wasn't I?

It was then that I had a brilliant idea. If I lost my virginity, then all the other stuff would go away. If Mendoza's legendary hunch was correct, then no virginity meant no clan, no drugs and no more weird stuff in my life, except for my job. I took my tray to the cafeteria's trash bin and went looking for Sam with a firm intent.

I found him working in the back of the E.R. He was attending to an elderly woman with Alzheimer's disease who was insisting that she needed a bedpan. He seemed to be trying to tell her that they'd catheterized her when she arrived, so that all her urine problems were over.

"But Doc, I have to pee." I heard her say.

Sam winced. "Now, Ms. Weathers, as I explained two minutes ago, we inserted a tube in your urethra that takes your urine to a bag. You don't even have to think about peeing. Our catheter does all the work for you."

"Oh, well thanks, Doctor. I hate those bedpans you know." Ms. Weathers smiled gratefully at Sam, and then she demanded, "What happened to your face, young man?"

I was standing across the room, and Sam's eyes met mine. "Bad luck, Ms. Weathers. And it looks like more just walked in the door." He started to turn away from Ms. Weathers' stretcher when the elderly woman shouted shrilly, "Can someone help me? I've got to pee!"

Sam slapped his head in frustration. He paused and debated for a moment, then chose to ignore Ms. Weathers and came to my side.

"Are you waiting for me?" he asked.

Ms. Weathers continued to wail for help behind him.

I gestured toward Ms. Weathers. "Is there anything we can do for her?" I asked, hoping he could hear my question over her wailing.

"No, she's hopelessly confused. Even if we provided a bedpan, she'd forget that she was sitting on it within seconds."

"Oh," I said thinking, that I'd prefer to have someone just smother me with a pillow if I ever ended up that confused.

"So how was lunch?" Sam asked.

"Interesting," I replied.

His eyes took on a hard glint. "How so?"

I sighed. "Look," I said, "I don't know why you've got such a nasty attitude about Mendoza. You have nothing to be upset about. Our relationship is strictly professional."

"Then what was he doing at your apartment so late last night?" Sam countered grimly.

"Honestly?" I asked.

"Honestly," he answered.

"He came back to question me because, if you remember, he thought I was a druggie criminal and he wanted to ask about my relationship with Adam Petrovich."

"Adam?" Now Sam looked thoroughly confused.

"Yes. Apparently Adam reviewed the results of my blood test and cleared me of any illegal drug use. So, Mendoza wanted to know if I was sleeping with the guy."

Sam looked incredulous. "Are you?" he asked bluntly.

I stomped my foot. "NO!" I said a little too loudly, but with Ms. Weathers' shrill pleas for urinary assistance I doubted anyone could hear me. "I haven't ever slept with *anyone*—which is why Mendoza wanted to have lunch with me today."

Sam grinned and waggled his eyebrows. "I guess so. I mean a virginal preacher's daughter? You're hot - but damn, that's every man's wet dream."

"Including yours?" I asked unabashedly.

Sam gave me a wicked leer. "Of course!"

"Good!" I said. "Meet me at my place tonight, and I'll make all your dreams come true."

"Huh?" he asked, a look of confusion spreading across his face.

"You heard me! You get first dibs on this virginal preacher's daughter. Be there at 7 o'clock sharp," I ordered as I walked away.

"But Charlie!" he called after me.

"But nothing," I called back over my shoulder. I was resolute in my determination to get my life back on track and at the moment I felt there were much worse things than having sex with the delectable Dr. Macgregor.

The rest of what was left of the day passed in a blur. It was still the height of flu season, and I was continually running for pink basins and calling housekeeping. Sandy was still in the waiting room, but she remained quiet and only stared at me silently as I did my job. Seeing her reminded me of the nightmare I'd had when I was sleeping on Haley's couch, and I tried to shake the resulting unease I felt at the memory.

As I clocked out later that day, I congratulated myself on surviving yet another day at Cedars and rushed home to prepare for my planned deflowering. I envisioned a candlelit dinner—after all, I still had a fridge full of the Chinese food Sam had brought over, didn't I? Then I realized I needed clean sheets, so I had to do laundry before Sam got there. I hummed as I swung into my building and headed for my door.

## Chapter 28

After closing the door behind me, I quickly loaded up my dirty clothes and sheets, intending to head for the laundry room, which was in the basement—not my favorite place in the building. The room was dark, dank and musty. Usually I'd just take my clothes down to the bright and airy Buff and Fluff down the street. They had a TV, fairly recent magazines, a coffee machine and a little old lady who made sure the place stayed nice and tidy. I liked nice and tidy, I did not like dark and musty.

After changing into navy sweats, I looked for my laundry detergent and remembered I was out of it. I decided dishwashing soap was the next best thing and grabbed the bottle off the kitchen counter along with my dryer sheets with the little bear on the box. Experience told me that the dryer sheets would pretty much ensure that, no matter what I did, everything would come out smelling pretty much okay.

I gathered my courage and marched downstairs to the laundry. I felt for the wall switch in the dark and flicked it on. The low-wattage bulb illuminated a room with a cement floor and a tired-looking washer and dryer in the corner. I flipped open the lid and did a double take when I realized there was something already in the washer.

I peered in closer. A rotten smell, like that of a dead, wet dog, wafted from the machine. I was gazing at stuff that looked like matted hair. I was pretty sure it was some sort of a rug or a dead animal. I wanted to lean toward the rug idea but I couldn't be sure. I grabbed a broom that was leaning against the wall and poked at the thing. It didn't move. I poked at it some more until I was pretty sure it wasn't going to jump out at me, then debated about what to do. Usually, I'd just call Alfred. But Alfred was no longer available. Besides, I was in a hurry. I took a deep breath, reached in and grabbed the thing with both hands.

I quickly realized what it was and flung it away across the room. It was a dead cat. A dead black cat in the washing machine was not a good omen. I tried not to think about that and stuffed my laundry in the machine with a good amount of dishwashing soap, hoping to wash away any remnants of the dead cat woogies and started the machine.

Knowing I needed to do something about the cat, I decided to see if Haley had a shovel, and started up the stairs.

When I knocked on her door, she opened it almost immediately. Haley was her usual colorful self, made all the more so by her sun babe bronzed tan that hadn't seemed to fade the least bit.

"Hi, Haley."

"Can I help you?" she asked.

"Um," I replied. "You wouldn't happen to have a shovel, would you?"

"A shovel?" she repeated. "What on earth for?"

"Well, I kind of need it to shovel up a dead cat."

Haley looked surprised, and then turned a bit green. "What cat?"

"The dead one down in the laundry room."

"You killed my cat?" she asked in shock.

"You have a cat?" I asked. We had a strict rule prohibiting pets in the building. I honestly had no idea that Haley had a cat.

"Yes I have a cat. I mean, I *hope* I still have a cat; he's been missing for a few days."

"He wasn't black was he?" I know it was a stupid question. If Haley, of all people, had a cat, of course it would have to be black. It went with her being a seer and all the crystal ball stuff.

"As a matter of fact, ..." she said before she was able to grasp what I had told her. "He's in the laundry room? Are you sure he's dead?"

"Yes and yes," I replied.

"You killed my cat?" she asked again.

"No, not me. I just found it in the washing machine when I went to do laundry. I swear I didn't kill it!"

Haley sighed. "That rotten bastard."

"Yeah, he's been dead for a while if the smell is anything to go by."

"Not the cat." Haley rolled her eyes. "I mean Alfred."

"You think Alfred killed your cat?"

Haley nodded, tears welling up in the corner of her eyes. "Who else? He hated animals and he especially didn't like De ..."

"You mean he knew you had a cat?" I suddenly remembered Alfred's last message—about the laundry room being out of service, and wondered if he had indeed killed Haley's cat.

Haley waved her hands in exasperation. "Never mind. Take me to my cat."

I led her to the laundry room and pointed to the corner. Haley immediately went over, gathered the cat in her arms and held him to her bosom. I couldn't imagine how she could stand the smell.

"His name was Demon," she offered.

I nodded and tried to look sympathetic. "Why would Alfred kill your cat? Why not just evict you or tell you to get rid of it?"

"He couldn't," she replied. "I had too much on him and...." She stopped talking and choked on a sob.

"Too much what?" I asked.

"Never mind. It doesn't matter now that he's dead."

I was a little perplexed. "Now that Alfred's dead or now that the cat's dead?"

"Both," Haley answered, still hugging her cat.

"What are you going to do with Demon?" I asked. I was a little worried she'd gone off the deep end and wondered what she was planning to do with the fur-clumped corpse.

"Why, I'm going to have him cremated, of course. That way I'll be able to keep him near me always." Haley looked at me like I was off my rocker for even asking the question.

"Huh." I would have never thought of a cat crematorium. I mean, when I was a kid and our pets died, my father would just put it in a black trash bag, say a prayer over it and toss it in one of the metal cans to be picked up with the trash.

I noticed the washer winding down on its last spin. I was anxious to continue preparing for my planned evening activities, so I flipped open the lid and started pulling out the wet clothes to put in the dryer. I tried not to notice the cat hair that was clinging to everything. I hoped the hair would disappear in the dryer vent and stuffed about 12 of the dryer sheets in the load for good measure.

I looked into the washer for errant socks and undies, and noticed some loose change. I leaned in to scoop it up and I stopped cold. I was staring at what I was almost positive was one of the Trufalic coins. I picked it up and held it under the low-wattage light bulb for a better view and tried to figure out how the coin had gotten in there. I glanced back at the open dryer door and noticed the shirt I'd worn to work on my first day. I remembered the day Alfred was brought in as a code blue and recalled going through his pockets. I remembered slipping his change into my shirt pocket, and I felt my heart speed up in my chest at the memory. I swung the dryer door shut and flipped the machine on, anxious to get back to my apartment and study the coin more carefully.

When I turned back toward Haley, she held out her hand. "Give it to me."

"Give what to you?" I asked.

"Don't be a moron. The coin, stupid."

This was not the Haley I knew. I figured she was probably so overcome with grief over her cat that she didn't know what she was saying. "It was in Alfred's pocket. It doesn't belong to you," I replied.

Haley stood there silently for a moment, and then lunged for the hand that was holding the coin. I sidestepped her and turned quickly to avoid contact. She was still clutching Demon in her other arm.

"Give it to me, Charlie. You don't know what you've got there."

"No," I answered. "I have to get it back to the hospital and log it in," I said, trying to reason with her. Haley made another lunge for my hand and nearly dropped Demon in the process. She managed to grab his tail just as he was about to hit the cement. She looked down at Demon and then at me, and I saw a wicked look cross her face.

"Don't even think about it, Haley," I said.

Haley just smiled and started swinging Demon by his tail.

I reached into my sweatpants and stuffed the coin inside my underwear. "There, it's nice and secure in my undies. Just try and get it." Haley continued to swing the cat, gaining more momentum.

"I know you can't possibly be thinking of clocking me with your beloved, dead cat," I said.

Haley smiled and swung the cat higher. "Give me the coin, Charlie. If it gets in the wrong hands...."

"Sorry, no can do," I interrupted her.

I did the only thing I could think of and turned and ran up the stairs. The cat went sailing past my head, missing me by about an inch. He landed halfway up the steps and started tumbling back down toward me. I jumped and avoided the cat and sprinted to my apartment, closing and latching the door just as what sounded like a dead cat thumped against the door. "Jeez, what is wrong with you?!" I yelled to Haley. The only response I got was the sound of Haley's apartment door slamming shut.

I tried to think of a good hiding spot for the coin and decided to tape it under the hood of the stove. I'd seen that in a movie once and it had worked. I realized that I was shaking and spied the wine that Sam had brought with him on his first visit. I poured a glass and drank it down in two gulps. I poured another glass, took it into the bathroom with me and ran my bath.

An hour later, I was feeling pretty good, thanks to the wine, and quietly stepped into the corridor in a furtive attempt to retrieve my laundry. I tiptoed down the hall to the basement, unloaded the dryer and quickly tiptoed back. There was no sign of Haley. There were, however, clumps of cat hair stuck to my door, on the spot where poor Demon had made contact earlier. I didn't want to linger in the hall and left the clumps where they were.

After putting clean sheets on the bed (I was pleased to note that they had few cat hairs on them), I chose my outfit for the evening. I decided the black miniskirt couldn't hurt my plans and, in an attempt to be festive and full of the holiday spirit, decided on a red silk shirt. I thought it was probably a pretty good idea to forgo the nylons in light of prior difficulties in that area and slipped on the Hepburn boots. A quick fluff of my hair, a swipe of mascara, some lip-gloss and I was ready—with 10 minutes to spare before Sam was due to arrive. I poured myself another glass of wine and carried it and the bottle into the living room along with another wine glass for Sam when he arrived.

I had to admit I was nervous. It didn't help much that Haley had tried to clock me with her cat. Even though I thought Haley was weird and eccentric, I had always enjoyed her deep down. The change in her behavior along with the drug thing had me confused and doubting my own judgment with regard to people—not to mention that now I had to worry about being clobbered every time I stepped foot from my apartment.

I switched on the television and tried to find a program to distract me. Everything on the tube, including the commercials, had a holiday theme. The commercials all showed chic holiday revelers buying chic things for their chic holiday festivities. I looked at my Charlie Brownish Christmas tree standing in the corner. It wasn't exactly chic, but it was festive in its own wilted, needle-less sort of way. I tried to remember the last time I'd watered it and decided that, since I couldn't remember, it was time to water it again. I got up to get water from the kitchen and noticed that I was a little woozy from the wine. I got myself some water too.

More needles fell off the tree as I watered it and I hoped I wasn't too late. I didn't want Mendoza adding tree slaying to my list of crimes. I settled back on the couch and left the channel on that was showing "It's a Wonderful Life," and that's the last thing I remember about the evening.

The next thing I knew, I was waking up in my bed with my tongue stuck to the pillow. I tried to figure out how I'd gotten there, but the pounding in my head kept getting in the way. I wished my bottle of Advil would magically float to my bed along with a glass of water. My head thumped harder at even the thought of actually getting up and trying to make my way to the kitchen.

I lay there with my eyes closed and realized I was suffering from all the symptoms of a massive hangover. It was then that I remembered the wine. I remembered pouring a third—or was it a fourth—glass after watering the tree. Then nothing. I had no memory of anything after that. Did I pass out? If I did, how did I get into bed? I slowly lifted the covers and peeked down. I was wearing nothing but underwear. Well, obviously I'd gotten partially undressed somehow. I lay there trying to remember, but nothing was coming to me. I stared at the ceiling, trying not to panic, and counted my breaths. Something was off with that as well. I was counting four breaths for every two I was taking. It was then that I realized someone else was breathing in my room.

## Chapter 29

I kept my eyes on the ceiling and slowly moved my arm toward the center of the bed. Sure enough, I made contact with another person. I turned my head and looked to my right. It was dark in the room but there was just enough light to make out someone lying next to me. I tried not to panic. After all, whoever it was, the person was just sleeping, right? I mean, other than a pounding head, I didn't seem to have been ravaged or anything, which had been the point of the whole evening anyway. I frowned, wondering why I hadn't been ravaged.

I summoned enough courage to lean over and flick on the bedside lamp. After all, I decided, lying there *wondering* whom I was sharing my bed with wasn't helping matters. I flicked on the light, gasped and flicked it back off.

The pain in my head was even worse. It was Mendoza who was sound asleep next to me. I felt every nerve ending in my body go into high alert and stared hard at the ceiling again. I had the town's hottest, sexiest detective in—I mean, on—my bed. I had to smile just the teensiest bit at that.

Just then he shifted, reached out—still asleep—and pulled me to him. He wasn't under the covers with me and was fully clothed, but the warmth of his arm around me, and his breath in my hair was doing extremely strange things to me. I was reminded of the pictures I'd seen of lava flows.

I groaned under my breath in frustration at my inability to remember the evening and wondered what had happened to Sam. I groaned again when Mendoza's hand jerked in his sleep against the covers over my belly. Lightning—liquid lightning—kept trying to interfere with my reasoning capabilities. The fact that I really had to go to the bathroom made it even harder to think straight.

I tried to ignore the call to the bathroom, but it was impossible. I really wanted to lie there and enjoy the liquid lightning sensation, but my bladder was making it impossible. Plus, I really wanted to know why I'd lost the evening. I decided it was either wet the bed or try to slither away from Mendoza, whose heat was seeping through the covers and infiltrating the nether reaches of my body.

I inched my way away from him and slipped one leg out from under the covers until my foot touched the floor. Mendoza didn't move. I inched away some more until my other foot touched the floor. Now I just had to slip my torso away from his arm—his lovely, warm, snuggly arm. I slipped from underneath it and I was free. I stood on wobbly legs, my head still throbbing, and tiptoed across the floor toward the bathroom.

Once in the bathroom, I sighed with relief and did my business. I caught sight of myself in the mirror and stopped dead in my tracks. I looked terrible. My eyes were bloodshot and my hair was sticking up at impossible angles. I did my best to repair the damage, using eye drops for my eyes and water for my hair. I decided to brush my teeth too, since it felt like I'd swallowed something dead.

Finally finished, I debated about going to the kitchen for an Advil and a glass of water or trying to snuggle back into bed with Mendoza. I had a guilty flash of Sam and decided that pain relief was the better option. Still clad in just a bra and undies, I swung the door open to head for the kitchen, but seeing Mendoza, his eyes still heavy from sleep, standing in front of me when I opened the door sort of nixed that idea. I shrieked and slammed the door shut in his sleepy face. I mean, I was almost naked, wasn't I?

Mendoza knocked on the door. "Who's there?" I asked rather stupidly.

"Me," came back his answer.

"Who's me?" I was stalling for time.

"Mendoza. Come on. I've got to pee, Charlie."

"But I'm almost naked."

"As if I care," Mendoza answered.

Ouch, that hurt. After all, most guys I knew would care if I were naked or not.

"You don't care?" I asked through the door.

"Not at the moment. Do you want me to care?"

"Most guys care." I answered.

Silence.

I decided to change the subject. "Okay, so close your eyes, and I'll come out and you can get in."

"My eyes are closed," came his reply.

"Promise?" I asked.

"On my life," he answered dryly.

"Okay, I'm opening the door. You'd better swear your eyes are closed." I opened the door and saw that, true to his word, Mendoza's eyes were scrunched tight. He really looked cute with his hair all mussed up and his eyes scrunched shut like that. He looked almost like a little boy—except for the 5 o'clock shadow, that is.

I squeezed by him and fled to the bedroom for my clothes.

When he emerged from the bathroom, I was dressed in my cozy blue sweats and was in the kitchen getting a glass of water. I chugged it with about four Advil tablets. My heart was beating a little rapidly. I'd checked the clock and it was almost 4 a.m. I'd lost a huge swatch of time and was anxious to find out what had happened to my plans to get deflowered. I mean, I was pretty sure I hadn't accomplished that feat. I'm sure I'd feel different somehow if I had, and I felt exactly the same as I always did—except for the headache, that is.

Mendoza stood in the entrance to the kitchen and ran a hand through his rumpled hair. "How are you feeling?" he asked

"Well my head's pounding and I can't remember much about last night, except that I was drinking wine and watching 'It's a Wonderful Life' on T.V. Do you suppose you could fill in some of the blanks?" I asked anxiously.

Mendoza motioned for me to follow him, and we both sat down at the dining room table. "Well," he began, "I showed up at about 8:30. You didn't answer the door, so after a while, I tried the knob and it was unlocked. I opened the door, and you where halfway to it, on your way to answer it. You looked like you'd been sleeping, and, oh yeah, you were swaying on your feet."

"Swaying?" I asked.

"Yep, kind of like the town drunk."

"Oh," I answered.

"Then you asked me where Macgregor was."

"I did?"

Mendoza nodded. "Apparently you were expecting him to ... how did you say it? Oh yeah, you were expecting him to deflower you."

"I told you *that*?" I asked in complete embarrassment.

"Yes, among other things." Mendoza grinned.

"What other things?" I asked. I kind of felt like I was choking, but I had to know what I said.

"Oh, only that you thought I was sexy."

"No, I didn't."

Mendoza waggled his eyebrows. "Oh yeah—and hot."

"No."

"Yep, and that's not all."

"Oh, God!"

"You said I'm a stud and you wouldn't mind if I took Macgregor's place in the deflowering thing."

"Please tell me you're kidding."

Mendoza's grin got wider. "Nope, that was right before you wound yourself around me and tried to give me a big sloppy kiss."

"Oh *puh-lease*. You expect me to believe that?"

"Would you believe you bit me?"

I shook my head in consternation. "Absolutely not."

Mendoza pointed to a definite bite mark on his neck. "It's true."

I buried my head in my arms on dining room table. "Oh God! Oh God! Oh God! This can't be happening."

"You were sloppy drunk and determined to get rid of your virginity."

"I almost never get drunk. I don't know how that could have happened."

"Probably the empty bottle of wine on the living room table."

I uncovered my face and looked at him. "I drank it all?" I asked incredulously.

"The evidence appears to support that fact."

"Um, did you happen to take me up on my offer?"

Mendoza had the nerve to laugh. "What do you think?"

"Well, I was nearly naked when I woke up."

"That's because you threw up all over yourself after you bit me."

I groaned and covered my face with my hands this time. "Yuck, I'm sorry."

"Actually, it's for the best. Up until you yakked I was more than a little tempted to take you up on your offer."

"Really?"

I peeked at him from behind my hands. Why did his eyes have to be so impossibly blue?

"Of course. I'm a man, aren't I? I don't know many red-blooded men who wouldn't be tempted at an inebriated offer for sex with a very long-legged attractive woman."

I think I may have blushed at that assessment. "What happened after I yakked?" I asked.

"You passed out. I cleaned you up and put you to bed. Your clothes are hanging in the shower."

Now I know I was blushing. The thought of Mendoza undressing me and putting me to bed would usually have been enough to bring on a seizure at the very least. In my present state, the thought could have potentially lethal consequences.

"You stayed," I stated.

He shrugged nonchalantly. "Yeah, I didn't want to leave you passed out and vulnerable like that. Who knows? Macgregor might have shown up and taken advantage. I don't think he has the will power that I do."

I rubbed my temples. "That was the whole point though. I figured if I could lose my virginity, all the other stuff would go away."

"Like?" he asked.

"You know the cult, the coin... Speaking of which, I found one of those in my laundry earlier."

Mendoza sat up straighter in his chair. "You did?"

I nodded. "I think it was Alfred's. I accidentally ended up with it after he coded in the E.R."

"How's that?" Mendoza wondered.

"I stuck it in my shirt pocket along with the other stuff that was in his pockets while I was trying to I.D. him. Then I passed out in the E.R. and totally forgot about it until I did my laundry and found it in the washer."

"Where is it?" Mendoza asked.

"I hid it in the kitchen. Hang on." I got up to retrieve the coin and noticed with some relief that my headache seemed to be ebbing a bit. I went directly to the stove and looked under the hood. The coin was gone! I frantically searched under the hood, on top of the stove, around the burners, on the floor. The coin was nowhere to be found.

I walked into the dining room and looked at Mendoza, who was looking at me expectantly.

"It's gone," I stated.

"Gone?" Mendoza stood up to go look for himself. "Where was it?"

I walked back into the kitchen with him and showed him the area. "It was here." I pointed to the spot where I'd taped it. "I learned that trick in a movie."

Mendoza did a quick search of the kitchen, including all the areas I had just checked.

"You're sure it was here?"

I nodded.

"You're sure you didn't move it after you'd started drinking?" Mendoza looked upset.

I nodded again. "I don't know what could have happened to it ... unless ..."

"Unless what?" Mendoza was leaning against the stove in his favorite position, with his arms crossed over his chest.

"Well, Haley knew I'd found it, because she was in the laundry room taking care of her dead cat when I did. When she realized what I had, she sort of went psycho on me and tried to get it away from me."

"Dead cat?" Mendoza asked. His eyes had narrowed and he was looking at me as though he thought I were crazy or something.

"Yeah, I found her cat in the washing machine. His name was Demon."

Mendoza shook his head as if to clear it. "So Haley was in the laundry room, because you found her dead cat whose name was Demon, and while you were there, you found one of the Trufalic coins and Haley tried to take it," he summarized.

I nodded. "She threw the cat at me and chased me back into my apartment."

"Oh." Mendoza stared at me in wonder while he tried to digest this new information. "Haley was the only one who knew you had the coin?"

"Yes," I answered.

"Then she must have taken it somehow."

"Oh wait, you said the door was unlocked when you got here?" I asked.

"Yeah it was."

"How could that be? I've been anal about locking that thing since I got the new locks installed after the break-in." My heart felt like a lead weight in my chest.

"You had been drinking and you were expecting company. Maybe you peeked down the hall once or twice and forgot to lock the door again."

I shook my head no. "After Haley tried to clock me with her cat, I was all the more paranoid about locking it. But still, I *was* drunk."

"Very," Mendoza added dryly.

I stared at my hands, feeling like a chastised second-grader.

"By the way," Mendoza spoke again, "the whole reason I came by tonight is because you said you had information to share with me."

"Oh yeah." I got up and went to the bedroom to get the shoebox. At least the box was right where I had left it.

Mendoza was still sitting at the table when I got back, and I set the box on the table.

"The mystery box." He smiled as he said it.

"Yep. I came across it in Haley's apartment."

"Came across it?" Mendoza repeated.

"I'm not elaborating on that since it might incriminate me." I took out the mini-recorder and the tapes. "Listen to this." I rewound the tape I'd been listening to and pushed the play button. I sat down and buried my head in my arms, too hung over and embarrassed by what Mendoza was about to hear to look up.

## Chapter 30

Mendoza listened to the tape quietly. I looked up when the audio got to the point where I had turned off the recorder when I first listened to it. Haley's voice was saying "Doctor! It would help if you'd take your hands off her."

There was the sound of rustling and Haley was saying, "I think that's enough. You got what you came for." And the tape clicked off.

Mendoza sat staring at the recorder.

"Well?" I asked. I was dying of embarrassment.

Mendoza stretched lazily and looked at me, "You really are a virgin, then."

"That's it?" I asked surprised. "That's all you got from that?"

Mendoza looked at me with a curious smile. "No, of course not. You were obviously drugged. Haley's in it up to her eyeballs for sure, but most importantly, there's a doctor out there somewhere who's also involved. What's on the other tapes?"

I shrugged. "I don't know. I haven't had a chance to listen to them."

Mendoza selected one of the tapes labeled "KH" and stuck it in the recorder. There was a bunch of voices chanting. Then the chanting stopped and there was absolute silence. A male voice started speaking in what sounded like a foreign language. This went on for quite a while, and then there was silence again. There was a whirring noise in the background that sounded like some piece of electric machinery running. The silence was broken by a piercing scream. Then, all hell seemed to break loose, with where several people shouting and the sound of a crash and more screaming. The tape ended abruptly.

"Weird," I commented.

Mendoza nodded and stuck the other tape marked "KH" in the recorder. The audio on this tape was more intelligible. A female voice that I did not recognize came through the speakers. "Kimberly, are you with us?" she asked.

Mendoza sat up in his chair as though a bolt of lightning had struck him.

What I'm assuming was Kimberly's voice answered, "Yes, who are you?"

My mind was frantically trying to associate the name. I knew I'd heard the name before, suddenly, I remembered that was the name of the young lady who'd caused the rift between Mendoza and Macgregor. No wonder Mendoza was sitting on the edge of his chair in front of me!

"I'm a friend, Kimberly," the woman answered. "And this is my friend. You may refer to him as Doctor."

"Nice to meet you, Doctor," Kimberly answered. "What's up?" She had that same slurry sound I had in my voice when I was talking on my tape.

"We have a few questions," came the voice of the so-called doctor. "Are you okay with that, Kimberly?"

"Sure," she answered gamely.

"Well, Kimberly, how's your sex life these days?"

My jaw nearly dropped on the table. Even Mendoza looked about ready to fall out of his chair.

"Is it...?" I started to ask.

"Shh!" Mendoza cut me off.

"What do you mean?" Kimberly asked sleepily.

The mysterious woman's voice answered, "You might want to get straight to the point, Doc."

"Oh, okay. Are you a virgin?" he asked.

An embarrassed giggle came from the little tape recorder.

"I think that's all we need. Thank you, Kimberly." The male voice sounded happy. The tape ended.

"Did I miss the answer?" I asked Mendoza.

Mendoza sat quietly for a moment. "I think she must have answered by nodding."

"Oh!" I reflected for a moment. "Was it your Kimberly?"

Mendoza nodded his head yes. "It certainly sounded like her. Jeez, Charlie, when you said you had information, you weren't kidding. Do you know what this means?"

I shook my head no.

"It means we're going to have to reopen Kimberly's case on top of everything else."

"But we can't prove it was her voice on the tape. We're not even supposed to have the tapes."

"Look," Mendoza said, tapping the tape case. "It's marked 'K.H.'—Kimberly Hawthorne." He tapped another tape case. "Here's one that's labeled 'C.M.'—Charlie Meadows."

"I see your point, but we still aren't supposed to have these tapes. I've watched enough "Law and Order" to know that illegally obtained evidence isn't admissible or something like that."

"True," Mendoza answered and did the Colombo head scratch thing. "You realize, don't you, that this means you're in even more danger than I previously imagined?"

"Why?" I asked with a dumb expression on my face.

"Kimberly was asked the same questions you were, and she disappeared. The screams on the other tape could very well have been hers. It certainly sounded like some ritualistic activity was going on." He looked at me with a seriousness I wasn't sure I liked.

"I'm still having a hard time believing all this stuff," I answered. But really, as I thought about it, the evidence was quickly stacking up in favor of the idea of the Trufalic clan and its ritual. I was definitely starting to feel extremely weirded out.

"The ritual is supposed to take place during the winter solstice. That's December 21—four days away," Mendoza informed me.

I gulped. "You sure you don't want to just take care of the virginity thing for me?" I joked.

Mendoza stood and walked over to squat on his haunches in front of me. He brushed back the errant hair that had fallen across my eyes. "I honestly would love to, but I don't think it's in either or our best interest, right now."

His face was so close that I could feel his breath on my cheek. His eyes were intense and serious. I knew we were treading in deep water, and I finally had to admit to myself that I was intensely attracted to this man—and it wasn't just my hormones acting up. I also admitted to myself that he was right. If I had sex with him it would go much deeper than that. I looked at the bite mark on his neck and touched it with my index finger. "Sorry about that," I stated lamely for lack of anything better to say.

"Why?" Mendoza grinned. "I'm not." He stood up and walked into the kitchen, calling over his shoulder. "What's for breakfast?"

A half-hour later we were eating Sam's Chinese food and drinking coffee. "Why do you suppose Macgregor didn't show for your date?" Mendoza asked.

I shrugged. "Maybe he did and I scared him away," I answered. "It sounds like I was in a rather ferocious state of mind last night."

Mendoza rubbed his neck and I grimaced. "Yeah, true, but I can't imagine that would scare him off."

I shrugged. "I guess only time will tell."

Mendoza glanced at his watch. "Speaking of which, I have to get home. Claudia will wonder where I've been all night."

"Claudia?" I asked. So Mendoza had a live-in girlfriend?

"Yeah, she's the love of my life. She gets upset when I'm out all night on a case."

My heart sank further. I finally admit to myself that I have feelings for this guy and he up and tells me he's got someone named Claudia waiting for him at home!

Mendoza laughed. "Are you jealous?"

I stared at him stonily. I just couldn't help it.

"You are! You *are* jealous!"

"Am not," I muttered.

"Are too," he grinned and happily ate some more lo mien.

I shoved another egg roll in my mouth. I was feeling much better physically. The mental side of things was at an all-time low, though. I changed the subject. "So where do we go from here?"

"You and me?" he asked with raised eyebrows.

"No with the clan thing."

"Oh that." He sat back in his chair and wiped his impossibly sensual mouth. "I'd like to bring Haley in for questioning, but it's risky. It could alert the whole clan organization that we're on to them. We should put you under constant surveillance for your own safety."

"Oh yeah? And just how are we going to do that?" I asked.

"Well, I could move in for a while," Mendoza stated simply.

"*Puh-lease.*" I knew he had to be joking.

"I'm serious. I don't think you should be alone, especially at night."

"Well, I'm sure Claudia would have something to say about *that*," I replied.

"Claudia?" Mendoza grinned again. "Oh, she's not a problem. I'll just bring her along with me."

I felt my mouth starting to hang open but I willed it shut. I stared at him in disbelief. "You'd bring her *here*?"

Mendoza nodded. "Either that or farm her out to one of my buddies."

At first my mouth wanted to hang open again, but then it dawned on me that, unless Mendoza was a total Neanderthal, he wasn't talking about a girlfriend. "Okay," I said. "What exactly is Claudia?"

Mendoza's broad grin disappeared a little when he realized I was on to him. "She's an Irish setter with the most beautiful red hair and soulful eyes you've ever seen."

I smiled, feeling a little foolish that I'd been jealous—however briefly—of a dog. "We have a strict no pets rule here."

"Who's going to enforce it?" Mendoza asked.

"Good question." After all, no more Alfred, no more rules. "Still," I said, "I don't want to be a bother, plus I don't think it's necessary. I think you should question Haley. If the rest of her buddies think you're on to them, maybe they'll think twice about trying to perform any hoo hoo clan thingy."

"That's the point. If the clan backs off, we have little or no chance of catching the rest of them. I strongly believe that they had something to do with Kimberly's disappearance as well, and frankly..."

"And frankly?" I interrupted him.

"Well, I'd love to catch the whole lot of them. I have a feeling we'd be able to solve Alfred's murder and Kimberly's disappearance or murder as well as the mystery surrounding all the strange things that have been happening to you lately."

I could see his point. "Okay, so we don't question Haley. But I'm also refusing your offer to move in. That might make them wary as well. I'd like this thing over and done with—the sooner the better."

Mendoza nodded. "I won't argue with you, although I think you were just a wee bit tempted at the thought of having me around all the time."

I shook my head. "I'm not sure you, your ego and I would all fit in this small apartment." Plus the thought of waking up next to him earlier was bringing back that liquid lightning sensation. I could feel my body temperature rising and my nipples getting hard. I was sooo glad I was wearing baggy sweats.

I glanced at the clock and noted with some relief that it was time to get ready for work. "It's time for you to go. I've got a job to go to."

Mendoza stood up to leave. "Okay, but I'm taking this with me." He scooped up the shoebox and its contents. "Call me if anything the least bit suspicious happens. I'll try not to be too far away."

Thinking of work reminded me of Horace and his fingers, which led me to another thought. I followed Mendoza into the living area and asked, "Besides the coins and the virgin, what else do these guys need for their ritual?"

Mendoza threw on his jacket and looked at me. "I'm not sure. There's some sort of recipe for a potion, but I didn't read it. Why?"

"I'm just wondering if they need a finger, because when I gave Horace back his fingers, one was missing."

"Good thought. I'll check when I get back to the office."

"Thanks," I said as Mendoza was heading out the door. He paused and turned back toward me. "Oh, and Charlie?"

"Now what?" I asked.

"If we want to catch these guys you might want to nix the idea of losing your virginity. I'd hate for them to disappear until they've found another target."

I blushed. "Is that the only reason? I mean it wouldn't have anything to do with your competitive relationship with Sam would it?"

Mendoza studied me for a moment. "No, I'd say it had more to do with the fact that as soon as this is over I intend to take care of that myself. And it has nothing to do with Macgregor but with the way I want you."

My mouth dropped open at his audacity. Mendoza just grinned and walked out the door. I made sure I locked it behind him.

## Chapter 31

Later, when leaving for work, I felt a thrill of relief at not having to worry about being hit by a flying cat. After all, I was 99 percent sure that it was Haley who'd taken the coin out of my kitchen. I could only assume that I must have left the door unlocked at some point the previous evening and maybe even told her where I had hidden the coin. Even so, I opened the door slowly and peeked into the hall. It was empty.

It was Friday and that in itself was a relief. After today, I would have two whole days of not worrying about Cedars' E.R. Christmas was only a week away, and I knew I'd spend most of the weekend doing last-minute shopping. I smiled to myself. Despite all the weirdness and mayhem, at least I didn't have a boring job.

The first person I ran into at Cedars was Sandy. She was coming out the door to the E.R. as I was walking in. She stopped as I held the door open for her and stared at me in her usual vacant way. She was wearing a Santa cap that had little jingle bell balls on the end. A look of recognition crossed her face, and she put her hand on my shoulder. "Be careful, Ms. Charlie," she said in greeting. "I heard the king talking to the witch."

I stared at her in surprise. I couldn't believe she remembered my name. "What did the king say to the witch?" I asked, trying to be polite.

Sandy stared at me for a moment. "The king wants to take you," she said. "I don't want him to. You've been nice to me." She removed her hand from my shoulder and jerked her head to the left, making the bells on the cap tinkle. She appeared to be listening attentively to something. "I won't let anyone stick a knife in you either."

"Huh?" I asked. But Sandy's vacant look was back, and she was moving on through the door, jingling with each step.

I shook my head and briefly wondered if I should worry about the king and the witch but tossed the thought away. As for the knife, I decided that Henrietta was probably still talking to her. Sandy was Sandy, and I knew that not much of what she said or did made sense to the rest of us. Besides, I had enough to worry about with a virgin-thirsty clan on the loose, as it was.

I stowed my stuff in my locker and picked up my hospital phone and made my way to my little desk in the E.R. I sat down and tried to concentrate on signing in patients, but it was difficult because of all the thoughts banging around in my brain. I glanced around the semi-crowded E.R. and groaned when I saw Joyce walk in and make a beeline for my desk.

She came to a stop in front of me and took up her Daphne pose, so I knew it wasn't going to be a pleasant conversation.

"Good morning, Charlie," she said in a way that suggested it was going to be anything but pleasant.

"Good morning, Joyce," I replied. "Is there anything I can help you with?"

"As a matter of fact, there is." She flipped her hair and stared hard at me.

"And that would be?"

"That would be the department's Christmas party," she stated flatly.

"Oh. Do they need help with decorations or anything?" I asked innocently.

"No. I'm just here to tell you that *I* am being escorted to the party by Dr. Macgregor."

I raised my eyebrows. "You are?"

She nodded.

"Did he ask you?" I felt a twinge of jealousy. Okay, admittedly I still had a thing for Macgregor in addition to the new thing for Mendoza. It was all very confusing at the moment.

"First thing this morning," she smiled smugly.

"Oh? And what's your gynecologist girlfriend going to have to say about that?" I asked, flashing a smile.

The smug look disappeared from Joyce's face. "You know what, Charlie?"

"What?" I kept the smile on my face.

"You're a bitch, and I don't like you." She turned on her heel and walked out.

"Funny, but the feeling's mutual," I whispered under my breath. I gazed off into space, trying to figure out why Sam would suddenly ask Joyce to the party. It also made me wonder what had happened to Sam last night and why he hadn't shown up. I mean, at least I *thought* he hadn't shown up.

My little black phone started trilling and I answered it, praying it wasn't about a code blue being brought in. "Charlie?"

"Yes," I answered.

"It's Adam Petrovich."

"May I help you?" I asked in a very businesslike tone. The guy gave me the willies.

"I'd like to have lunch with you today, if you're available."

"Why?" I asked. The surprise in my voice was apparent.

"Because I like you and want to spend some time with you," he purred on the other end of the line.

Yuck, yuck and more yuck. I was so creeped out that I couldn't even think of a good excuse to say no.

"You mean like a lunch *date*?" I inquired bluntly.

"If you want to call it that," he purred back.

"I don't," I said before I could stop myself. Then I quickly tried to do damage control. "That is, I'm sort of involved."

"Do you mean you don't want to have lunch because you're involved in work or you don't want a lunch *date* because you're sort of involved with someone else?"

"Um, the last one."

My reply was met with silence on the other end of the line. "Well, a little lunch wouldn't hurt between coworkers. Besides, among other things, I'd like to discuss Horace's missing finger with you."

My mind was racing. How did he find out about that? Adam was the head of pathology lab and on the hospital's board of directors. I probably didn't want to piss him off if I wanted to keep my job, and I really needed my job right now.

"Lunch between coworkers would be nice, Adam." I was struggling to sound pleasant. I felt like I was being blackmailed somehow. "But that's all it is, right?"

"Of course." Adam's voice was dripping with sweetness. "Say noon in my office?" I'm having something special catered and brought in."

"Your office? Catered?"

"Yes, from Kenichi. That way, everyone who comes through the cafeteria won't interrupt us. You wouldn't believe the gossips in this place."

Oh yes I would, I thought. I also thought about Kenichi. The restaurant's food was divine and uber-expensive. I hoped that I'd be able to enjoy it in Adam's presence.

"I'll be there at noon," I replied and hung up before he could purr again. How did he find out about Horace's finger? Then I remembered the paperwork. Horace had signed for his fingers minus one. Adam must have read the paperwork I'd sent via interoffice mail the day before. Damn, I thought. I never even considered that I might get into trouble that way. I felt like thumping my head on the desk again but thought better of it. My head already hurt too much anyway, and I buried it in my arms instead.

I might have dozed off for a moment, I'm not sure—after all, I had had an extremely uncomfortable evening and early morning. I started when I heard a male voice say, "Excuse me?"

I looked up to find a pleasant-looking man in his 50s standing in front of my desk. A horrible odor hit my nostrils about two seconds later.

"Yes?" I winced as I breathed in the contaminated air. "May I help you?" I wondered if the odor was coming from him. He looked so neat and clean, it didn't seem possible.

"I need to see the doctor," the man replied. "There's something wrong with my foot."

"Oh, okay, sure." I picked up a pen to take down his information and asked him to have a seat until the nurse called him. He did as I asked, and I took the form to the triage window and handed it to Katy Dee. She had changed the color of her hair from gothic black to neon red. "Nice hair," I called through the window. "Very festive."

Katy Dee just stared at me like I was an alien from outer space. I let it go and went back to my desk. The odor was still there. I looked around and couldn't fathom where it was coming from.

I decided to try to ignore the stench. Another patient came up to my desk and asked to see the doctor. She sniffed the air in an obvious way and looked at me with her face scrunched up. "Is that *you* who smells?" she asked bluntly.

"Nope, not me," I replied. "Your name?" I asked attempting to get her sign-in sheet started.

"Amanda Miles," she answered and continued to stare at me with her face still scrunched up.

I continued filling out the form, and she answered the questions, stating that she was there because of a migraine headache. "That smell is really making me sick," she stated bluntly.

"Me too. I don't know what it is. Your date of birth?" I asked.

"It's got to be you," she accused.

"It's not," I answered. "Date of birth?"

"It is too you. Why won't you admit it and do something about it? It's disgusting!" Her voice was starting to rise.

"Ms. Miles. It's not me. I'm just as grossed out about it as you are. Date of birth?"

"November 7, 1965. You stink."

"I do *not* stink." I gritted my teeth.

"I'm going to puke and it's your fault." She glared at me, then made good on her threat and threw up in my lap.

I sat there in stunned silence. She took a tissue from her purse and daintily dabbed at her mouth. "Well, if you didn't stink before, you sure do now." She turned on her heel and took a seat in the waiting room.

I looked at my lap. I was wearing a forest-green skirt and a white sweater. I had pinned a dancing Santa on the sweater in an attempt to get into the Christmas spirit. It hadn't worked then, and now Santa just appeared to be mocking me. I grabbed a paper towel from the stash that was under my desk and tried to mop some of the mess off my skirt before I stood up and made my way to the ladies' room. I dropped Ms. Miles' intake form off at the triage window as I passed it.

I threw the paper towel in the wastebasket in the bathroom, took off my skirt and did my best to clean the soiled area. At least, Ms. Miles hadn't had a huge breakfast. My phone started ringing and I answered it.

"Hey Charlie, it's Sam. We need you in the resuscitation room, STAT; a code blue is on the way in. He hung up before I could answer. Well, isn't that nice, I thought. No hello, sorry about last night? Jeez, could this day get any better? I looked down at my half-naked self. Nope, my day wasn't going to improve. How was I supposed to go to the resuscitation room with no skirt on? I dialed the triage, desk thinking that perhaps Katy Dee would let me borrow her lab coat. I figured if I could button it up, no one would know I wasn't wearing a skirt.

"Triage," Katy Dee answered.

"It's Charlie, Katy Dee. I need help."

"You want me to help you after what you said about my hair?"

"What?" I answered, "I told you I liked your hair."

The door to the ladies' room swung open and a woman in her 70s walked in. She stopped dead when she saw me standing at the sink in just heels, pantyhose and a sweater, and talking on the phone. Her mouth dropped open. I smiled and gave her a little finger wave.

"You were being sarcastic," Katy Dee accused.

"No, I wasn't. I really think your hair is cool."

The little old lady gave me a little wave back, then turned and bolted out the door as fast as her little old legs could carry her.

"Really?" Katy Dee replied.

"Absolutely, I wish I had the nerve to do something like that to my hair," I said sincerely.

"Thanks. Hey, some little old lady just tripped coming out of the ladies' room. I have to go." Then she hung up.

I dialed her number again, but she didn't pick up her phone. The phone number for the triage office was the only one I had memorized in the hospital. I looked at my skirt and did the only thing I could do. I picked it up, stuck it under the hand dryer for about a minute, put it back on and headed out to the resuscitation room. I noticed a group of people, including Katy Dee, gathered around the lady who had run out of the bathroom. She was sprawled on the floor with what looked like a badly twisted ankle—at least I hoped it was only twisted. She glared at me from where she lay on the floor, and I gave her another little wave with my fingers as I hurried past her.

I entered the resuscitation room and the patient was already there. Everyone was busily doing their part, and I walked over to Sam, who was studying the screens showing the patient's vital sign. Actually there was a definite lack of vital signs showing up on the screens over the bed.

"What can I do?" I asked. I tried to put the little old lady in the waiting room out of my thoughts. I kind of felt bad about what had happened to her.

Sam didn't so much as glance at me. "His duffel bag is on the counter. Find out who he is and log in his belongings, please."

"Sure," I said and went to work. I decided that Sam wasn't being deliberately curt. After all, he was trying to save a life. Besides, if he didn't look at me, he wouldn't notice my dripping wet skirt.

I located the patient's wallet in the duffel bag and found out that his name was Thayne Williams. He was a 34-year-old blue-eyed blond, who, according to his license, was six feet, one inch tall. I called out the information to the nurse who was charting his case and I went about logging in his belongings. His bag contained a clean T-shirt, a pair of clean socks and a pair of what appeared to be clean underwear. I found a notebook that looked as though it was used for work-related purposes. Its pages were covered with what looked like mini-blue print sketches and lists of lumber, nails and other items. The only other thing in the bag was a half-empty box of condoms.

I put everything in the bag that was used to hold a patient's personal belongings and stapled my log to the outside of the bag. "Does he have family on the way?" I called out to no one in particular.

By now the activity in the room had calmed somewhat and, according to the screen above the bed, Mr. Williams' heart was beating again. Sam looked at me and walked over. "The E.M.S. said that his wife was on her way. They called her from the scene." Sam wrinkled his nose a bit. "Um, I hate to say this, but you don't smell very good. Oh, and it looks like you wet yourself."

"I know," I replied. "I got yakked on in the waiting room. By the way, what happened to you last night?"

Sam turned those impossibly green eyes on me. "I tried to tell you before you rushed off yesterday, then never got a chance to see you again before you left work. I had to work late and then had to go by my parents' house. By the time I left their house, it was late. You can't imagine how sorry I am that I couldn't take you up on your offer. I'd like to take you to my parents' Christmas party tonight, though." He gave me a wicked grin, and I found myself transfixed by his dimpled smile. "I hope the offer still stands," he added.

I hesitated. My virginity wasn't on the table anymore, at least not until we caught the people with an ulterior interest in it. I stalled. "Didn't you ask Joyce to the department's Christmas party?" I asked.

Sam nodded and sighed. "It's complicated but I assure you that my escorting Joyce to the department party has no bearing on our relationship. Joyce and I are not dating. It's more of a work obligation."

I considered this new information and was still confused. I didn't have any other plans for the night, though, and a party sounded like a nice change of pace. "Sure, I'll go," I answered. "But some really weird things have been going on that I need to tell you about."

Sam lost the devilish grin and looked serious again. "What kind of weird things?"

"There's too much to talk about now. I'll tell you about it later."

He nodded and stroked my cheek lightly with the palm of his hand. "I'll pick you up around 7 o'clock tonight."

I nodded. My phone started trilling and I clicked it on. "Cedars, may I help you?" I inquired.

It was Katy Dee. "Charlie, there's a woman here who says she's the wife of the guy you have in the resuscitation room."

"Oh, thanks," I answered. "Tell her I'll be right there."

"Sure thing. Oh, and by the way, you might want to call Housekeeping."

"Why" I asked.

"Well, the guy with the foot problem has gangrene oozing out of the seams of his shoes and he's leaving a trail of putrid odor wherever he walks."

"Whew! So that's where the smell was coming from."

"Yeah, it's pretty obnoxious."

"Could you do me a favor and explain that to the lady with the migraine?" I asked.

"Sure, why?" Katy Dee asked.

"Because she threw up on me and seemed to enjoy it," I replied.

"If you say so." Katy Dee hung up and I grabbed Thayne's belongings and headed toward the E.R. waiting room.

## Chapter 32

Mrs. Williams was a petite, dark-haired woman in her early 30s. She was wearing jeans and a sweater that had snowflakes embroidered in the fabric. She had three children with her, who looked like they were about a year apart from one another, starting at age of three.

I escorted her and the three children to the consultation room and asked her to have a seat. She and the children crowded onto the small sofa, and I took one of the chairs. She looked around her and her nose wrinkled up.

"Do you smell something?" she asked.

I debated about trying to explain the odor and decided to play dumb. "Umm, as a matter of fact, I do. I wonder what it is?"

"Smells like vomit," she stated.

"Sure does. Or doo-doo." I looked pointedly at her young children, trying to redirect her scrutiny away from me.

She flushed and looked accusingly at the youngest. Did you doody your pants?" she asked. The child looked at her blankly. Then Mrs. Williams seemed to remember why she was here. "Is Thayne going to be okay?" she asked.

"I'm not sure," I replied. "The doctor will be in to speak with you in a moment."

"Oh God, that means he's dead, isn't he?" she wailed. The children looked startled. I was sure, however, that they were all too young to understand what was going on.

"No," I answered immediately. "It means he's very ill."

Ms. Williams wrung her hands and stared at me hopelessly. "He's the only man I've ever loved. He's got to be okay."

I nodded. "Would you like me to call someone to be with you?" I asked, "maybe a family friend or a minister?"

She nodded. "Could you call our priest? We go to St. Mary's down the road."

I pulled out my phone. "Do you have a phone number?" She immediately recited the number to me, which told me that she must be very active in the church to have the number memorized. I dialed the number and spoke to the church secretary, who assured me that Father O'Malley would be on his way immediately.

I hung up and turned my attention back to Ms. Williams. "I have the things he came in with, Ms. Williams. Would you like them?"

She nodded, and I handed the bag over to her. I remembered the box of condoms too late. For some reason I was pretty sure they were going to cause a problem. The box was the first thing she pulled out of the bag.

Her eyes widened as she stared at the box. "I think you gave me the wrong bag. These must belong to someone else," she said, holding out the offending box. Then she reached back into the bag and pulled out the notebook. "This is his, though." She continued going through the bag. "Everything else is his." She stopped rifling through the bag and stared up at me. "How did this box get in there?"

I thought fast. "Um, maybe he was holding them for a friend?" I suggested.

"Why?" she asked.

I shrugged.

She stared at the box like it was going to suddenly jump up and bite her.

I decided to excuse myself. "Ms. Williams, I'm going to let the doctor know you're here and see if he's available to speak with you."

Ms. Williams just continued to look at the box.

I walked back into the resuscitation room and found Sam. He was still monitoring Mr. Williams' vital signs. "Ms. Williams is here. Do you have a few minutes to speak to her about her husband?"

He turned away from the monitor and nodded. "Sure, I'll be there in a couple minutes."

I walked back to the consultation room and opened the door. Ms. Williams was counting the condoms in the box.

"Dr. Macgregor will be with you in a moment," I stated as I sat back down.

"Thirteen," Mrs. Williams announced.

"Thirteen?" I asked in a confused tone.

"This is a 25-count box. There are only 12 left, which means he's cheated on me at least 13 times," she stated.

"But they might not be his." I was trying to help both of them.

"What are you, stupid?" She stood up and started pacing. "How is the asshole anyway? God help me, if he isn't dead, I'm going to kill him."

I glanced at the children, who appeared to be oblivious to what was going on. The youngest sat in the corner of the couch sucking her thumb. The two older children were busy destroying a magazine that had been on the end table. At that moment, there was a knock on the door. I answered it and sighed in relief at the sight of a man in priest's garb standing outside the door. "Father O'Malley?" I inquired.

"Yes," he replied.

"Please come in. Dr. Macgregor will be joining us in a moment."

Mrs. Williams stopped pacing when she saw Father O'Malley. "Get out!" she yelled at him.

Father O'Malley seemed taken aback by her greeting. "But Rita, why? Don't you want to say a prayer for your husband?" I had to assume Rita was Ms. Williams' first name.

"No, I don't want to say a prayer for my husband," she ground out between gritted teeth. "He's a cheat and a bastard."

Sam walked in, looking crisp, extremely handsome and professional in his suit and lab coat. Ms. Williams sat down next to her children, who had moved on to the demolition of a second magazine. "Is he dead?" she asked Sam bluntly. Then she swung her gaze to Father O'Malley and yelled, "I said, get out!" Father O'Malley scurried through the door without so much as a peep.

Sam gave me a questioning look, then turned back to Ms. Williams. "I'm Dr. Macgregor," he stated, "and no, your husband is not dead."

"Damn!" Ms. Williams stood up quickly. "Take me to him then, so I can do the job."

Sam looked stunned. I guess that's not the usual reaction he got from distraught wives who found out that their spouses were okay. "Whoa there, now!" he said, as Ms. Williams headed for the door to the E.R. "Let's talk a little first."

Ms. Williams stared at Sam as though she thought he was off is rocker. "Thirteen!" she shrieked. "Thirteen times! Just try and explain that!"

Joyce had joined us by now, and she quickly assessed the situation after seeing the condom box in Ms. Williams' hand. "There, there," said Joyce, "you don't know that for sure. Perhaps some of them broke before he got them on. You don't know that he actually used them 13 times. Maybe it was only a few times."

Ms. Williams stared hard at Joyce and said exactly what I wanted to say, "You must be even stupider than you look."

"Could someone please fill me in on what we're talking about?" Sam looked totally confused.

"Ms. Williams discovered a box of condoms in her husband's belongings," I explained. "Thirteen are missing. From what I can gather, it appears the Williams' don't use condoms."

"My husband is a devout Catholic. He doesn't believe in birth control," Ms. Williams explained a bit more. "I mean, look, we've been married four years, and what do you see here?" She gestured to the children next to her. "A child for almost each year of marriage! Do you think that was *my* idea?" She started crying, and I sighed in defeat. I still didn't know where the tissues were kept.

Sam knelt in front of Ms. Williams and took her hands in his. "I understand you must be confused. But right now we need to make sure your husband survives his heart attack. Later, when he's better and no longer under my care, well, you can kill him then if you still want to, okay?"

I wanted to laugh out loud. At that precise moment I knew that Sam was a real treasure.

Ms. Williams looked into Sam's eyes and nodded. "He . . . he had a heart attack?" she asked.

Sam nodded. Ms. Williams looked at me. "Could you ask Father O'Malley to come back in?"

I nodded and left the room. Father O'Malley was standing just outside the door.

"Ms. Williams wants you to come back in," I told him.

"Is it safe?" he asked.

I considered the situation for a few seconds, "Yes. I think she wants him to get better so she can take him home and finish off the job there. That way there won't be any witnesses."

Father O'Malley looked at me as if I were nuts, but he went back into the consultation room anyway.

I decided that, with Sam and Father O'Malley there, my presence was no longer needed, so I made my way back to the Emergency Room. The odor there hit me like a ton of bricks, and I quickly called Housekeeping. Apparently, the foot guy had made a few laps around the waiting room. He was nowhere to be seen, so I assumed that he had been taken him to an examination room. The migraine lady was still there, though, and when she saw me, she quickly feigned interest in the magazine that was on her lap.

Well, she had been right about one thing. I *did* stink now and I didn't know quite what to do about it. Plus, it was time to meet Dr. Petrovich for lunch. My skirt was practically dry by now, but I could still smell the lingering aroma of vomit. I hoped the smell was just stuck in my nose and made my way to Dr. Petrovich's office, which was on the fourth floor. I took the stairs up. I wasn't exactly sure where it was located and read the nameplate on each door as I walked down the hall. I finally located his office. The nameplate read Dr. Adam Petrovich, Director of Pathology and Dr. Samuel Macgregor, Sr., Director of Oncology. I assumed that meant that Adam shared an office with Sam's father, whom I'd had yet to meet.

I knocked on the door, and a voice told me to come in. The office was rather large and plush. It was lined with bookshelves and featured two large mahogany desks on either side of the room. Adam sat at one and an older-looking version of Sam sat at the other.

Adam looked up when I came in and smiled. "Hello, Charlie. Please come in and have a seat." He gestured to one of the armchairs facing his desk. "I'd like you to meet Sam Macgregor, Sr., he's our head of oncology." I looked at Sam, Sr., who had risen from his desk and was taking a seat in the other armchair in front of Adam's desk. Sam, Sr., was about the same build as Sam, Jr.—maybe a little heavier—and his blond hair had quite a bit of silver running through it.

The senior Doctor Macgregor held out his hand, and I shook it while taking my seat. "Good to meet you, Charlie. I've heard quite a lot about you."

"I hope it was good," I commented.

"Well, let's just say that you're definitely an interesting addition to our staff," he replied. "I understand you'll be coming to the Christmas party at our home tonight."

I folded my hands in my lap in an effort to keep them still. I was suddenly nervous and had a huge case of the willies. Something about his voice sounded familiar. I couldn't decide if he sounded like his son or if I'd heard that voice somewhere else. "Yes, your son invited me this morning."

"Good, good!" Sam, Sr., answered. "It's nice to see he's coming out of his shell again."

"I hope you don't mind that I invited Sam to join us," Adam said to me.

I turned my gaze from Sam, Sr.. and managed to direct a nervous smile at Adam. "Oh no, of course not," I said, thinking that I vastly preferred this to being alone with Adam.

There was a knock on the door, and Adam answered it. He returned with several large bags with the Kenichi logo across them. He set the bags on his desk and started doling out the food—tempura vegetables and shrimp, a papaya salad and a pasta entrée. It all smelled heavenly. He handed each of us a bottle of designer mineral water to drink with our meal.

"This is so nice, Dr. Petrovich. Thank you," I said as politely as I could muster.

He handed me a fork and said, "You're more than welcome. Go ahead, dig in."

We all ate in silence for a few minutes. Then Dr. Petrovich wiped his mouth and began, "One of the reasons I wanted to have lunch with you was to offer you a project."

"A project?" I asked. That was news to me. I had thought that we'd be discussing my immediate dismissal because I had lost a patient's finger.

"Yes. It's a study we'll be doing in the E.R. Our patient satisfaction rate in that department is well below the average rate of the rest of the hospital. We want to do a survey that will give us feedback on ways to improve service down there."

"It sounds interesting," I replied. I wondered if I was off the hook with regard to Horace's missing finger.

"We'd like to start conducting the survey on Monday. I've already drawn up the questionnaire. Your job would be to call the patients a day or two after they've been discharged and ask them the questions." He paused to take another bite of his salad.

I thought of the large number of patients who visited the E.R. each day. "All the patients?" I asked.

"Oh no. One of every five."

That still seemed like quite a few, but at least it wasn't every patient. "Sure," I replied, "I'd love to help."

We discussed the survey while finishing the meal. I realized that Sam, Sr., wasn't doing much in the way of participating in the conversation. As a matter of fact, every time I glanced his way, his eyes seemed to be riveted on me. And that was making me distinctly uncomfortable. I wished he would speak, eat his food or pick his nose— anything but stare at me.

Dr. Petrovich took the last bite of his pasta and leaned back in his chair with a satisfied expression on his face. "If you have any questions once you start working on the surveys, you can call me."

"Thank you, Doctor," I replied a little stiffly. I had just snuck another peek and saw that Sam, Sr., was still staring at me.

"Sound good to you, Sam?" Adam asked.

Sam, Sr., finally tore his eyes off me and acknowledged Adam. "I think she'll be perfect, " he replied. "Are you with us, Charlie?"

I started choking on the bite I was chewing and grabbed for my bottle of water. I took a huge gulp and tried to regain my composure. I suddenly knew where I'd heard that voice before. What Sam, Sr., had just said were exactly the same words and it was the same voice that I had heard on Haley's audiotape.

"Oh, sorry," I choked. "The food went down the wrong way. Yes, of course, I look forward to the addition to my duties."

"Good, good, then we're all agreed." Adam announced enthusiastically.

Sam, Sr., stood up and tossed his still almost full plate and fork into the wastebasket next to Adam's desk. "I'm quite excited to see what the results of our little experiment will yield." He smiled at me and excused himself, stating he had to make his rounds.

After the door had closed behind him, I asked Dr. Petrovich, "Is he always so um…?"

"Intense?" Adam finished my sentence.

I nodded as my mind raced. Sam, Sr.? He was the one who had drugged me? I couldn't fathom the possibility. Maybe the similarities were just coincidental. Maybe I was just crazy and imagining things.

"Yes, he is," Dr. Petrovich was still speaking. "He's very dedicated to the healing arts. We're lucky to have him." He paused, and then continued, "Did you enjoy your lunch?"

"Yes, very much," I answered.

"Good. Now we have to discuss the matter of the fingers."

"Fingers?" I asked. My mind was still on Dr. Sam, Sr.

"Horace Schmidt's fingers," Dr. Petrovich reminded me.

"Oh yes, Horace's fingers. Sorry, my mind was somewhere else."

"The paperwork shows that one was missing when you returned them to Mr. Schmidt."

"I can explain," I answered.

"Please do." He smiled, but his eyes were fixed and stern.

"Well, remember how you gave them to me to keep until Horace could pick them up?" I started to explain.

"Yes. Go on."

"Well, they disappeared for a while, and then someone returned them to me minus the one finger. I'm so sorry."

Dr. Petrovich studied me from his side of the desk. "Somebody took all four of them and returned only three?"

"Yes sir," I answered a bit sheepishly.

"Was Mr. Schmidt okay with just the three fingers?" Dr. Petrovich asked.

"Well, no."

"Is he going to sue?"

"No, he wants a date."

Adam looked surprised. "A date?"

"Yes," I sighed. "One date for one finger. One date with a very large, very scary guy."

"Oh," Dr. Petrovich studied me carefully. "And are you going to go on this date?"

"Maybe. I'm still hoping his finger will turn up somewhere."

Dr. Petrovich burst out laughing. "Charlie, I don't think it's going to turn up. I'm going to give you the benefit of the doubt and assume that you didn't take it yourself, though. As long as Horace doesn't sue, we're okay. However, I don't want you to go on any dates. I mean any dates with Horace. Tell him that employees of the hospital cannot date patients and that he should see me if he has any questions about that."

"Yes sir," I answered. "Thank you."

"You're welcome."

"May I be excused now?"

"Sure. Get back to work," Dr. Petrovich was still smiling. "Oh, and Charlie."

I was heading for the door and turned back. "Yes?"

He stared at me intently. "I want to apologize for my earlier advances. I didn't know you were involved with Sam's son."

I know I looked surprised at what he admitted. "It's okay."

Dr. Petrovich's smile turned wicked. "Let me know if it doesn't work out, though. I'd like to be next one up to bat."

"As if that will ever happen," I mumbled under my breath as I all but ran out of his office.

## Chapter 33

I hurried back to my desk in the waiting room and dialed Mendoza's number. I got his voice mail and left a message for him to call me at the hospital as soon as possible. I wanted to tell him about my suspicions concerning Sam, Sr.

I suddenly felt extremely tired and realized I'd been up since 4:00 a.m. A nap sounded good, so I decided to do the next best thing and made my way to the Starbucks kiosk in the cafeteria. Dr. Caudill was there, ordering for himself and when he saw me he motioned me over. "What would you like, Charlie? It's on me."

"A three-shot, grande, toffee-nut latte. Thanks."

"You're welcome. You look like you could use a lift. How's your day going?"

"Oh it's been interesting. Dr. Petrovich told me about the surveys we'll be doing of the E.R. patients."

Dr. Caudill stirred his coffee and looked at me quizzically. "Surveys?"

"Yes." The barrista handed me my latte and I took a sip. "They want me to survey one out of every five patients in an effort to find ways to improve patient satisfaction."

"That's odd. No one told *me* about that." Dr. Caudill looked perplexed. "Anything like that concerning my department should at least be discussed with me before it's implemented."

"You weren't consulted?"

"No. Hang on a second while I call Dr. Petrovich." Dr. Caudill used his own hospital-issued phone and dialed Dr. Petrovich.

We walked over to one of the little café tables and sat down. "Adam, it's David. What's this I hear about Charlie surveying our patients?" Dr. Caudill listened carefully, then spoke again. "Don't you think it would be a good idea to let me in on these things? After all, it's my department."

Dr. Caudill was silent while he listened to the response, but he didn't look very happy.

"Well, I'd still like to discuss this in more depth and at least review the questionnaires before you start," Dr. Caudill spoke again.

He paused again and listened intently, then he said, "Sure. Thanks, Dr. Petrovich."

Dr. Caudill ended the call and looked at me seriously. "Charlie, he says he didn't intend to start until he spoke to me. Those guys upstairs make me nuts. They think they're God and have no regard for anyone else."

I didn't quite know what to say and studied the logo on my coffee cup. Dr. Caudill spoke again, "Sorry, Charlie. I've been under a lot of stress lately. You certainly don't need to hear me ranting and raving about hospital politics."

"It's okay, I don't mind. It's not as though I've lightened your stress load at all since I started working here." I thought it was interesting that Dr. Caudill seemed to dislike Dr. Petrovich just about as much as I did. My phone started ringing and I answered it.

"Hey, Hoochie girl!" It was Sherrie.

Dr. Caudill was standing to leave, so I told Sherrie to hold on a minute.

"Dr. Caudill," I called after him. I felt bad for inadvertently upsetting him and wanted to say something to cheer him up.

Dr. Caudill raised his hand to stop me from speaking. "It's okay. I'm sure it was just a misunderstanding." He left the cafeteria and I went back to my phone call.

"Hey, Sherrie. You still there?" I asked.

"Yeah, how's it going? I haven't heard from you since the other night."

"Oh Jeez, Sherrie, things are getting weirder and weirder."

"You want to meet me for a drink and tell me about it?" she asked.

"I can't, I have to go to Sam's parents' house for a Christmas party tonight. Why don't you come over and help me get ready and I'll tell you about it then?"

"Great! I'll bring the makings for cosmos, and we'll loosen you up a bit for your date," she replied, full of enthusiasm. "Maybe I'll get to meet this Sam guy. If he's as easy on the eyes as Mendoza is, it'll be a treat."

"Sounds good," I said in a less than enthusiastic tone. The thought of cosmos after my wine binge the night before sounded anything but good. I also realized that I was less than excited about going to Sam's parents' house. My first encounter with Sam, Sr., had been creepy, and I felt like my relationship with Sam, Jr., was less than stellar at the moment as well.

"Jeez, girl, you do need some livening up. I'll see you around 5 o'clock okay?"

"Okay." I tried to muster up some enthusiasm. "See you then."

I went back to the E.R. and decided to check on the Williams'. I found Sam at the nurse's station where he was reviewing charts. He looked up at me when I approached and smiled warmly. My heart did a little roll in my chest.

"How's it going, Charlie? I heard you had lunch with my father," he said.

"I did. You look just like him," I replied. I thought about the way Sam's father had stared at me through the entire lunch.. "He seemed, um, very interested in me."

"Of course!" Sam grinned. "He knows I like you."

I sat in the empty chair that was next to him. "How are the Williams' doing?" I asked, remembering why I'd sought him out in the first place.

He reached under the station desk to caress my thigh. "As good as can be expected. It's going to be a while before he's released, but by all accounts, given his wife's state of mind, I'd say that's a good thing."

I tried to take my mind off Sam's hand and smiled. "I guess he didn't have a good explanation for the condoms then."

"No." Sam smiled back. "And to make matters worse, his girlfriend showed up shortly after you left. We almost had another E.R. patient by the time Ms. Williams was through with her." The hand that had been caressing my thigh gave it a gentle squeeze.

"Whoops!" I exclaimed.

"Yeah, whoops!" Sam repeated. He leaned in and whispered in my ear, "So are you looking forward to our date tonight?" His lips brushed my earlobe and that, along with the hand on my leg, sent a quiver through my stomach.

"Of course," I replied in a slightly breathless voice. "Now that I've met your father, I'm wondering what your mother is like."

"Is that the only reason?" He leaned over again and brushed an errant hair from my face.

"Hmm, whatever do you mean?" I asked coyly.

Sam smiled wickedly. "You know what I'm talking about."

"Oh that. Yesterday would have been good for that, but today might not be so good. You know, Aunt Flo?" I hoped he'd understand the metaphor for my menstrual cycle. Evidently he did.

"Damn." Sam said, but he winked nonetheless. "Well, Flo won't be visiting forever." He gave my thigh another gentle squeeze and stood up to leave.

I got up to leave as well and felt my heart beating a little too fast. How I could be so attracted to two such different men at the same time?

I went back to the E.R. waiting room and sighed in exasperation when I saw Mabel at my desk. She peered at me over the glasses that were sitting low on her nose and stuck her protuberant bottom lip even further out than I had remembered. "My desk!" She barked.

"I know," I barked back and went into the triage office. Katy Dee was still there. Her shift didn't end till 4 o'clock. "Anything I can help you with?" I asked her.

"Yes, as matter of fact, there is. You can go to Bed 15 and apologize to Ms. Murdock for scaring her nearly to death this morning."

"Ms. Murdock?" I asked, somewhat confused.

"Yeah, she's the lady who broke her ankle coming out of the ladies' room. She's been telling everyone that you were in the ladies' room naked and scared her so much that she tripped. She's threatening to sue the hospital."

"Oh God!" I whispered to myself.

"God can't help you out of this one," Katy Dee answered my quiet plea. "She said she wants an apology and, if she gets one, she may reconsider the lawsuit."

"E.R., Bed 15?" I asked.

"Bed 15," Katy Dee replied. She grinned and leaned in to whisper coyly, "By the way, what were you doing in there naked?"

"I wasn't naked, I swear. I had to rinse my skirt after the migraine lady yakked on me, and Ms. Murdock came in and found me in my underwear and a sweater.

"Sure," Katy Dee replied. She didn't seem to believe me.

I made my way to Bed 15, where Ms. Murdock was lying with her ankle propped up on a stack of pillows. Her eyes were closed, and she looked a bit like she was dead. I quietly walked up to the bed and peered down at her in an attempt to see if she was still breathing. Her eyes popped open, and I let out a little shriek in surprise. My shriek was drowned out by her high-pitched scream.

"Shh, shh!" I implored, patting her shoulder.

She stopped screaming and stared at me with wide eyes. Two nurses came barreling through the door. "What happened?" the first nurse asked. The second nurse started checking Ms. Murdock's vital signs.

"She scared me," Ms. Murdock said.

"Again?" The first nurse, a cute little redhead with freckles asked. "You didn't break anything this time did you?" The nurse shot me an accusatory look.

I wanted to drop through the floor.

"I didn't mean to scare her either time. It was an accident."

"Well, what were you doing naked in the ladies' room?" the nurse asked. "It wouldn't have anything to do with a certain doctor you've been seeing, would it?"

"Are you crazy?" I asked in surprise. "I wouldn't dream of doing something like that."

"Well, from what I hear," the other nurse piped in, "you're the one who's nuts around here."

The first nurse asked Ms. Murdock if she was okay.

"Yes, yes, I'm fine. She just startled me is all." Ms. Murdock waved toward the door. "You nice ladies can leave now." I started to walk out the door with the nurses. "I said the *nice* ladies," Ms. Murdock said. "I want to talk to you, Ms. Naked in the Bathroom."

I walked back to the side of her bed. "I'm so sorry," I said and tried to explain. "I had to take my skirt off because someone vomited on me. I didn't mean to scare you."

Ms. Murdock nodded and patted my hand. "I know. I really just wanted to talk to you, which is why I came to the E.R. in the first place. After I broke my ankle, I had to find a way to get a word with you, so I asked them to make you apologize."

"Oh, couldn't you have just said that you wanted to talk to me?" I asked wondering what she could possibly have wanted to talk to me about.

Ms. Murdock considered my suggestion. "Yes, I guess I could have. I think those painkillers they gave me made me a little stupid."

"Do I know you?" I asked.

"You don't," she replied. She lowered her voice to a conspirator's whisper. "I'm a friend of a friend, and I can't mention names right now."

"Oh, I see," I said, not seeing at all.

"Charlie, you have to be careful. There are things going on that could put your life in danger."

I stared at her in surprise. "Have you been talking to my neighbor?"

She smiled. "Like I said, a friend of a friend asked me to come see you."

"Can you tell me anything else?"

"Well, yes," she said. "I was told to tell you to absolutely stay away from the hospital at all costs. You need to quit this job and go on a trip for a few days. And don't tell anyone where you're going."

"I can't do that, Ms. Murdock." I wished I could. I wished I could just up and leave and make all this weirdness go away. But there was Alfred's murder and Kimberly's disappearance—and both were wrapped up together somehow. I couldn't leave town. I wanted to catch the people who were involved. Only then would this whole ordeal truly be over.

"My friend told me you might say that, but she wanted me to try anyway."

I stared at Ms. Murdock. "Your friend is a she?"

Ms. Murdock didn't answer immediately. "That's all I can say. I hope you'll change your mind."

"Well, thank you for trying." I laid my hand on hers. "I'm so sorry about your ankle."

"It's my fault. I don't know what possessed me to run out like that. I guess I was just startled."

"Well," I answered, "if there's anything I can do for you, please let me know."

"No, I won't do that. I don't know what you've gotten yourself into, but I don't want anything more to do with it." She paused and smiled. "I only got involved because it sounded fun—like playing secret agent. I always wanted to be a secret agent like Mata Hari." She smiled. "Well, that and the fact that my friend gave me a hundred dollars to do it. I've been spending a little too much at Bingo lately, if you know what I mean. Anyway, my husband's on his way and should be here soon to take me home."

I was surprised. Someone felt it was important enough for me to disappear to give Ms. Murdock money to talk to me. "Well good-bye then." I was oddly reluctant to leave. I liked Ms. Murdock.

"Take care, Charlie. Be careful!"

I told her I would and left the room.

When I returned to the E.R. waiting room, Mabel was gone as was most of the obnoxious gangrene odor that had permeated the room earlier. I stationed myself at my desk and tried calling Mendoza but got his voice mail again. I left another message, imploring him to call me back and hung up.

The waiting room was nearly full again, and I went around to check on each of the patients, assuring them that they'd be seen as soon as possible. Sandy was back, and I wondered if she was there for food or for voices today. Her eyes seemed to follow me, and I decided to check on her as well.

"How are you doing, Sandy?" I asked.

"We're fine. Got any juice?" she asked. She was still wearing her cap with the jingle bells, which tinkled merrily whenever she moved.

"Sure. Did you sign in?" I asked.

"No, we're just hungry," she answered.

I smiled and said, "Well, I'll take care of that." I decided to forgo getting her juice and crackers and went to the employees' lounge. It was the holiday season, so the table was laden with Christmas goodies that assorted doctors and pharmaceutical reps had been leaving for the E.R. staff. Today they had left cookies, a tray of cold cuts and cheese and a veggie platter with dip. I loaded up a plate and poured a cup of apple cider and took them back to Sandy.

Her eyes widened at the sight of all the food. She grabbed it immediately and started stuffing her mouth with carrots and cheese.

I set the cider next to her and went back to my desk.

I pulled out a piece of paper and started writing about the day's events. So much had been happening that I thought it might be a good idea to start keeping a journal.

I made a list of names—including Haley's, Alfred's and Sam, Sr.'s—and started to note what I knew about each one's involvement with the Trufalic clan. I was halfway through my notes when I glanced up and saw Mendoza walk into the waiting room. He was in his sinfully sexy jeans and was wearing a beat-up leather jacket. I gulped as I watched him saunter over to my desk.

## Chapter 34

Mendoza stopped at my desk and pinned me with his bright blue eyes. "You rang?" he asked.

"Answer your phone much?" I accused sarcastically.

"Ouch! Bad day?" He sat on the edge of my desk and smiled.

"Seriously, what if I'd been in trouble? How am I supposed to reach you, if you don't answer your phone?"

"I knew you were okay. I was busy," he replied.

I crossed my arms over my chest in an effort to cover my breast lest they betray the tightening sensations his nearness was causing. I glared up at him. "You knew I was okay? How?"

"Oh, I have my ways," he answered. "So how was lunch with the powers that be?"

"What? How'd you know about that?"

"And did you get Ms. Murdock to reconsider her lawsuit?"

My mouth dropped open. "Did you bug me?"

Mendoza just smiled.

"Spill it, Mendoza. I want to know."

"Let's just say I have some friends in the E.R. They've been keeping me posted."

I was still glaring at him. "Oh, you answer your phone for *them*, huh, but not for me?"

"I didn't want to talk to you while you were using your hospital phone. I know for a fact that the system they use has Big Brother capabilities."

"Big Brother?" I asked.

"Yes, they can listen in whenever you make or receive a call."

"You're kidding?" I was dumbfounded.

"Nope. They use the telephone system primarily to catch employees using the phone for personal reasons on company time and also to catch employees abusing the long-distance service."

I rubbed my temples. "I would have never thought of that."

"Anyway," Mendoza went on, "I don't think we can be too careful. At least one doctor is involved in this thing, and we don't know who he is. He could work here."

"As a matter of fact," I said, "that's one of the reasons I called."

Mendoza raised an eyebrow. "Really?"

"Yes. When I had lunch upstairs with Dr. Petrovich, I met someone whose voice I recognized as belonging to the doctor on the tape."

"Who?" Mendoza asked.

I glanced around the waiting room. I could see Joyce staring at us through the triage window. She must have relieved Katy Dee when her shift ended. "Do you think it's safe to talk here?"

Mendoza glanced around too. "It appears to be."

"It was Sam's father. Dr. Sam Macgregor, Sr."

Mendoza's eyes widened in surprise, "You're serious?"

I nodded. "At first, I just thought he reminded me of Sam—I mean Sam, Jr. But then he asked me the exact same question I heard him ask me on the tape, and I realized it was probably his voice.

Mendoza sat silently for a few seconds, then got up. "Let's walk. I think better when I'm in motion."

I stood and followed Mendoza out of the waiting room. I noticed that Sandy was gone—along with the food and the cider I had brought her.

"What question did he ask you?" Mendoza inquired.

"We were talking about this new project they want me to start working on, and once they had explained it to me, Sam, Sr., asked, "Are you with us, Charlie? I was so shocked that I started to choke on my papaya salad."

"Papaya salad? Was it from Kenichi's?"

"What does that have to do with anything?"

"Nothing, I'm just hungry and fantasizing about your lunch. You're sure it was Macgregor, Sr. on the tape?"

I hesitated just a moment before answering. "I can't be absolutely sure, but under the circumstances, I'm as sure as I can be."

We were walking down one of the long, little-used corridors in the back of the hospital, and a movement in one of the doorways caught my attention. I heard a jingle and looked closer and realized it was Sandy. She was sitting in the alcove; finishing the food I'd given her. I waved and felt her eyes follow us as we continued down the hallway.

"Friend of yours?" Mendoza asked quizzically.

"She's a regular in the E.R.," I replied. "She's a paranoid schizophrenic with homicidal tendencies."

"She has a tendency to kill people?" Mendoza asked.

"She's okay," I assured him. "I feed her and she seems to like me. She said she wasn't going to let the king and the witch hurt me."

Mendoza looked less than convinced. "Okaaaay."

"Do you think I'm crazy?" I asked Mendoza. "I mean, do you think I could have imagined the voice thing?"

Mendoza took a moment to think about it before answering.. "I think you're upset, but I don't think you imagined it. It's entirely possible that it was Sam's father on the tape and for now I'm going to assume it was. I don't think we can afford to discount any lead we have."

I sighed in relief. At least Mendoza didn't think I was imagining things. "There was something else I wanted to tell you about."

Mendoza stopped walking, and I stopped as well. "What's that?" he asked.

"Ms. Murdock," I stated.

"The lady who wants to sue the hospital?" he asked quizzically.

I nodded. "She's not really suing though."

"What does she have to do with anything?" Mendoza was staring at me intently and I felt myself melt a little.

"She said she came to the hospital because a friend of a friend wanted her to warn me."

"Really? Warn you about what?" Mendoza wanted to know.

"She didn't seem to really know what, just that I was in danger and should quit my job and leave town."

Mendoza did the familiar Colombo head scratch thing. "Did she say who the friend of the friend was?"

"No, I asked her and she wouldn't say. I got the impression the person was a woman, though, and that she had paid Ms. Murdock money to come see me."

"Wow! She wanted you to quit your job and leave town? Sounds serious. Sure you don't want me to move in?" He narrowed his eyes and winked..

"Are you laughing at me?" I inquired crossly. "You are! You think this is funny!"

Mendoza got serious. "No, I'm not laughing at you. I would like to be your evening bodyguard though. Everything points to you being in real danger."

"Well you can't," I replied. I was starting to get ticked off. I have a date tonight, and I don't think he'd be happy to find you as my new roomy."

Mendoza frowned. "A date?"

"A date," I confirmed.

"With who?" he asked and his eyes glinted dangerously.

"Are you jealous?" I asked coyly, remembering that he'd asked me the same question early that morning.

"Of course not!" he replied emphatically.

"Jealous," I stated simply.

It dawned on him that he recognized an earlier conversation, and he laughed. "Got me, didn't you?"

I smiled and nodded. "Yep, you're jealous."

"Really, though," Mendoza said. "Who's the lucky guy?"

"You're not going to like it," I replied.

"It's Macgregor," Mendoza stated coldly.

"Yes, Macgregor," I replied. "I'm going to a Christmas party at his parents' house with him."

"Are you crazy?" Mendoza snapped.

I jumped back at the heatedness of his tone. He looked furious.

"What are you so upset about?" I snapped back. I was glad we were nearly alone in the corridor. I was sure that, if anyone besides Sandy had been there, they would have taken a great interest in the little spat Mendoza and I were having.

Mendoza glanced around, realizing where we were, and lowered his voice. "You just told me you think it was Sam's dad on the tape. Now you're planning on going to a party hosted by the same guy? For all we know, he could have murdered Alfred and perhaps made Kimberly vanish. It's not safe!"

"I'm sure I'll be fine," I answered meekly. "Sam wouldn't let anything happen to me."

"Are you sure?" Mendoza narrowed his eyes at me. "What if he's involved too?"

I considered that for a moment, then discarded the idea. "No, I don't think so. The clan needs a virgin, and he's been pretty hot to rid me of that little problem."

Mendoza's face hardened into a cold frown. "He didn't show up last night when you offered it to him on a platter, did he?"

"No, but he got detained at his...." I didn't finish my sentence, realizing the implications of what I was about to say.

Mendoza stared at me, waiting for me to finish. "Detained where?" He finally asked when I didn't finish my sentence.

I studied Mendoza's angry face for a moment. "At his parents' house."

Mendoza and I were both silent for a moment.

"I guess I didn't think this through very carefully," I admitted, "but, in all fairness, Sam asked me to the party before I realized that it was his father's voice on the tape."

Mendoza scratched his head and looked down at his feet for a few seconds. When he looked back up at me, he no longer looked angry. "I think you should go to the party."

"Really? I was perplexed. Why are you changing your mind?"

"Maybe if you snoop around very carefully and keep your ears open, you'll find some answers to our puzzle. Just make sure Sam knows that I know you're with him. I don't think anything will happen to you if he knows that. In addition, the winter solstice isn't for a few days. I don't think they'd make you disappear that far in advance."

My stomach felt like a rock. Mendoza had just stated the very thing that had been niggling at the edges of my consciousness since we realized that Kimberly was involved in this mystery. She had disappeared and I was worried that I would disappear too.

Mendoza must have read the fear on my face. "I know this is all very scary. I wish I could say something to make it easier for you."

I grinned wryly. "It's okay. Believe me, it's scary, but the thought of not catching them is even scarier to me." The absurdity of the whole situation and the lack of sleep made me giggle in a somewhat delirious fashion.

"What's so funny?" Mendoza wanted to be let in on the joke.

"Oh, it's just that a few days ago I would have never believed in cults, rituals—all that stuff—and now... ," I trailed off.

"And now?" Mendoza inquired.

"Well now I've been thrown into this thing and I'm starting to totally believe it. What if we're wrong? What if all this has absolutely nothing to do with the Trufalic clan or with coins? What if Alfred was murdered simply because someone disliked him? What if Kimberly just ran away and is happily alive in another state somewhere?"

Mendoza nodded. "I see your point. But my job is to connect the dots. And all the dots seem to be leading to you and to the Trufalics' obsession with a virgin."

I glanced at my watch and noticed the time. It was already 4:30, and Sherrie would be arriving sometime after 5 o'clock. "Hey, my shift is over," I told him. "I've gotta roll. Sherrie is coming over to help me get ready for the party."

"She's going to help you get ready?" Mendoza asked blankly.

"It's a girl thing," I answered with a grin. "It includes cosmos, which are sounding pretty good all of a sudden."

Mendoza studied me with a funny smile playing at the edges of his sinfully sexy mouth. "Have you already forgotten about your run-in with the wine last night?"

"How could I? I'm just going to be more careful this time. I really have to go." I started to turn back toward the E.R. Mendoza reached out and grabbed my arm, and I turned back to him. The feel of his fingers seared through the knit of my sweater, and I gasped as he abruptly pulled me to him.

"What...?" He cut off my question with his mouth. His kiss was a combination of anger and passion, and I felt his teeth on my lips as his tongue pressed for entry. The full force of the onslaught had my mouth opening in response, and in seconds I was engulfed in a heated passion that had my head spinning and my knees threatening to collapse.

His hands moved from my arms to my hair, and his strong fingers caressed my scalp, sending even more waves of heat coursing through my blood. I whimpered with the impact and pressed my body closer to his, feeling a desire to blend with him— to become him. My arms looped around his neck, and I caressed it, my fingers mingling with the silken hair that fell to his collar.

His kiss grew deeper and even more ferocious. His teeth ground into my lips as his tongue caressed mine, and the pain that mingled with the passion lit delicious fires throughout my entire body. I felt my breasts swell and my nipples became hard and taut where they were pressed firmly against his chest. I whimpered again, and the sound of it seemed to reach Mendoza, who answered with a groan deep in his throat.

How long the kiss lasted I can't say, but the suddenness with which Mendoza ripped his mouth away and pushed me away from him felt like a bucket of ice water had been thrown in my face. We stood gasping and staring at each other—each seemingly rocked to the core at what had just transpired.

Mendoza spoke first. "I want you to take the memory of that with you tonight."

"Why?" I whispered.

"Because I want you to remember that I still intend to take care of that unfinished business when this case is closed," he stated matter-of-factly, then turned and strode down the hall, leaving me standing in the abandoned corridor with my mouth hanging open and my body throbbing.

I shook my self and tried to get my heart rate under control. I touched my fingers to my swollen lips, in wonder. "Now that wasn't very fair," I whispered. I wanted a moment to compose myself but realized I didn't have one and quickly made my way to the E.R on shaky legs. I had a party to get ready for!

## Chapter 35

An hour later, I was freshly showered and standing in front of my closet trying to decide what to wear, when there was a knock on the door. I looked at my watch. It was 5:35. I assumed it was Sherrie, so and I made my way to the living room and opened the door without asking who was there. It wasn't Sherrie but Haley who stood at the threshold.

I tried to close the door quickly, but Haley stuck her foot on the jamb to stop me. "I need to talk to you," she implored.

"You should have thought of that before you tried to beam me with your dead cat," I growled. "Move your foot or you might lose it."

"I'm sorry! Please, I promise to be good." Haley looked at me with pleading eyes.

"What could you possibly want now?" I asked.

"Just to talk for a minute. Please, may I come in?" She certainly looked sincere enough.

"Okay, but just for a minute. I've got plans this evening."

Haley nodded. "Okay, I promise to be quick." She was still sun babe bronzed and the color clashed with the red caftan she was wearing. She swept into the living room and planted herself on my couch. I sat in the seat opposite her and waited.

"Well?" I inquired.

"I wanted to apologize," she said. "I have no good explanation other than I was distraught over losing my cat and not thinking very clearly. When I saw you had that coin, well I just had to have it." She peered at me closely. "What happened to your lips? Did you get cortisone?"

I winced ruefully. My lips were painfully swollen. Mendoza's kisses sure did pack a punch! "An accident," I said, referring to my lips. "Why did you just have to have the coin?"

"It's personal," she replied. "The coin is very valuable and carries a significance that most people don't know about. I wanted to add it to my collection."

"You have a coin collection?" I was surprised to hear that.

"Yes, that's one of the things Alfred and I had in common—an interest in rare coins. Actually, that's how I met Alfred. We were both at a conference on rare coins. It wasn't until later, when I needed a place to live, that I moved in here."

"Well, you've got the coin now. What are you going to do with it?"

Haley looked surprised. "What do you mean I've got it now? I was going to ask you to reconsider letting me keep it for a while."

My mouth dropped open. "You don't have it?" I asked.

"No. Why?"

I studied her and decided that she wasn't acting. She seemed genuinely bewildered. "It disappeared the same night I found it," I told her.

Haley turned white under her tan and looked truly upset. "They got it?"

"Who are they?" I asked.

Haley got up abruptly. "Never mind. I have to go. I'm really sorry about the cat thing. You'll be pleased to know that he was cremated this morning," she said and headed for the door.

"Haley, wait!" I called after her. "Who are they?"

She ignored me and opened the door. Sherrie was standing in the doorway, poised to knock, and Haley pushed by her and disappeared into her own apartment.

"Wow! She really looks orange. Has she seen a doctor for that?" Sherrie asked as she came in, closing the door behind her.

"What?" I asked. My mind was on the coin and who "they" were.

"Your neighbor," Sherrie said, "she's orange. Has she seen a doctor?"

"Oh that—its just spray tan." I replied.

"I'd sue." Sherrie said removing her coat.

"Yeah, me too." I noticed that Sherrie had once again gone all-out with her outfit. She was wearing a fluffy, white angora sweater with a deep V-neck that ended at her ample cleavage, a red leather miniskirt and red knee-high boots with stiletto heels.

"Wow! You look like a playboy bunny for Santa," I said.

"Like it?" she asked. "I wanted to look nice in case your friend Mendoza shows up. I thought it wouldn't hurt to make a good impression on your doctor friend, as well."

"Oh, you'll make an impression alright," I stated dryly. "By the way, how are things with Eddie?"

"Oh, he's just too much!" Sherrie answered enthusiastically. "Remember the little package he promised me? Look!"

She held out her arm, and a beautiful diamond-and-ruby tennis bracelet twinkled merrily in the light.

"It's gorgeous, Sherrie." I grabbed her arm for a better look. "What does this guy do for a living?"

"He's a lawyer."

"Sounds like a real catch," I replied.

"Well yeah, but he's always working. I need to find someone who's a little more available, if you know what I mean."

I didn't think there was ever going to be anyone to satisfy Sherrie 100 percent. She seemed to need two or three men at a time so as to round out the edges. I grinned. I loved Sherrie with all my heart. "Yes, I know exactly what you mean."

Sherrie headed toward the kitchen with the bag she had brought with her. "I'll mix up the cosmos and meet you in the bedroom!"

I was back to studying my closet when Sherrie came in with the cosmos. She handed me one and raised her glass. "Cheers!" she said gaily.

"Cheers," I repeated somewhat less gaily. I took a sip of my cocktail and sighed in contentment. Sherrie made the best cosmos on the face of the planet. I turned away from the closet and sat down on the bed, careful not to spill my drink. "Why don't you pick out my outfit, and I'll just sit here and drink and talk?"

"Sure." Sherrie started riffling the clothes hangers. I told her the whole story of the past few days, starting with my intent to be deflowered. While I talked, I watched her pull out my black sequined pumps and a deep green dress with black piping that I'd worn two years ago for a NERT Christmas party. I went on to tell her about that day's events in the E.R. and ended with a description of Mendoza's ferocious kiss.

Sherrie plopped down on the bed next to me. "And I thought your lips looked like that because they were still swollen from your allergic reaction!"

"I'm telling you, Sherrie, I thought my head was going to either spin off or catch on fire."

"So you've got a thing for Mendoza now?"

I nodded and sighed. "I have had such a dull romantic life for the past few years, and now I can hardly keep up with who or what I want in that department."

Sherrie laughed. "I'm like that all the time. You get used to it. So what do you think of your outfit?"

"Let me try it on and we'll see." I quickly donned the figure-hugging dress and the heels and stood in front of the mirror. The green of the dress brought out the golden highlights in my hair and the V-neck was cut deeply enough to show the soft creamy skin of my breasts—but not enough to make me look less than respectable. The black piping on the dress tied into the heels, and the rhinestones on the shoes gave the whole outfit a festive air.

Sherrie studied me carefully. "It needs something." She began digging through my jewelry box. "Aha!" she cried and lifted a delicate antique necklace that had been handed down to me by my grandmother. It was a simple, gold chain adorned with a simple, emerald solitaire.

I put the necklace on and the emerald nestled perfectly in the barely exposed curve of my breasts. "Well, Sherrie, you've done it again. I think I'll do."

"You'll more than do," Sherrie replied. "You'll knock their damn hoity-toity socks off!"

I laughed. "I hope they're not too hoity-toity. That would be boring. What time is it?" I asked her.

Sherrie looked at her watch. "It's 6:15. You have just enough time for another cosmo." She grabbed our empty glasses and headed for the kitchen while I went to the bathroom to put on my makeup. I was applying mascara when she came in with the fresh drinks. She sat mine on the counter and took a sip of hers while she studied me reflectively.

"What? Is it too much?" I asked referring to the blush and lipstick I'd already applied.

"Hmm? Oh no," she replied, "I was just thinking about everything you told me. I'm worried about you, Hoochie girl."

I was worried about me too. "I know. It's creepy, isn't it?"

"More than creepy! Did you ever get a chance to check out Alfred's apartment?"

I shook my head no. "Everything's been happening so fast. I forgot about it."

"Do you want me to do it while you're at the party?"

"You'd do that for me?"

She shrugged. "What are friends for? Besides, Eddie's working late tonight."

"That would be great, but I don't want to get you into any trouble."

"I won't get into trouble. I'll be careful, I promise. And when I'm done, I'll just come back here and wait for you to get home. Maybe I could spend the night?"

I looked at Sherrie and realized that she really just wanted to stay close so that she could keep an eye on me. "That would be great," I replied.

We left the bathroom and went back to the bedroom, where I retrieved the skeleton key from under the mattress. I also gave her the article that Mendoza had given me to read about the Trufalic Ritual. "It'll give you a better idea of what we are up against." I told her.

She nodded, then looked at the bed. "Is that the side Mendoza slept on?"

I nodded, and she sighed dreamily as she collapsed onto the bed. "You're so lucky he's into you. He's dreamy."

I laughed. "Sherrie, you'll never change."

"And proud of it."

There was a knock at the door, and my heart jumped, realizing it was probably Sam. I took one last look in the mirror and headed to the living room to answer the door with Sherrie following close behind.

I opened the door and Sam stepped in. He was dressed in a tuxedo under his overcoat. He stopped and stared at me, his eyes warm and appreciative. "Wow! You look beautiful."

I smiled at him. He looked amazingly handsome in his tux and the stitches slanting across his cheek made him look like a complete rake. "Thank you," I replied graciously. "I have to give most of the credit to my wardrobe assistant." I gestured toward Sherrie. "Sam, meet my closest and dearest friend, Sherrie."

Sam's eyes went to Sherrie and widened. "Wow! Another beautiful lady!"

Sherrie stared at Sam with her mouth open, forming a little O. She was speechless. I'd never seen Sherrie speechless around a man.

"Ahem," I prodded for a response or some kind of reaction from Sherrie.

She sort of shook herself as if realizing that she was staring and said, "Um, Doctor, I mean Sam. It's nice to meet you too. I've heard a lot about you."

She moved forward and caught the toe of her boot on the rug and almost tripped. She stopped, and Sam closed the distance between the two of them, and they shook hands. "It's a pleasure," he said.

Sherrie actually blushed. "Can I get you two partiers a drink before you leave?" She inquired, batting her eyelashes at Sam. I wanted to laugh. Now that was the Sherrie I knew and loved.

"That's tempting, but we really should be going. Perhaps some other time?" Sam said.

"Absolutely," Sherrie gushed, "some other time."

Sam helped me on with my coat and we said good-bye to Sherrie. "Lock the door behind me, please," I told her and she nodded, her eyes still riveted to Sam.

Sam led me to a sleek sports car in the parking lot. I was expecting the gas-guzzling SUV that he was driving when I first encountered him, but I had to admit that this car was vastly more appealing. It was midnight blue and sported a scripted logo on the fender that read "Alfa Romeo." Sam opened the door for me and took my hand while I lowered myself into the leather seat. "It's a fun car but murder to get in and out of," he said apologetically.

"It's beautiful," I replied, feeling oddly shy. The Sam Macgregor in the tux and the sports car seemed completely different than the Sam I knew. He reminded me of Bond ... James Bond, that is, and once again, I realized that I really didn't know Sam very well at all.

"Your friend Sherrie seems very nice," he said as he started the car.

"She's the best friend I've ever had," I answered.

"Those are the best kind, but sometimes they surprise you."

I knew he was referring to his friendship with Mendoza and I decided not to pry.

"Earlier you said that you had something important to tell me," He said. Without taking his eyes off the road, he reached out and took my hand.

I didn't know where to begin and knew I could be making a huge mistake if Sam was indeed involved with the Trufalic cult. I decided to start slowly and gage his reaction as I went along. As we drove to his parents' home, which was located just outside the city limits, I told him about the Trufalics and what Mendoza and I suspected. I left out the part about Kimberly and his father. He listened intently and nodded, asking few questions. When I finished, he gave my hand a hard squeeze.

"It sounds crazy," he remarked.

I was relieved that he wasn't showing any indication of being involved. I don't know what his guilt would look like exactly, but the fact that he was acting normal, seemed to be a good sign.

"Crazy, but almost believable," he added. "I told you to be careful of Mendoza. I'm worried about you, Charlie."

I squeezed his hand back. "I am being careful, but, Sam, you have to remember that a lot of strange things have been going on and Mendoza's only trying to help."

"I see the way he looks at you, Charlie. There's more there than Mendoza's just doing his job. He looks at you the way I feel about you—as though he'd like to swallow you whole."

"All the more reason he wouldn't let anything bad happen to me," I replied glibly.

Sam abruptly released my hand, wrenched the steering wheel and stepped on the brakes. He stopped the car on the side of the road and turned to me, putting a hand on either side of my face. "I can't believe you're taking this so lightly, you don't know what he's capable of," he insisted.

"I'm not taking it lightly," I argued back, "I have no reason to fear Mendoza. Even though he can be annoying as hell, he's been doing everything he can to help me get my life back. Why..."

He cut me off with a kiss. Liquid heat flooded my veins as his tongue explored my mouth and his hands left my face to pull my body close. He twisted his hands into my hair so tightly that it hurt and I answered by slipping my arms beneath his overcoat and digging my nails into his broad shoulders. He lifted his head from mine for just a moment, looked into my eyes and, with a groan, captured my bottom lip with his teeth and suckled it, sending more fire through my body. I gasped as he released my lip and plunged his tongue back into my mouth.

I became lost in a hot swirl of eddying sensations and found I could happily drown in them. As Sam's mouth and tongue continued to plunder mine, his hands left my hair to delve under my coat in search of my breasts. They swelled under his touch, and I was convinced that I was going to either die of pleasure or explode into a million pieces at any moment. That was when a sharp rapping at the window rudely interrupted us.

We jumped apart like two kids caught necking on lovers' lane. Actually, I felt like I was a kid caught necking, especially when I realized that all the windows in the car were completely fogged up. I had no idea who was knocking on the window. Sam looked at me and tenderly brushed my mussed hair back into place. "Can we just drop the subject for now and enjoy the evening?" He asked.

I was still reeling from the impromptu make out session and could barely remember what the subject was so I nodded. Sam smiled and turned to buzz the window down by pressing the automatic button.

As the window moved down, I could see only a man's torso. The sports car was so low that the man had to lean down to peer into the car. When he did, a very familiar face came into view. It was Mendoza.

## Chapter 36

"Sorry to bother you, but I was passing and noticed you stranded on the highway here. Everything okay?" Mendoza's eyes widened in mock surprise, "Oh, hey there, Macgregor! Hey Charlie! Everything okay here?"

I gave him a little wave with a couple fingers. "Hey there!" I replied. I was glad it was dark so he couldn't see how flushed I was.

Sam nodded at Mendoza. "We're fine. We just pulled off to have an intense, uh, conversation."

Mendoza nodded and grinned. "Good, have a great night then," he said cheerfully and walked back to his car, which he'd pulled in behind us.

Sam buzzed the window back up and started the ignition. He let the car idle while he waited for the windows to defog. "You know," he said, "I can't help but to think that Mendoza interrupted us on purpose."

I had a tendency to want to agree, and remained silent as Sam put the car into gear and pulled back onto the road.

It took us a few minutes to reach his parents' house, which looked positively brilliant with twinkling lights hanging copiously in the surrounding trees. Lights blazed from the house as well, and as we got closer, music floated into the car. We'd been back on the road for only five minutes, and I was still trying to put myself back together mentally. I was torn between the two hottest men I'd ever encountered in my life. And it didn't help one bit that they had a history between them.

Valets were parking cars and they quickly opened the car doors for us when Sam pulled up. "Storm predicted for tonight, sir," one of them announced. "Would you like it in the garage?"

"Yes, please." Sam replied and handed the man a generous tip along with the keys. "If the storm starts, I'll take the Navigator home."

"Yes, sir." The man replied. Sam took my arm and escorted me to the front door. I hadn't heard about a storm and I hoped it wouldn't be a bad one. Christmas shopping was on my to-do list for tomorrow, so being snowbound would be a real problem.

I found myself growing even more nervous as we approached the door, and I wondered what the rest of the evening would have in store for me. If it was anything like the beginning, there were bound to be fireworks. I was also wishing that I had had at least one more Cosmo before we left—to calm my nerves, that is. I stopped suddenly, and Sam stopped beside me—a quizzical look on his face.

"I just need to gather my courage before we go in." I said. "I don't really frequent these kinds of functions."

Sam smiled as snowflakes began to drift in the air around us. "I can guarantee you that the worst thing that could happen to you is a slow, painful death by boredom. Most of these people are just a bunch of stuffy self-important types, who forgot to have fun a long time ago."

I took a deep breath and nodded. "Okay, I'm ready."

We moved forward, and a door attendant swung the doors open to let us in. I felt sorry for the poor guy. He looked cold, but he watched us pass with a stoic gaze. He nodded toward Sam and closed the doors behind us once we had stepped through.

I looked around curiously. The entrance hall was blazing with lights from two huge crystal chandeliers that were hanging from a vaulted ceiling. Christmas garlands hung from the walls, and poinsettias filled every available nook and cranny. Huge vases of red and white roses mixed with dark green ferns adorned every table. I'd never seen so much Christmas finery in one place. The effect was overwhelming and I grinned. I'd been transported to Christmas land.

Sam helped me off with my coat and handed it along with his to a young maid in a black-and-white uniform who had appeared out of nowhere. She disappeared just as quickly.

I looked at Sam and raised an eyebrow. "You grew up here?"

He nodded. "See the banister on that staircase?" He gestured toward the steps spiraling upward in the corner of the hall. "I broke my leg sliding down that thing," he chuckled. "The pain in my leg was nothing compared to the tongue lashing I got from my father for that."

I tried to imagine Sam sliding down the banister as a young boy. "Did you ever do it again?"

Sam nodded. "Broke my left arm the next summer. I was the ultimate wild child."

"You must have been a handful." I smiled at him.

"Let's just say I gave my parents a run for their money. I think I was the bane of their existence for the first 18 years of my life. Then I decided that I wanted to become a surgeon."

"A surgeon?" I asked. "I thought your specialty was emergency medicine."

"The broken left arm fixed the surgeon thing. You need to be very dexterous for surgery, and the fracture left the nerves in my left hand just a bit off. It was then that I realized my parents weren't just ridiculously overprotective. They were really trying to protect me from myself. I buckled down and studied and now I'm just a year away from completing my residency."

"Are you close to your parents?" I asked.

"Not really," Sam answered. "My father was busy building his career as an oncologist and my stepmother was pursuing hers as a gynecologist. "I really only saw them when I got into trouble for something, which is probably why I was always getting into trouble. I couldn't get their attention any other way."

"What about now?" I asked.

"Now?" he asked. "Well, now we have certain things in common. We're all a part of the medical community. My father and I work at the same hospital. We talk to each other a little more but usually on a professional level. The only time I can remember my parents taking any kind of interest in me was when I was planning on marrying my high school sweetheart."

"Oh," I said. "What happened there?" I asked innocently. I already knew what had happened but wanted to give him yet another opening to discuss it and his feelings toward Mendoza.

"It didn't work out," he answered curtly. "Shall we join the party now?"

It appeared that Sam had no intention of sharing the details of his failed engagement with me. It was also obvious that he hadn't dealt with his feelings regarding the matter. It had been years since Kimberly disappeared, and I found Sam's reticence in letting go disappointing.

Other couples had come in while we were chatting and they had already moved on to join the festivities. I nodded, and Sam took my arm and led me through an entrance to our right.

The room we entered appeared to be some sort of solarium with a glass roof and floor-to-ceiling windows, allowing a view of the snow that was falling outside. The winter scene outdoors was the perfect setting for the gilt Christmas finery displayed indoors.

Each corner of the room sported a huge Christmas tree decorated with shiny red apples, gold bows and holly. The buffet table along one side of the room displayed towers of food and a champagne fountain. A smaller table boasted hills of assorted fruit and a waterfall made out of dark and white chocolate.

Waiters mingled among the many guests and carried trays of champagne-filled glasses and trays of food. Smaller tables with chairs were set up throughout the rooms, each table sporting a miniature bouquet of red and white roses along with small boxes wrapped to look like gifts.

The men were dressed in tuxedos and the women all looked like they had stepped out of the best evening gown edition of *Vogue* magazine. I was horribly underdressed in my little green party dress.

I took a glass of champagne from a passing waiter and quickly drained it. Sam raised an eyebrow.

"I'm thirsty," I said and grabbed another glass as the waiter passed by.

"So it would seem," he said wryly. He face showed open amusement and for a moment I was struck dumb by his dimples.

A stout gentleman with a balding head and rosy cheeks came up and demanded Sam's attention. "Sam, Jr.! How the hell are you, boy?" he roared. He grabbed Sam's hand and started pumping it up and down. "Haven't seen you since… " He stepped in front of me, cutting me off from Sam. I stood there with my two champagne glasses, feeling oddly like a fifth wheel.

Several other men joined the bald man, and I was completely cut off from my date. I was just starting to think about heading to the food tables when I heard Sam say firmly but politely, "Excuse me, gentlemen." Within a few seconds he was by my side again, grabbing my arm and turning back to his acquaintances. "I would like you to meet my date tonight, Charlie Meadows."

He steered me into the men's midst. His eyes never left my face as he introduced the men surrounding him, but I didn't catch any of their names. I was too busy staring back at Sam and wishing that we were back in the Alfa Romeo so I could explore his dimples some more.

As Sam completed the introductions, I politely looked around and nodded at each of the men. They were all older, and each one carried them selves in a distinctive fashion that shouted their feeling of self-importance. I knew they had business to discuss and didn't feel like trying to make small talk, so I excused myself as graciously as I could. "Please enjoy my escort," I said. "I'll catch up with him later." Sam frowned, but my mind was made up. I was heading for anything that had dip.

I wandered over to the buffet table and found the dip. Yep, I had a feeling the dip was going to be my best friend tonight. I took a small glass plate and started loading it up with crackers, veggies and dip. A woman joined me at the table, and I sensed her quizzical glances as I finished filling my already overloaded plate.

"Are you Sam's date?" she inquired. I turned to face her. She was stunning. She was about my height and had a delicate build. Her amazing topaz-colored eyes, framed by thick dark lashes, danced merrily in her face. Her emerald-green silk gown was cut in a Grecian style and outlined her willowy body perfectly. Her jet-black hair was streaked with brilliant silver and was pulled back gently into a Grecian knot, accentuating her perfectly sculpted cheekbones.

I felt like a big bumbling oaf next to her delicately graceful presence and immediately upset my plate on the table. "Oops!" I said and began to put the food back on my plate nervously. "Yes, I'm Charlie Meadows," I replied, remembering that she had asked me a question.

She put her hands on mine. "It's okay. You don't have to clean that up. That's what we hired the help for."

I stopped fumbling and looked up at her again. Her eyes were still laughing, and a gentle smile teased her lips. "Sam isn't the best at the dating thing. I must apologize for my son. He can be quite rude at times."

"You're Sam's mother?" I questioned. I know I must have looked stunned. I don't know what I had expected, but this gorgeous willowy wisp of a creature was not how I'd pictured Sam's gynecologist mother.

"Why, yes I am," she laughed. "Actually stepmother would be the correct term. I married Sam's dad when Sam was eight years old. But, at the moment, I'm not sure if I should admit that. I can't imagine how he allowed himself to become separated from such a lovely girl."

"Actually, I separated myself from him," I came to Sam's defense. "He's talking business with some friends of his. So I decided I'd rather make friends with the dip for the moment."

"I see." She took my arm and led me away from the table. "Let's sit and talk a little until he's finished."

We sat at one of the smaller café tables. She nodded and smiled at passing guests but still managed to make me feel as though I were the center of her attention.

"Sam tells me he met you at the hospital?" she prodded gently.

"Yes, in the E.R."

"Ah yes, the day you fainted in the resuscitation room." Apparently she'd heard the whole story.

I blushed. "I wasn't myself that day."

"It happens. I had to do a C-section on my first day as a resident. I hate to admit it, but I fainted that day as well. All the studying in the world doesn't prepare you for the real thing. I'm surprised I haven't run into you at the hospital yet, but then again I'm usually on the sixth floor, managing our fleet of baby doctors."

"Are you a part of Dr. Reece's group, then?" I asked in surprise.

"Yes. Actually I guess you could say I'm Dr. Reece's boss." She smiled. "Why?"

"Oh, it's just that Dr. Reece is my gynecologist."

"Well, I'll be sure to tell her to treat you well."

I blushed. "That's not necessary. That's not what I meant."

"I know. I promise I won't say anything to her. She's a good doctor, who doesn't need prompting to do a good job."

"Thank you," I said and tried to stifle a yawn. "I'm sorry. It's been a long week and I guess I'm a little tired."

"And what a week it's been!" She patted my hand. "From what Sam has told me, you've certainly had a time of it."

I wondered if she was referring to the drug ordeal, the finger ordeal, the Alfred ordeal or all of the above. I decided that it really didn't matter. I'd survived my first week and was still employed, wasn't I? "It certainly isn't a dull job," I countered.

"Well, I'm very pleased that Sam brought you here tonight. I've been looking forward to meeting you. You're every bit as lovely as he told us."

"Thank you," I replied. I wasn't sure what else to say.

She pulled her hand away from mine to wave at a passing waiter. He stopped and she took two glasses from his tray and handed one to me. "Let's toast to the beginning of what I hope in a beautiful relationship."

I felt guilty, thinking of the hot lip lock I'd had with Mendoza earlier and flushed a bit more when I remembered my hot lip lock with her son on the way to her house. I wondered if kissing two men in less than 24 hours made me a smooch whore. I nodded to myself, thinking it probably did, and Alayna took my inadvertent gesture as my consent to the toast. We clinked glasses and each took a sip.

"I hate to bring this up," she said as she set her glass down on a nearby table, "but I feel it's important that you know something."

I remained silent and waited for her to continue.

"My son hasn't had the best luck in the romance department. As a matter of fact, his heart was broken quite badly when he was a senior in high school. Apparently, the girl he was planning to marry had been having an affair with another man—Sam's best friend."

I tried to look surprised. "Oh?"

"He hasn't told you about it, I gather?"

I shook my head no. Mendoza had but Sam didn't, so it didn't count as a lie.

"Well that's his business, I suppose." She played with the stem of her glass for a moment. "Sam's dad is rather protective of him in that area. He may give you the third degree. If he does, try not to be offended. It's just Sam Sr. watching out for Sam Jr."

I smiled and nodded. A moment later, the subject of our conversation was standing beside our table. "Hi Mom, I see you've met my date," he said, flashing a wide smile.

Alayna looked up at her son. "Yes, Sam. You should be ashamed of yourself, letting such a pretty girl leave your side."

Sam grinned even wider. "I've seen her in action, Mom. She's pretty good at taking care of herself."

He leaned down and took my hand. "Now Mom, if you'll excuse us, I'd like to dance with my date."

I hadn't even noticed that an area had been cleared for dancing. A small ensemble was playing Christmas music, and several couples were on the dance floor moving to the strands of "White Christmas."

I thanked Alayna for rescuing me from the buffet table and followed Sam to the dance floor. He pulled me close to him, and we moved across the floor, surprisingly graceful for a couple that had never danced together before. "So what did you think of my stepmother?" he asked, his breath caressing my ear as he spoke.

"She's lovely," I replied, trying to ignore the shiver his very breath created when it touched my skin. His cologne was exquisite and I inhaled deeply.

"I'm sorry I left you alone like that. That was one of the hospital's major financial contributors and some of his friends. What were you and my mother talking about?"

I grinned. "Wouldn't you like to know?"

He laughed and gently nipped at the ear he'd been speaking into, turning the shivers I was feeling into goose bumps.

The song ended, and the rocking rhythm of "Jingle Bell Rock" rose around us. "Do you want to keep dancing or should we eat?" Sam inquired.

I was feeling a little light-headed from the champagne and thought that food was probably a better choice. "Food first," I replied.

We made our way to the buffet table, stopping several times along the way to speak to some of Sam's friends. A few of the women looked pointedly at my dress, but, other than that, everyone was very pleasant and showed great enthusiasm for meeting Sam's date.

Sam handed me a plate from the table, and we both filled our plates with smoked salmon, Cornish game hens, grilled pineapple kabobs and assorted gourmet vegetable dishes. The spread smelled and looked heavenly, and I dug in as soon as we sat down at the table.

My mouth was stuffed with the Cornish game hen and pineapple when Sam's father came up to the table. "So how are you two doing?" he asked warmly and patted me on the shoulder. I felt my skin crawl, and the food that had tasted so good a moment before now turned to ash in my mouth.

## Chapter 37

Sam stiffened perceptibly as he looked up at his father. "Hello, Father," he said in a careful voice. If I didn't know better, I would have thought that Sam was greeting a casual acquaintance—and one he didn't like too much at that.

Sam's father ignored the cold response and took a seat at our table. "Great party, isn't it? Alayna certainly knows how to put together festive occasions."

Sam simply nodded and took another bite of his salmon.

"Are you enjoying yourself, Charlie?" Sam, Sr., asked me.

I nodded. "It's a lovely party, and your home is beautiful."

"Thank you." His gaze was intense. He looked like a child eyeballing a favorite dessert. "You look lovely."

I flushed and said, "Thank you, sir."

"Not exactly what you're used to, huh son?" He slapped his son on the back. I didn't like the undertone of that comment. What the heck was that supposed to mean?

Sam glanced up at his father. "Thank God for small favors. What my father means Charlie, is that of late, if I take someone out, it's usually strictly business related. You, on the other hand, are a breath of fresh air."

I smiled at the compliment and looked at Sam, Sr., warily. I wondered again if it I had really heard his voice on the tape I'd found in Haley's closet. He took a sip of the drink he'd brought with him. His face was flushed, leading me to wonder how much he'd had to drink.

I decided to try to rattle him a bit. "I know I've met you somewhere before today," I stated, "but I just can't seem to put my finger on where."

Sam, Sr., raised an eyebrow in surprise. "I'm quite sure you're mistaken."

"No, no. I don't think so. At first I thought it was because Sam resembles you so much, but now I could swear we've met before. It's sort of a hazy recollection, but it's there. I never forget a face." I pretended to study him carefully.

A fine sheen of perspiration appeared on his forehead. "Maybe you saw me somewhere in the hospital," he countered. He pulled out a handkerchief and dabbed at his forehead.

I pretended to consider the possibility. "No, I don't think so. I think it was some other sort of setting—like perhaps a friend's house." I paused for a moment. "Funny, but my friend Haley's apartment keeps popping into my head." I shook my head as if to clear the thought. "Odd. I'm sure it'll come to me."

Sam, Sr., stared at me for a moment. "Well, if you two will excuse me, I need to attend to the rest of our guests," he said and left abruptly.

I started vacantly at my plate of food. My appetite seemed to have fled. I looked at Sam, who was staring at me in wonder. "Is something wrong?" I asked.

Sam picked up his champagne glass and drained it before answering, "No, not at all," he replied, and then changed the subject. "Did you get enough to eat?"

I nodded, suddenly feeling the need for some air. "Would you please tell me where I could find the restroom?" I asked.

"Sure. Just go back the way we came in and take the corridor on your left. It's the second door on the right. I can show you, if you want."

"That's okay. I can find it," I replied and stood up. "I'll be back in a few minutes."

Sam nodded and stood up as well. "Can I get you anything while you're gone. The chocolate waterfalls look amazing."

I managed a smile. "One thing you should know about me is that I never turn down chocolate."

"I'll definitely make a note of that," he said and headed toward the dessert table as I made my way to the restroom.

I found it exactly where Sam had said it would be. The room looked like a little sitting room. It was furnished with several stuffed chairs and a coffee table. A large mirror framed by globe lanterns hung on one wall. There was a counter below the mirror and several stools beneath the counter. The actual bathroom was just off that room. I quickly made use of the facilities and washed my hands. I was just about to open the door to leave when I realized that someone else had entered the other room. I could hear her speaking animatedly to another person and stopped to listen the minute I heard my name.

"Well, if you ask me, Charlie has no fashion sense whatsoever. I mean, who wears a dress like that to a party like this? I mean, really! Has Sam lost his senses?"

"I think Charlie looked very nice." I recognized Alayna's soft voice. "I think you're just upset that he brought her instead of you."

"Well, of course. I mean, I thought he was told to stay away from her."

"He was," Alayna replied, "and he chose to disregard that. He's a grown man. We can't dictate to him who he sees and who he doesn't see."

I gasped silently. Alayna had warned Sam not to see me? She'd seemed so ... well, so nice. What could she possibly have had against me when she didn't even know me?

"Well, I hope you know what you're doing," the other woman replied. "I think Sam's getting way too much exposure with her."

"I know," came Alayna's soft reply. "Now why don't you go on and enjoy the party. You've earned it."

"I will, but first I have to use the restroom."

I jumped when I heard the doorknob rattle.

"Someone's in there," the unidentified woman said in hushed voice.

I jumped again when she tapped on the door and called, "Excuse me! Are you almost finished in there?"

I gulped. I was trapped. If I walked out, they would know I had heard them. I was mortified at what had been said, but the thought of them knowing that I had heard them was too much to bear.

I tried to disguise my voice and ground out, "Nooo. I'm shick. Too much champagne." I made a loud retching noise.

"Ewe." I heard from the other side of the door. I made another retching noise.

"Well, I'm certainly not going to use *that* restroom," the woman said to Alayna.

I heard Alayna say, "You can use the restroom on the second floor. Do you remember where it is?"

"Sure," the other woman said, then I heard the door open and close. I prayed that both of the women were leaving not just the one whose voice I did not know. I listened and waited. I imagined Sam was probably wondering why I was taking so long.

I jumped when I heard another knock on the door. "Miss. it's Alayna Macgregor. Is there anything I can do for you?"

I made another retching noise, stalling for time. Then I got an idea. "Ginger ale," I moaned.

"What was that?" Alayna called back.

"Please, ginger ale....thirsty," I rasped out.

"Sure, I'll be back in a moment. Will you be okay for that long?"

"Yesh," I called back, trying to sound drunk. Then I made yet another retching sound just for good measure.

I heard the door open and close and I congratulated myself for my quick thinking. I waited a moment and quickly left the restroom. I opened the second door a crack and peeked into the corridor. It was empty. I fled down the hall and peeked into the main entrance area. I jerked out of sight when I glimpsed Alayna headed my way with a can of ginger ale in one hand and a glass of ice in the other.

I ran back down the hall and went through the first door I came to and listened for the click of Alayna's heels on the marble floor to pass by. While I waited, I looked around me. The light was dim, but I could tell I was in a study of sorts. Huge bookshelves lined the walls, and a fairly large desk occupied one corner of the room. A computer monitor, which was turned on, sat on the desk and emitted the only light in the room. I could also make out assorted books and writing pads on the desk.

My curiosity got the better of me, and I wandered over to the desk. One of the writing pads boasted a preprinted line of type that read "From the Desk of Samuel Macgregor, Sr." So; I was in Sam, Sr.'s study. The thought gave me the willies.

I turned to leave the room, figuring Alayna must have passed by now, when the title of one of the books on the desk caught my eye: *Healing Power of the Ancients*. I picked it up and read the title of the book lying beneath it: *Life and Death Through History*. I started leafing though the pages and was in the middle of a chapter on ritual sacrifice when the door to the study opened. I quickly placed the books back where I had found them and moved away from the desk.

An overhead light flicked on, and I saw Alayna standing there and staring at me curiously. "What are you doing in here?" she asked.

"Oh," I answered quickly. "Sam directed me to the restroom and I got lost. I thought he said this room, but I can't find a bathroom in here."

"You're right, you can't. The restroom is the next door down the hall."

"Oh, I'm so sorry. I didn't mean to intrude... I mean, I hope you don't think I was snooping," I said with as much innocence as I could muster.

Alayna stared at me skeptically.

"Well," I said, "I guess I'll just head on over to the restroom then."

"Wait," Alayna said as I headed for the door. "You were on your way to the restroom?"

I nodded.

"You didn't see anyone in the hall, did you? I mean someone who may have looked ill?"

I shook my head no. "Someone who looked ill?" I inquired, trying not to betray that I knew what she was referring to.

"Yes, there was someone in the restroom getting sick. I left to get her something to drink, but when I returned she was gone."

I did my best to look blank. "No, I didn't see anyone," I replied. "It sounds like I was lucky I didn't find the bathroom right away, though. Did you happen to notice if it's okay to go in there? I don't have a very strong stomach when it comes to vomit."

Alayna smiled at that. "Yes, it's fine. Odd, though, because she sounded like she was getting really ill in there."

"Better her than me," I said and headed out the door of the study.

Alayna followed, but I noticed that she stopped for a moment to press the button lock on the doorknob before she closed the door. "Just in case someone else gets lost," she said, and we parted ways.

I reentered the bathroom, waited a few minutes, flushed the toilet, and left again. I quickly made my way back to the party and found Sam still waiting at our table. "Get lost?" he teased.

I sat down and smiled. "As a matter of fact, I did. Alayna found me in your father's study, where I was looking for the restroom."

"Oh?" he asked.

"But she steered me in the right direction."

"Good," Sam replied.

I looked at my plate of strawberries, pineapple, and mango—all coated with a rich layer of chocolate. I picked up a strawberry and took a healthy bite. "Umm," I sighed, "these are heavenly."

"No," he winked, "watching you eat them is heavenly. I could watch you eat strawberries all night."

I flushed, remembering what Mendoza had said about the way I ate donuts. I wondered if Sam was referring to the same thing.

"Would you like to dance again?" he asked.

"Love to," I answered.

The combo was playing another slow song. Sam pulled me close and rested his chin on my head. His warmth once again seeped through me, and I felt warm tingles spreading throughout my body. I wondered if all contact with males did the same thing to me. Then I remembered the hug I'd given to Horace Schmidt and immediately rejected the idea. Apparently, my tingles were reserved for Sam and Mendoza.

I felt Sam stiffen. He raised his chin from my head and muttered, "Oh great! It's the nurse of doom." I looked up at him questioningly. He was looking at someone behind me. That someone tapped my shoulder, and I turned to find Joyce staring at me malevolently.

"May I cut in?" she asked.

"Maybe later," I replied and turned back to Sam. Joyce tapped my shoulder again.

"I must insist," she hissed.

"I said no," I replied calmly.

Joyce thought about what to do next. She looked really beautiful in a sequined red gown. It was really too bad the ugly look on her face ruined the picture. She considered her options for a few seconds, seemed to reach a conclusion, and then punched me in the nose.

## Chapter 38

The pain from Joyce's punch made me see stars, and the unexpectedness of the blow sent me to the floor. I put my hands to my nose and, when I pulled one hand away, it was wet with blood. Joyce sure knew how to pack a punch. She stood over me, a satisfied expression on her face. What Joyce didn't know was that I could pack a punch too. I kicked out at her and landed a stiletto heel on her kneecap, and she went down like a ton of bricks.

In the next instance Joyce was on top of me, pulling my hair and shouting curse words that would have made the most seasoned sailor blush. I grabbed a fistful of her hair, trying to pull her off, and then we were off and rolling around the floor, hissing, scratching and spitting in the mother of all catfights. I was wondering how I was going to get out of this mess alive when Sam grabbed my waist and tried to pull me away from her. At the same time, Sam, Sr., grabbed Joyce and started to haul her away from me. Joyce had a hold of my neck, and I was positive that my head was going to pop off when she finally let go, sending all four of us flying and landing in a heap.

I lay on the floor and summoned enough strength to glance to my right. Sam, who had fallen next to me, grinned at me like a little boy. "What's so funny?" I asked.

"I haven't had that much fun at one of these parties since the year I let my pet rat loose on the dance floor. That was in 1989, I believe," he laughed, then got up and helped me to my feet. My legs were still a little wobbly, and I leaned against him. He pulled a handkerchief from his pocket and started dabbing at my nose.

Most of the guests were standing around us and staring with various expressions of horror. Joyce was still sitting on the floor, weeping into Sam, Sr.'s shoulder. He was patting her head and murmuring words of what I supposed were comfort.

Alayna stepped forward and motioned to the band to start playing again. "Please, everyone," she called, "enjoy the party. I think this situation has been resolved." She looked completely serene, as though catfights happened at her parties all the time.

Sam, Sr., was helping Joyce to her feet. She saw me watching them and pointed her finger at me. "She started it!" she yelled. The people who'd started to drift away took a renewed interest in the goings-on.

I looked at her incredulously. "You PUNCHED me in the NOSE!" I yelled at her.

"Well, you wouldn't let me cut in." She stepped closer, and Sam, Sr., put a hand on her arm as if he wanted to be ready in case she made another lunge at me.

"Who's your date tonight, anyway?" I asked.

She stopped in her tracks. "My dad."

"Your dad?"

"Yes, you got a problem with that?" She planted her hands on her hips.

"Where is he?" I said and glanced around the room.

Adam Petrovich stepped out of the crowd. "What's going on here?" He looked at Joyce. Can't I even leave you alone for a minute without your getting into trouble?" he reproached her.

My jaw dropped. "*You're* Joyce's father?" I asked, completely dumbfounded.

"Of course. I'm surprised you didn't know that."

I shook my head as if to clear the thoughts buzzing around in my brain. Now I knew who had been speaking with Alayna in the bathroom. Joyce was the woman complaining about Sam's taking me to the party. I couldn't believe I hadn't recognized her snotty voice. Given Adam's position in the hospital, dating Joyce could only mean good things for Sam's career. No wonder they'd warned him about bringing me to the party. I sighed and suddenly felt very tired.

"You are in so much trouble," Joyce said. "Isn't she, Daddy?" she asked her father.

Adam shrugged. "Why? She's the one who's bleeding, and you look just fine. I think I'll stay out of this one."

Joyce stomped her foot and pouted. "Can't you fire her or something? I mean, she's been nothing but trouble at the hospital, and we don't need her anymore af… "

Adam raised a hand and cut her off. "I think we'll discuss this matter in greater length at home, dear. But since you brought it up, I don't plan to do anything to Charlie. Her position at the hospital has nothing to do with *your* punching her in the nose."

Joyce balled her fists but remained silent. She stared daggers at me.

"I think it's time we made a graceful exit," I told Sam.

He nodded in agreement. "I think we need to take you home and get some ice on your nose. It's looking kind of swollen."

I could only imagine how I looked and I rolled my eyes, but even that small effort shot new daggers of pain up my nostrils. Sam took my hand and led me from the ballroom. He retrieved our coats while I headed to the restroom. When I got there, I looked in the mirror and cringed. My nose was about three times its normal size. Blood was splattered on my neck, chest and dress. I thought about sending Joyce my dry cleaning bill.

I did my best to clean away most of the blood, immensely grateful that my nose had stopped bleeding. Then I washed my hands and combed my hair. Feeling that at least I looked a tad bit more presentable, I went back to the entrance, where Sam was waiting with our coats and speaking to Alayna. They were focused on each other and didn't notice my approach.

"All I'm saying is, the next time you might want to listen when I tell you something. You know how important Adam's support at the hospital is to your father and me," Alayna was telling Sam quietly.

Sam looked at his stepmother with barely concealed contempt. When he noticed my approach, he decided to bid her farewell. "Good evening, Alayna. Thank you for your hospitality."

Alayna turned her back on her stepson, then approached me and patted my arm. "I hope your nose feels better soon. I can't imagine what got into Joyce."

"It's okay," I offered. "She hasn't liked me much since I met her. I'm sorry I bled all over the dance floor."

Alayna waved us off with a smile, and I gave her a slight wave as we stepped out into the cold snowy night. The snow had fallen steadily since the party began, and now a thick blanket of the white stuff was covering the ground. Sam had apparently asked the valet to bring the Navigator around. The snow was still falling, and I wondered how much we'd get by morning. The cold air stung my already abused nose, and my eyes were watering. Much to my amusement, I realized that the car we were in was the one I'd nicked with my bug that first day.

"Do you live with your parents?" I asked.

Sam shook his head no. "I live *next* to them. I took what used to be the caretaker's cottage attached to the estate and had it remodeled. It's near the hospital and comfortable, and it works for the time being."

I could see the tension in Sam's jaw and knew he was still upset by his conversation with his mother. The roads hadn't been plowed yet, so Sam had to concentrate on driving through the thick wet stuff. I leaned back, taking great delight in the heated seat—it felt so good that I considered trading my bug in for a Navigator one day. Before I could think of anything else, I fell fast asleep.

I woke up when we pulled into the parking lot of my apartment building. It was after 11:00 p.m., and the quiet snow-covered night was eerily peaceful as Sam and I made our way to the door. He was holding my elbow, and a funny little smile was playing at the corners of his mouth. I was glad he seemed to have gotten over his spat with his stepmother.

"Did you enjoy yourself?" he asked. "I mean, other than getting punched in the nose by Joyce?"

I grimaced. "It certainly was an interesting evening."

Sam nodded and grinned wickedly. "I'd say—especially the part before we got to the party."

I looked up as him as he held the door open for me, and we continued down the hall toward my door. I paused to dig the key out of my coat pocket, and Sam continued to stare at me with that odd smile. I unlocked the door and turned to face him. "What's so funny?" I asked.

Sam's smile widened. "Nothing. I was just thinking how adorable you looked all conked out in the car like that."

"Did I snore?" I asked. I was terrified of snoring in front of other people. I remember when I was a kid and my dad would pass out from turkey overload on Thanksgiving and all the visiting family would make fun of his snorts while he slept—totally unaware of our laughter.

"As a matter of fact... " Sam started. I cut him off by punching him in the arm.

"I did not!" I said adamantly.

"Maybe it was the punch in the nose you got from Joyce. You can't help snoring if your nose is messed up."

I blushed, realizing that he was telling the truth. I had probably snored like a freight train all the way home. I didn't have much time to be embarrassed, though, because the next moment Sam was kissing me. It was a gentle, teasing kiss, as his lips nibbled mine. His tongue gently prodded, this time asking instead of demanding entrance. I sighed and let him in.

Fresh tingles surged through my blood as his tongue gently explored mine. The only problem was that my nose was plugged up, so that I couldn't breathe. As much as I was enjoying the kiss, it was more important for me to breathe, and, thanks to Joyce and her fist, I wasn't getting much air.

I pushed Sam away, breaking the kiss and gasping for air. "Sorry," I panted. "I can't breathe through my nose." I pointed to it and grimaced. "Joyce sure knows how to put a damper on things."

Realizing what I was trying to say, he laughed and kissed me on the cheek. "Maybe I should just nibble here," he said, teasing an earlobe, "or here." And he started down my neck.

"Oh," I said softly, "that's nice." I closed my eyes while his kisses trailed liquid fire down my throat. I was starting to really enjoy myself when the door I was leaning against was yanked open. My eyes flew open as I stumbled backward into my living room. Sam, who had been leaning into me, came flying in after me. I barely managed to keep from falling on my butt and looked around in confusion.

Sherrie, hair mussed from sleep and clad in nothing but undies and one of my T-shirts, stood at the door with her hand on the knob. Sam stared at her open-mouthed. Sherrie stared back at him with the same expression. Then she realized what she was wearing and, with a high-pitched squeal, ran into the bedroom and slammed the door shut.

I had totally forgotten that Sherrie was spending the night, and I looked at Sam who was still standing there with his mouth still hanging open. Sherrie came back into the living room, having quickly donned a pair of my sweatpants.

"Sorry about that," she said casually and plopped down on the sofa. "Did you guys have a good time tonight?" she asked nonchalantly.

Sam helped me out of my coat. "Yes, it was a good party," he replied and glanced at me with amusement. "Unfortunately, though, Charlie needs rest. Besides, the snow's getting pretty deep so I'm going to have to call it a night."

I would have liked him to stay just a bit later, but I knew he was right. I sighed and nodded. "Does this mean I won't see you until Monday at work?" I asked.

He looked surprised. "You're not going to the department's Christmas party tomorrow?"

I shook my head no. "I don't have a date, plus I think I've had enough of Cedars for one week."

"I'm not really looking forward to it myself," he answered soberly.

I nodded. "I overheard your mother talking about how important your parents' relationship is with Adam. I'm guessing that's why you agreed to take Joyce."

Sam nodded and said, "Still, I wish you'd go." "I'm sure I can lose Joyce the moment I get there."

I touched my nose and gave him a wry smile. "Try telling *her* that."

Sam stepped closer to me and took my hand. "Please, go to the party," he said. "It might give you an opportunity to get to know the other employees a little better. The department's parties are usually a lot of fun." He glanced at Sherrie, and his eyes brightened. "Why don't you take Sherrie? I'm sure she'd enjoy it as well."

Sherrie grinned. "Sure! I'd love to go. Who knows, I might meet a handsome eligible doctor or something." She winked at Sam.

I was too tired to argue. "I'll think about it," I promised.

Sam nodded and waved at Sherrie. "Make her go, Sherrie. I'll see you two girls tomorrow."

He kissed me on the cheek, touched my nose gently and said. "Put some ice on that before you go to bed."

"Doctors' orders?" I asked.

He nodded with a grin and turned to leave. I closed and locked the door behind him, kicked off my shoes and coat and plopped down next to Sherrie on the couch. "What happened to your nose?" she asked. "You look like that dwarf. You know, the one that's always sneezing."

I grimaced. "Joyce from the E.R. punched me because I wouldn't let her dance with Sam."

"Wow! She must have quite a temper," Sherrie replied. She got up, went to the kitchen and came back with a bag of ice. I put it on my nose and winced.

"Did you get into Alfred's apartment?" I asked.

Sherrie nodded. "I was so nervous. At first I didn't think I was going to get up the courage to do it, but then I had two more cosmos, started humming the theme song from 'Mission Impossible' and off I went."

I laughed. It was just like Sherrie to have to have mood music to go along with what she was doing. "Did you find anything?" I asked.

Sherrie got up and went to the bedroom. She came back with a file folder. "I don't know how the detectives missed this. It was under a stack of pizza boxes in the living room."

"What is it?" I asked.

"It's a file on you." She stated bluntly.

"What? Let me see that."

I grabbed the file out of her hand and started going through its contents. When I saw that the file included photos of me, a chill ran through my body. The pictures were not just of me here in town. There were also pictures of me as I was leaving my mother's house, which was a three-hour drive away. There was a picture of me at the Dairy Queen in the mall. That one was terrible: my mouth was wide open, and a spoon of peanut buster parfait was poised in flight to my lips. I felt nauseous, realizing that someone had been following me for quite some time. I couldn't remember the last time I had had a peanut buster parfait.

Sherrie was watching me as I studied the pictures. "That's a terrible shot. You look like a pig."

I glared at her. "How was I supposed to know that someone was taking glossies of me? Jeez, these days a girl can't even have a private moment to pig out."

I set the pictures aside and continued to look through the file. There were notes on my activities going back to October—when I was first laid off from my job at NERT. I continued leafing through the file and came to a several pages that looked similar to the charts they used at the hospital. The paper was a photocopy of my medical records from my gynecologist's office. The letterhead read "Cedars Gynecologist and Obstetrics. I stared in astonishment. These were my records from my gynecologist office. I glanced through the pages and noticed lines marked in red. They were discussion notes that the Dr. Reese had written after my gynecological exam: "The patient has a hymen, fully intact, leading this doctor to believe that the patient has not had sexual intercourse."

I felt like the couch was tilting beneath me. How had Alfred Tenny obtained my medical records? Had he paid someone? Was there a mole in the office? Then it occurred to me that Alayna worked in that office too. Not only that, but it was her husband's voice I'd heard on the tape I found in Haley's apartment. Could Alayna and her husband be a part of this ridiculous clan? If they were, was Sam, Jr. in on it as well? I thought of the gentle kiss he'd given me earlier. I remembered that he had not shown up the day I'd offered him my virginity on a silver platter.

Sherrie yawned and stretched. I placed the file on the coffee table and looked at her. "Do you know what this means, Sherrie? It means that they've been watching me for months!" I shivered. "My gynecologist's records are here too. That's how they knew I'm a virgin!"

Sherrie nodded. "Who would have thought that being a good girl could get you into so much trouble? I still can't believe you're a virgin, though. I mean, I thought Skip Townsend took care of that a long time ago."

"He was gay," I told Sherrie, and her eyes widened.

"He was?" she asked in shock. "How come you never told me that before?"

"It was embarrassing," I replied dryly.

"For him maybe, but not for you. How'd you find out?"

"I caught him in a lip lock with his golf caddie behind the tenth hole at the country club."

"Oh!"

"Yep. I dated him for three and a half years, and, if I hadn't caught him, I probably would have married him. Marrying a preacher's daughter is great for a senator's son with his own political aspirations."

"That jerk! I mean, just think of all the great dating opportunities you missed in college while he was off sinking holes on the golf course."

I grimaced. "Yuck."

"Yeah, yuck," Sherrie agreed.

I looked at the file again. "I need to get that to Mendoza. I still can't believe they missed that in their search."

"I can," Sherrie replied. "That place is a dump. I don't think he ever threw anything away. The only reason I lifted those boxes is because I thought I saw a mouse run under them, and was I going to try to swat it with my shoe."

I remembered the scurrying creature I'd seen when I stuck my head in Alfred's door the day he died. "I remember that mouse."

Sherrie looked at me like I was crazy. She stood up, yawning again, and said, "Time to hit the sack. I have to work in the morning."

I stood up too. I was exhausted as well. "Thanks, Sherrie. I don't know what I'd do without a friend like you."

"Well, you're the only friend I'd do something like breaking and entering for. If anything happened to you, I'd miss you something awful." She gave me a quick hug and headed for the bedroom.

After looking through the file one more time, I quickly changed for bed and climbed in next to Sherrie, who was already snoring. At least I wouldn't be the only one snoring tonight. I sighed and fell asleep almost immediately despite the noisy snorts next to me.

## Chapter 39

A persistent pounding on my door woke me up in what felt like a few seconds later. I opened my eyes and tentatively explored my nose. It felt just about its normal size.

Sherrie was already gone, and I checked my clock on my bedside table. It was 9:00 a.m. I had fully intended to sleep at least until 10:00 a.m., so I pulled the covers over my head and tried to ignore the banging at the door. Whoever it was, though, wasn't giving up. I finally groaned and rolled out of bed, slipped on my fuzzy slippers and went to the door. "Who's there?" I called.

"Mendoza," came the curt reply. "Open up."

"I'm SLEEPING!" I yelled back. "Come back later."

"You're not sleeping," he called back, "you're talking to me."

"Go away," I said firmly.

"I brought you breakfast."

"You did?"

"Uh-huh."

"What'd you bring?" My stomach started growling at the thought of breakfast.

"You'll never know if you don't open the door."

I quickly opened the door. Mendoza stood in front of me. His cheeks were rosy, and his blue eyes were dancing merrily. But I didn't see any evidence of food.

"Where's the food?" I asked.

"I lied," he replied, sticking his foot in the door before I could close it.

"Bastard!" I tried to shut the door on his foot. He yelped but didn't move his foot.

"Come on, Charlie," he said. "Don't make me run you in for resisting an officer—especially me, because we both know how irresistible I am."

"Good to see you didn't forget your ego this morning," I replied, opening the door so he could come in.

"I never leave home without it." Mendoza came in and removed his leather jacket. He raised an eyebrow. "Nice bunnies," he said, referring to my slippers.

"They're not bunnies, their kitties. See? The ears are shorter than a bunny's ears," I said and stuck a foot toward him so he could examine my slippers more closely.

Mendoza grinned, "I sure like the leg they're attached to."

I looked down and realized my nightgown reached only the top of my knees, and at the angle that I had pointed my leg toward him the, fabric became translucent in the light. "Err, make yourself comfortable while I get dressed, okay? While you're at it, why don't you see if you can make breakfast magically appear or something." I went into the bedroom, where I grabbed some clothes, then headed for the shower.

Fifteen minutes later, I had finished my shower and was fluffing my hair with a blow dryer. Then I swiped on some mascara. The blue V-neck sweater I had on accented the gold highlights in my hair, and I had my comfiest jeans on. My nose almost looked normal. When I emerged from the bedroom, I found Mendoza in the kitchen. He was fixing scrambled eggs and toast.

"Where'd you get that?" I asked. I hadn't gone shopping, and I knew I didn't have eggs or bread on hand.

"I borrowed it from your neighbor, Haley. She wanted me to tell you 'good morning,'" Mendoza replied. "She also said that she didn't approve of young men spending the night in your apartment."

I groaned. "You mean she thinks you …?"

Mendoza tossed the eggs onto two plates. "She did. I quickly relieved her of her assumption. After all, we can't have her thinking you're no longer a prime virgin sacrifice, now, can we?"

I sighed. "No. Thanks for saving my reputation—I guess."

"De nada." He buttered the toast and placed it next to the eggs. There was something supremely endearing and about Mendoza's fixing breakfast in my kitchen. My heart did a little jumpity jump in my chest.

We moved into the dining room with our plates and two steaming mugs of coffee. At least I still had coffee in my kitchen cupboard.

"So," Mendoza said between bites of egg, "How was the party last night?"

"Well, let's see, " I began, "the party was beautiful. The food was great. The music divine and…."

Mendoza raised a hand to cut me off. "I think you know what I mean. I'm not interested in the fripperies."

I grinned mischievously. "Oh, okay. I had a conversation with Sam's dad, and I think I really flustered him."

"Oh?" Mendoza responded.

"Yeah. I pretended that I sort of remembered seeing him in Haley's apartment."

"How did he react?" Mendoza asked.

"He broke out in a sweat and walked away from me."

Mendoza picked up his toast. "Interesting, but it doesn't prove anything. He might have just had a sudden diarrhea attack or something."

I grimaced at the thought. "True, but still he was acting awfully biggigity. I really felt that what I said had upset him. He didn't come near me the rest of the night, you know—not even after my catfight with Joyce."

"You had a fight with Joyce? Joyce who?"

"Joyce from the E.R." There was a blank look on Mendoza's face. "You know, Joyce, the nurse with the needle who inflicted a great deal of pain while drawing my blood for a certain drug test?"

Mendoza's eyes lit with recognition. "Oh, *that* Joyce."

I nodded. "I also found out that she's Adam Petrovich's daughter."

"I knew that. How did you end up in a fight with her?"

"I wouldn't let her dance with Sam, so she popped me in the nose. The next thing I knew, we were rolling around on the floor trying to do each other in."

Mendoza was laughing. "What a picture that must have been."

"It sort of ended the festivities for me. We left shortly after that happened."

"So you didn't find out anything else?" he asked.

"Oh no. I found some other things." I went on to tell him about the books that I had seen on Sam, Sr.'s desk.

Mendoza had finished his breakfast and was studying me carefully. "If everything you've told me is true, it certainly implicates Sam, Sr., and perhaps Alayna too."

"Oh, I definitely think Alayna is involved." I finished my last bite of scrambled eggs and toast.

"How so?" Mendoza asked.

"Hang on," I said and left to retrieve the file that Sherrie had found the night before. "Gorman and Stefansky missed this in their search of Alfred's apartment. I tossed the file to Mendoza. He opened it and started leafing through the pages. He paused when he got to the picture of me eating the peanut buster parfait and laughed out loud.

I yanked the photo out of his hand and crumpled it into a ball.

"Hey that's evidence!" he exclaimed.

"Oops," I said and tossed it in the trash. I walked back to the table and pulled the gynecologist's report from the file and handed it to him. "This is better evidence."

He looked it over, his eyes widening when he realized what it was. "Who works in that office?" he asked.

"Dr. Alayna Macgregor," I stated flatly. "She's the head doctor there."

"Well, this file certainly implicates her."

I nodded.

"I'm not even going to ask how you came about this file."

"Good, because I'm not going to tell you." I sat down again and looked at Mendoza. "The winter solstice is in three days."

Mendoza's gaze softened. "I know. I promise you I'll do everything I can to keep you safe." He did the Colombo head scratch. "It's getting close enough that I think you need to be under constant surveillance. What are your plans for today?"

"Oh, God! " I replied. "I have to do my Christmas shopping. Later there's the department Christmas party, *if* I choose to go."

"Why wouldn't you go?" Mendoza asked.

"No date," I said. "I mean, Sherrie said she'd go with me, but until Sam almost insisted that I go last night, I hadn't planned to go."

"Sam insisted? Why isn't he taking you?"

"He's taking Joyce—office politics, you know."

Mendoza rolled his eyes.

I shrugged. "Well, that's what he said, but he was pretty insistent that I go anyway."

"So how did Sherrie come into the picture?" he asked.

"Oh, she was here last night when we came home and she offered when the subject came up."

"She was here?" Mendoza asked. "So you and Sam weren't alone?"

"What does that have to do with anything?" I asked. Then it dawned on me that Mendoza was curious about how the evening had ended.

"Are you concerned that Sam relieved me of my virginal status?" I asked glibly.

"Of course not! I thought we'd already established that was my job," Mendoza grinned lazily, "although I'll confess I didn't like finding you on the side of the road with the windows steamed up last night."

"How did that happen? You didn't happen to be following us, were you?" I asked.

Mendoza narrowed his eyes at me, which made my pulse rate speed up. "As much as I would have liked to, no, that wasn't the case. I was on my way back from a crime scene when I noticed a very fancy sports car seemingly stranded on the side of the road. I called in the plate number, and it turned out it was registered to a

Dr. Sam Macgregor. Because you were supposed to be with Sam, I wanted to make sure everything was okay."

"We were fine," I replied lamely, flushing at the memory of how fine we were.

"I could see that," Mendoza replied grimly but chose not to elaborate. He stood up and started gathering dishes. "I think I should be your date to the Christmas party tonight."

"Huh?" I asked.

"I can keep an eye on you and I can get a look at all these other players. It's an E.R. party, so I'm not sure the senior hospital staff will be there, but if they are, I'd like to check them out. This whole thing seems to be centered on employees at Cedars."

I sat and considered what he'd said. I knew I'd feel a lot better having Mendoza there with me, but I didn't want to hurt Sherrie's feelings, and I was positive that Sam wouldn't be too happy about my coming with Mendoza. Plus, when I thought about my inability to control myself around Sam and Mendoza in the tingle department, I knew I was positively asking for trouble.

"What do I tell Sherrie?" I asked as I followed him into the kitchen. "I mean, she's my best friend. I can't very well dump her in favor of you, now, can I?"

"We can both be your date," Mendoza said.

I started running water into the sink and added soap. "Oh boy," I responded, "I bet you'd like that!"

"Well, I certainly don't mind escorting the two of you. I would be the envy of every guy there." He wiggled his eyebrows in a mock leer and started drying the dishes as I washed them.

"I'm still not sure…" I began.

Mendoza cut me off. "I insist. Have you forgotten our agreement? I could still run you in for possession, you know."

"Oh great! Now you're blackmailing me into dating you?" I glared at him.

"Whatever it takes honey," he responded gamely and touched my nose with the tip of his finger. "What time should I pick the two of you up?"

"The party starts at 7:00—probably around then. Are you sure this is a good idea?"

Mendoza leaned against the counter while I put the dishes away. "I think it's as good idea as any. At least I can keep an eye on you this way. I'm also putting a patrolman on you while you're shopping. He'll be as inconspicuous as possible."

"Is that necessary?" I asked.

"I'd rather be safe than sorry."

After the dishes were put away, we left the kitchen, and Mendoza picked up his jacket and the file I'd given him. He glanced at my little Christmas tree standing in the corner of the living room. "That's a fire hazard, you know."

"Shh," I said, "You'll hurt its feelings."

Mendoza rolled his eyes. "You're worried about its feelings?"

I nodded. "It's doing the best job it can to spread Christmas spirit. It's not the tree's fault that I forgot to water it a few times, is it?"

Mendoza looked at me like I was crazy. "I'm sure you wouldn't worry about its feelings too much if your apartment went up in flames."

"What are you, some kind of Ebenezer Scrooge? I'll bet you haven't even put up a Christmas tree yet."

"Sure I have. My dog loves the holidays. She particularly likes chewing on the bottom branches. Do you think I would deprive my dog of such a treat?"

I laughed. "Okay, so you're not a total Scrooge. Now, get out of here so I can do my shopping."

Mendoza finished putting on his jacket, and I followed him to the door, closing and locking it behind him.

I gathered my purse and coat and checked my cell phone for messages. I'd missed several calls—most of them from my mother and one from Sherrie about a half-hour earlier. I called Sherrie first. "What's up?" I asked.

"I wanted to know what I'm supposed to wear to this party tonight. It's not going to be a tuxedo thing like your party last night, is it?"

"No, I think it's just regular corporate casual or something. I'm sure anything you choose would be fine. By the way, Mendoza's going to escort the two of us."

"Whoa! No kidding? How did that happen?"

I explained my morning breakfast meeting with Mendoza.

"Wow, cool! But how do you think Sam's going to feel about that?" she asked.

"I'm sure he won't like it," I said with a sigh. I still wasn't sure about my feelings for him, and I didn't want to screw things up. "Mendoza really didn't give me a choice," I added.

"Okay," Sherrie replied. "What time should I be at your place?"

"Any time before 7:00. We might want to finish off those cosmos you left in my fridge before we leave."

"Good thinking, Hoochie girl," Sherrie replied. "I'll be there about 6:00."

I hung up and called my mother. "Hi, Mom," I said when she answered the phone. "How are you?"

"Good, good, a little drunk," She replied.

"Drunk?" I asked. "Good god, Mom! It's not even noon!"

"How'sh I shpose'd to know Madeline spiked the eggnog at our Ladies' Club's Christmas brunch?"

"Mom, everyone knows Madeline spikes the punch at all her parties," I stated.

"Oopsh, forgot," Mom answered. I had to admit that she sounded pretty loopy. "Maybe you should call me later," she said. I thought I heard a man's voice in the background.

"Mom?" I asked. "Is there a man there?"

"Why, yesh, sweetie. You remember that nice Mr. Oppenheimer from church? He gave me a lift home, and we're jush having a little cup of Christmas tea."

"Mom, not Mr. Oppenheimer! You said yourself that he's only got one thing on his mind."

"Did I say that? Hmm. Must've been shomeone else. Gotta go, shweetie."

"But Mom!" I began, but she had hung up. Apparently, she was too busy spreading Christmas cheer to talk.

I shook my head, trying to clear get rid of the thought of my mom and Mr. Oppenheimer together, and headed for the door. I thought maybe I'd buy my mom a vibrator for Christmas.

The mall was packed. I had to drive around for at least 45 minutes before I found a parking space. Just as I was about to pull in, a gray sedan tried to steal the spot from me. I got the nose of my little bug in just far enough to block the other car, but it was also blocking me. We were at a standoff. I rolled down my window and yelled, "Hey, I was here first!"

The other driver rolled down the window and gave me the finger but didn't move the car. I opened my car door and marched over to the driver's window, which was rolled back up, and banged on the window. "That's my spot!" I yelled.

The driver didn't roll down the window and I couldn't make out who was behind the tinted glass. I wasn't sure what to do when I felt a tap on my shoulder. I turned around to find Officer Stefansky. "You need some help here, Charlie?" he asked.

"This idiot is trying to steal my parking spot," I explained. "Maybe you could ask them to move their car."

Stefansky surveyed the scene. Both cars were blocking the aisle, and angry drivers were lining up and down each end, honking horns and shouting curses in true Christmas spirit.

Stefansky tapped on the other driver's window and showed his badge. The driver rolled down the window just a teensy bit. "Can I help you officer?" came a feminine voice.

"Hey wait!" I yelled. "I know that voice. Get out of my space, Joyce!"

I couldn't believe it. Was I destined to be tortured by this woman wherever I went?

## Chapter 40

Joyce rolled down her car window completely. "I was here first," she stated firmly.

Stefansky looked at me, then looked at Joyce. "Ms. Meadows here says that she was here first."

"She's lying," Joyce said.

I'd had enough. I reached through her car window and grabbed a fistful of her hair. "How'd you like a punch in the nose?" I asked.

"Officer, she's trying to hurt me! Do something!" Joyce cried.

Stefansky grabbed my arm and tried to pull it back out of the window. At the same time, Joyce was rolling the window back up, so that my arm was painfully stuck between the glass and the metal door.

Stefansky still had a hold of my arm and was trying to pull it out. I looked at him in pain and wonder. "Can't you just shoot her or something?" I asked.

He looked surprised and tapped on Joyce's window again. "Miss, I'm warning you, if you don't open this window, I'm going to have to give you a ticket for resisting an officer." He put his hand on his gun belt.

Nothing happened for a moment, then she started to roll down the window. I immediately pulled out my arm and shook it to get the circulation going again.

"Are you crazy?" I yelled.

"Don't you call me crazy, you bitch!" Joyce yelled back.

Stefansky stepped into the fray. "Ladies, I'm going to have to ask both of you to move your cars. You're blocking traffic."

"But who gets the parking spot?" Joyce asked.

"I do," Stefansky replied and pointed to his cruiser, which he'd parked behind my bug. I saw Gorman sitting in the passenger seat and realized that they were the officers Mendoza had sent to keep an eye on me.

I sighed and went back to my car. I waited for Joyce to move, then slipped my car smoothly into the space. "Ha! Take that!" I said to no one in particular. I stepped out of the car, locked it and headed into the mall. Both Stefansky and Joyce were staring through their car windows at me with astonishment. I didn't care. I had exactly four hours to do Christmas shopping for my entire list. I was on a mission.

Three and a half hours later, I was sitting in the food court at the mall and devouring an extra-large order of crispy fries. I had one Christmas gift to show for my efforts—the vibrator for my mother (it was small and colorless and I didn't think it would scare her too much)—and no patience left. It was impossible to shop when there were so many last-minute shoppers in the mall.

To make matters worse, some creative type working in the mall had hired a bunch of people to dress up like elves and to spread Christmas cheer. You couldn't move from point A to point B without being accosted by one of the little buggers. As I was eating, one of the elves targeted me and jingled up to my table. "Merry Christmas!" he called. "For a donation of only a dollar, I'll give you a carnation."

I ignored him.

He moved closer to me. "It's for a good cause."

I munched on another fry and explained for what felt like the hundredth time that day, "I am extremely allergic to carnations. Go away!"

"You could just give me a dollar and not take the carnation."

I gave the elf the finger.

The elf made a sound expressing his outrage and disappeared back into the crowd.

"Now that's Christmas spirit for you!" A voice behind me said. I turned to face Stefansky. I gave him the finger too.

"Not having much luck with your shopping, huh?" he asked.

I shook my head no. "I hate Christmas," I muttered.

He sat down next to me. "Give me your list and some money, and I'll take care of your shopping for you."

"Are you serious?" I asked.

"Sure, I love shopping. Mendoza said to make sure you were out of here in time to go to some party tonight. Besides, I figure you have enough to worry about. Gorman's here. He can follow you home, then swing back and pick me up later."

I decided there was a Santa Claus after all. I handed him my list and some money. "Don't give any to those dumb elves. I think it's a racket."

Stefansky grinned. "Before I became a cop, I used to be an elf at Christmas time."

I looked at him quizzically. "You're kidding."

"Nope. I was an elf—a very large elf." He flushed a bit as he confessed this.

"Uh-huh." I didn't know what else to say.

He waved me off, and I made my way out of the mall to my car. Someone had keyed my car: "BITCH" was scratched in large letters across both sides of the car. I sighed and wanted to cry. I felt like my poor, innocent little bug had been raped. I was truly beginning to believe Joyce was insane.

I took my "BITCH" buggy home and showered and dressed in just enough time to answer the door when Sherrie knocked. "How was shopping?" she asked. She took her coat off and tossed it onto a chair. She was wearing a red mini dress and red stilettos.

The dress had a square neckline that fully accentuated Sherrie's ample breasts. She looked understatedly fabulous.

I looked down at my little black dress. It was passable and did justice to what little bosom I had, and it certainly displayed my legs to their best advantage. I'd also chosen black stilettos. I guess I wasn't feeling very merry, and my outfit reflected my mood. "It was grueling until Officer Stefansky offered to do it for me," I answered.

"Officer Stefansky?" she asked.

"Yes. He and Gorman were assigned to follow me today. Stefansky saw me give the finger to an elf and decided to step in."

"Was it one of those obscenely merry elves they hired down at the mall?" Sherrie asked. I'd followed her into the kitchen, and she was busily mixing the cosmos for us.

"Yep."

"Good, I hate those little bastards." She handed me a drink and we toasted. "Here's to Christmas," she said.

"Yeah, Fa la la la la—and all that," I replied. I told her about my run-in with Joyce and the graffiti on my car.

"Remind me to watch out for her," Sherrie replied. "She doesn't sound like someone you want to piss off."

"I've been finding that out," I said as I savored the flavor of cranberry and vodka. I could feel the tension between my shoulders starting to melt. "She's Sam's date tonight, remember?"

"Oh yeah. I can't wait to meet her." She rolled her eyes.

There was a knock at the door, and I assumed it was Mendoza. "Do you want to get that?" I asked Sherrie. "I want to put some lipstick on." She nodded and I headed to the bathroom.

When I came back to the living room, Haley was sitting on the couch. I looked at Sherrie questioningly. She shrugged. "She said she wanted to talk to you," Sherrie explained.

I looked at Haley. She was dressed in Christmas red and green, which clashed horribly with the color of her skin, and looked as though she was headed to some event herself. "Can I speak to you alone?" she asked.

I looked at Sherrie, who rolled her eyes and headed into the kitchen.

I sat down next to Haley. "What's up?" I asked.

"I want you to stay home tonight," she said simply.

"Why?" I asked.

"Because you're in danger," she replied.

"Haley, you've been telling me that all week."

"Well it's been true all week," she answered matter-of-factly.

I sighed. I knew that Haley was involved in the clan up to her eyeballs and I was sure she knew what she was talking about. I just wished she would enlighten me.

"I can't stay home, Haley. I promised I would go to this party. Besides, I would have gotten all dressed up for nothing." I looked at her curiously. "What makes you so sure I'm in danger?"

"The spirit guides…"

I raised a hand to cut her off. "I don't want to hear any more. You know I don't believe in that stuff."

Haley looked at her hands and nodded. "I know. And I knew you'd go out anyway, but I had to try." She stood to leave and looked at me as though she were seeing me for the last time. "Take care, Charlie. I hope the next time I see you it's here and not on the other side."

Her words sent a shiver down my spine. "Merry Christmas to you too, Haley!" I tried to lighten the mood.

"Hope it's not your last." she called back over her shoulder and walked out the door.

Sherrie came back into the living room.

"Did you hear that?" I asked.

"Sure did. I had my ear to the door for every word. She gives me the creeps."

I took another drink of my cocktail and tried to shake off the chill that permeated my body. "Me too," I said.

There was another knock at the door, and Sherrie opened it to admit Mendoza. He looked stunningly handsome in pleated slacks and a button-down shirt that was the color of the sea, matching his eyes exactly. He didn't wear a tie, but I couldn't imagine Mendoza with a tie on.

"Good evening, ladies." He grinned. I knew he was set to enjoy the evening thoroughly—clan or no clan.

Sherrie batted her eyelashes. "Can I offer you a cocktail, Officer?" she purred.

"You can call me Roman," he answered. "After all, I'm your date tonight."

Sherrie batted her eyelashes again. "Would you like a cocktail, *Roman.*"

"No, thank you. Even though I intend to have a great time, I think I'd better keep a clear head tonight. But thank you, anyway. Are you ladies ready to go?" He hadn't taken his eyes off Sherrie since he'd arrived, and I was feeling a little jealous.

"Absolutely," I replied quickly. Sherrie and I put our coats on and headed out the door.

We followed Mendoza to his Jeep Cherokee that was in the parking lot. I decided to let Sherrie have the front seat of the car. She and Mendoza kept up a lively banter all the way to the hospital. Mendoza was asking about her work, and Sherrie was asking him about what it was like to be a tough city detective. As we pulled into the lot at Cedars, my temper was simmering. I felt like a fifth wheel and didn't like the sensation one bit.

Mendoza hopped out of his car, came around to the passenger side and opened Sherrie's door. She offered him her hand, and he helped her out of the car. I decided to forgo his chivalry and climbed out of the car myself. And it was a good thing I did, because they had apparently forgotten me and were already headed toward the hospital entrance by the time I got out of the car. I fumed even more. I was wondering if Mendoza had perhaps forgotten that he was there partially as my bodyguard.

I followed them through the entrance, where they had paused to wait for me. "Where is this thing?" Mendoza asked.

"In the cafeteria," I replied curtly and led the way to the elevators. We paused to wait for the elevator door to open, and Sherrie reached over and squeezed my hand. "I don't care what Haley said, everything's going to be fine."

Mendoza raised an eyebrow. "Oh? You talked to Haley?"

"It's more like she talked to me," I answered.

We stepped into the elevator and the doors whooshed shut behind us. "What did she say?" he asked me.

I didn't answer immediately, so Sherrie piped up with an answer. "She said she didn't want Charlie to go out tonight—that she was in grave danger."

"And you didn't think it was important to tell me this because . . . ?" Mendoza looked irritated.

"The two of you were rather busy talking. I didn't want to spoil your fun." I replied, sarcasm oozing from my mouth.

Mendoza's eye's laughed at me. "Jealous?" he asked.

Sherrie looked at me, wide-eyed. "Are you?" she asked.

I felt stupid for saying something, and now not only was Mendoza laughing at me, but my best friend was also looking at me like I'd thoroughly wounded her.

"No, of course not!" I replied a little more sharply than I had intended. "I'm just nervous is all. I'm tired of everyone telling me about how much danger I'm in. It's getting a little stressful."

The elevator doors opened, and I could hear the sound of Christmas music coming from the direction of the cafeteria. I sighed. "Let's just forget about all the doom and gloom and have some fun, if nothing else."

Mendoza and Sherrie both looked at me a little cautiously, as though I were a powder keg about to go off. Mendoza said. "Okay, then, let's go in."

We walked through the cafeteria doors, and the music hit us full force. The cafeteria tables had been cleared to create a dance floor, and the disco ball that was hanging from the ceiling was giving off bright specks of light. Several couples were already there, boogying to a techno-jingle bell beat. Red and green helium balloons were scattered throughout the room, which boasted a buffet table at one end and a bar set up at the other end. The whole scene reminded me of a senior prom, and I muffled a little giggle at the thought.

I surveyed the room and didn't see Sam or Joyce anywhere. It was early, so I assumed that they hadn't arrived yet. I saw Katy Dee, Joey and a few other familiar faces. Even Mabel was there, glaring across the room at everyone.

We hung up our coats on a rack by the door and found a table halfway between the buffet table and the dance floor. "Can I get you ladies a drink?" Mendoza asked.

I nodded. "Vodka rocks, please."

Mendoza raised an eyebrow but didn't say anything. Sherrie asked for a cosmo, and Mendoza headed for the bar.

Sherrie looked at me, her face filled with concern. "I hope you don't think I'm trying to horn in on Mendoza."

I shook my head no. "I'm just irritable, Sherrie. Too much excitement and trying to shop on top of it today didn't help matters any."

Sherrie nodded. "That's why I always have my Christmas shopping done by October."

"Smart girl," I replied.

Mendoza returned with our drinks, and we sipped them while we watched the couples on the dance floor for a little while. I wasn't much in the party spirit and felt rather bored. I wondered why in the world I had let myself be persuaded to come.

Mendoza was watching everyone carefully, occasionally asking me the identity of one person or another. We saw Sam and Joyce enter. Sam's eyes swept the room, coming to a rest on our table. He frowned when he saw Mendoza and looked even unhappier at his presence than I imagined he would. I watched him help Joyce off with her coat. She also spied us. My eyes met hers, and the look in hers indicated that she was ready for war.

Sherrie leaned over to me and whispered. "I'm assuming the girl who's with Sam and has the scowl on her face is Joyce."

I nodded.

"She'd be pretty if she wasn't so unpleasant looking." Sherrie commented.

I giggled. To anyone else, that statement would have made absolutely no sense. I finished my vodka and swirled the ice in the glass.

Mendoza spoke up. "What are you two whispering about?"

"Joyce," Sherrie answered. "You know, it's mean, slightly vicious girl talk."

"Oh," Mendoza replied. He looked amused. I was glad he seemed to be enjoying himself.

At that moment, the object of our scrutiny approached our table with Sam in tow.

"Merry Christmas!" She greeted us gaily as she reached our table.

"Merry Christmas!" I returned the greeting and looked at Sam, whose attention was on Mendoza. Sam looked furious.

"So, how did you manage to get invited to our little department get-together?" Sam asked Mendoza.

Mendoza shrugged. "These two lovely ladies didn't have a male escort, so I volunteered to do the honors."

Sam arched and eyebrow. "Oh?"

"Oh," Mendoza replied.

Sam looked anything but happy. "Well, I certainly hope you enjoy yourself." Anger was simmering behind his emerald eyes.

"I intend to," was Mendoza replied.

Joyce directed her gaze at me. "Did you finish your Christmas shopping?"

"As a matter of fact, I did," I replied. I knew she was digging, trying to get a rise out of me, but I wasn't going to go there. I hoped to leave the party unscathed tonight.

Sherrie piped in, though, "Would you believe someone graffitied her car? I'm telling you, it's not even safe to go shopping these days."

Joyce had the grace to redden a bit and changed the subject. "It's those pesky elves I can't stand."

Sam took Joyce's arm and started leading her away from the table. "Let's go find a seat. This place is filling up fast."

## Chapter 41

We watched Sam and Joyce walk away, and I realized that the cafeteria had definitely become more crowded. Nearly all the tables were taken, and the dance floor was now packed. I glanced toward the food table and my stomach rumbled. "Should we get something to eat before it's all gone?" I asked.

Sherrie and Mendoza nodded. "Why don't you wait here, Charlie, and we'll fill up a plate for you. That way we won't lose our seats," Sherrie suggested.

I thought that was a good idea. "Make sure you get me some of those coconut shrimp and those little meatballs. Oh yeah, and don't forget the dip."

Mendoza gaped at me.

"What? I'm hungry!" I said somewhat defensively.

"Obviously," he said, and off they went.

I fiddled with my empty glass and waited for them to return. Katy Dee wandered over. "Enjoying yourself?" she asked.

I nodded. "Would you like to have a seat?"

She nodded and sat down. "So are you with Mendoza or is the redhead here with him?" she asked.

"Both of us." I answered.

She smiled somewhat wickedly. "Gosh, I didn't know you were into that kind of thing."

I laughed and said, "It's not like that."

"Sure," she teased. "I'm here with the guy standing over there by the bar." She pointed to an amazingly handsome man with dark hair and an athletic build. "His name's Simon and he plays tight end for the Redskins."

"Nice," I said. "How'd you meet him?"

"Thanks to a dislocated shoulder. He came through the E.R. about a month ago, and we've been seeing each other ever since."

I looked at her in surprise. "Why, Katy Dee, it sounds like one of your Harlequin romances."

She flushed. "I know I seem tough at times, but I'm a romantic at heart. I love roses, flowers and moonlight—the whole nine yards," she sighed. "At times Simon seems too good to be true."

"I'm happy for you," I said.

"Yeah, I'm happy for me too," she paused. "I wanted to let you know that Ms. Murdock seemed satisfied when she left the E.R. I don't think she's going to sue the hospital."

"I felt so bad about her broken ankle," I said.

"Accidents happen," Katy Dee replied and glanced over at her tight end, "thank God!"

I grinned. She got up to leave, wished me a Merry Christmas and rejoined her date. I continued to fiddle with my empty glass until Mendoza and Sherrie returned with the food.

"Where's the shrimp?" I asked.

Sherrie shrugged, "They ran out of it."

"I see you've got some on your plate," I pointed out.

"That was just before they ran out," she said unapologetically.

I grabbed a shrimp off her plate and munched on it. Mendoza was digging into his food, and I noticed he had shrimp too, so I grabbed one of his.

"Hey!" he exclaimed.

"It's nice to share," I said.

He popped the other shrimp on his plate into his mouth and smiled. "Sharing is good, I like sharing." He looked from me to Sherrie and back again.

I ignored that. "I'm going to get another drink. Anybody want anything?"

"A cosmo," Sherrie replied.

"I'm good," Mendoza answered.

I approached the bar and ordered drinks. The bartender looked pointedly at his tip jar when he handed them to me. "Get you next time," I said with a big smile and noted that it would probably be better for Mendoza to get future drinks. I'd given the last of my cash to Stefansky for the Christmas shopping he was doing for me.

I returned to the table and handed Sherrie her drink.

"I saved you another shrimp," she said a little too graciously.

"Gee thanks, you're a true friend, Sherrie," I said and sat down. The little meatballs were disappointing, but the dip was good and I munched on carrot sticks loaded with the stuff while I watched the people on the dance floor. I saw Sam and Joyce dancing. Joyce was staring at me with a smug look on her face. I didn't understand why she hated me so much.

I caught a glimpse of Katy Dee and her boyfriend among the other couples and I was truly happy for her. It was nice to see her with a smile on her face. Even Mabel was on the dance floor with an elderly gentleman I'd seen around the hospital but hadn't met.

Mendoza finished his food and watched me watching the revelers. Joey, the tech from the E.R., approached our table and asked Sherrie to dance. She eagerly accepted, and Mendoza and I watched until the music changed to a slower beat.

Mendoza stood up and offered his hand. "Would you like to dance?"

I hesitated. I recalled my previous reactions and what usually happened to my senses when I got too close to Mendoza.

"Come on," he said. "I promise not to step on your toes."

"It's not my toes I'm worried about," I said as I stood up and allowed him to lead me to the floor. I stepped into his arms and Mendoza pulled me close against his lean, muscular body. The warm, musky scent of him sent a warm shiver down my spine. It was the best I'd felt all day. I looked up at him and he smiled.

"See," he said. "Not so bad, huh?"

"Hmm," I replied. We gently swayed together as the music swelled around us. Mendoza was a surprisingly good dancer, and I found myself swiftly carried away by the music. I was starting to finally relax for the first time all evening when I saw Sam come up behind Mendoza and tap him on the shoulder. Mendoza glanced around and Sam asked to cut in.

Mendoza released me, gave me a little mock bow and allowed Sam to take over. "Having fun?" he asked, drawing me into his arms.

I shrugged, "I haven't been in the best mood today."

Sam smiled. "I'm going to assume it's because I'm not your escort tonight."

"Speaking of escorts … where's yours?" I asked, glancing around quickly. I didn't want to get punched in the nose again.

"In the ladies' room," Sam answered.

"That's a relief," I said and laughed. "I'd kind of like to avoid getting punched tonight."

Sam's fingers tightened on my back as he pulled me closer. "I swear I won't let anything like that happen to you again," he whispered in my ear.

I felt the warmth flow through my body, which was starting to tingle. I was getting more confused about the two men in my life with each passing minute.

The slow dance ended and a fast one started to play. "Would you like to keep dancing?" Sam asked.

"No, I think I'll sit this one out. Besides, your date's headed our way. Thank you, though."

Sam reluctantly released me just as Joyce reached his side. I made my way back to Sherrie and Mendoza with warm shivers running through my veins and my head spinning. I rejoined them at the table and took a deep gulp of my drink.

"How'd that go?" Sherrie asked.

"Okay," I replied. "At least I didn't get maimed or anything."

"That's always a plus," she replied.

The music stopped, and our glances were drawn to the dance floor. A man dressed as Santa had taken center stage and started speaking into a microphone.

"Merry Christmas!" he roared into the mike.

"Merry Christmas!" the crowd roared back.

"Have you been good this year?" he asked the crowd at large.

"Yes!" the crowd roared back.

"Well then," Santa said. "Have I got a surprise for you!" He clapped his hands and a troupe of elves came running onto the dance floor, each carrying a sack. Great, more elves, I thought and watched while Santa approached the first elf and reached into his sack. "What have we here?" he roared and pulled out an envelope.

"It says it's for a nurse named Katy Dee! Is Katy Dee here tonight?"

Katy Dee stood up, and Santa handed the envelope back to the elf, who, in turn, took it to Katy Dee. She sat back down, opened the envelope and smiled. Apparently, the E.R. staff was receiving their bonuses. Santa continued to pull out envelopes, and the elves ran them over to the staff member if that person was present. I didn't think I would be getting a bonus because I was such a new member of the E.R. staff, so I took the opportunity to excuse myself to use the rest room. Sherrie and Mendoza were laughing at the elves' antics and seemed to barely notice my exit.

I left the cafeteria and made my way to the rest rooms. Seeing the empty corridors, I assumed everyone was staying inside so they wouldn't miss their gift from Santa. I felt a little woozy from the vodka and decided that I'd had enough to drink that evening.

When I walked into the bathroom, I found that it was empty as well, and I quickly entered a stall and sat down. I heard the bathroom door open when someone else entered. I finished my business and headed to the sinks to wash up. Mabel was standing in front of the mirror. She turned to look at me as I turned the water on.

"Merry Christmas!" she barked.

"Merry Christmas to you, Mabel," I replied.

"I have a present for you," she said.

I looked at her curiously. Why on earth would Mabel have a gift for me? "Oh?" I said and tried to smile.

Mabel nodded. She reached into her bag and pulled out something. It was a rather large gun, and she aimed it directly at me.

The smile I had tried to muster instantly vanished. "What the hell, Mabel?" I blurted out.

"You need to come with me," she barked.

I stood still, rooted to the spot. "Is this about the desk?" I asked. "You can have the desk if you want."

She held the gun steady and trained it right between my eyes. "It's not about the desk," she replied curtly. "I want you to walk out of this bathroom in front of me and sit in the wheelchair that's just outside the door."

She motioned for me to go first. When I stepped in front of her, she poked the nozzle of the gun in my back. It felt cold, hard and deadly. "Make a false move and it's over, you hear me?" she warned.

I nodded and she poked the gun harder into my back. "Get moving," she commanded.

I stepped out of the ladies' room and into the deserted hallway. Just as she had said, there was a wheelchair outside the door. "Sit down in that chair," Mabel barked.

I sat down and desperately tried to figure out a way out of the situation. Mabel was behind me with the gun to my neck, now pushing the chair with her other hand. We hadn't gone too far before I saw a door down the corridor swing open. It appeared that someone was waiting for Mabel.

"Can't we talk about this?" I asked.

Mabel didn't answer. She quickly wheeled me into the dark room and closed the door behind her. I peered into the darkness, trying to make out who had opened the door for Mabel, when I suddenly found myself gasping for breath. Someone had thrust a rag in my face. The rag had a horrible smell of some strong chemical. I tried to pry away the hand that was holding the rag over my nose and mouth, but my assailant was stronger than I was. I tried not to breathe, but I was already getting woozy. Familiar little bright sparks invaded my vision, and I realized I was going to pass out. Then everything disappeared into total darkness.

## Chapter 42

I don't know how long I was out cold. When I came to, I was still surrounded by darkness, but I was no longer sitting in a wheelchair. I was lying on something hard and smooth. My head was pounding, and my dry mouth had a nasty taste in it. I felt like I'd been on the mother of all benders. Memories of what had happened started to return to me, and I couldn't believe that Mabel, of all people, had done this to me.

I gingerly tried to sit up but only rose a few inches when my head hit something hard. I stretched out my arms and felt smooth walls only inches away from my side. I reached out with my toes and touched yet another smooth wall. Then I realized it was my toes that had touched the wall. Where were my shoes? I ran my hands over my chest and abdomen. Where were my clothes? I was lying completely naked in a very small space.

My heart was hammering in my chest, and my breath was coming out in gasps. I knew I was hyperventilating and willed myself to calm down before I passed out again. I put my hands over my mouth, my elbows bumping the sides of my prison and encountered some sort of plastic object over my face. As I felt around it, I felt the straps that were holding it in place. It was an oxygen mask.

Wherever I was, there wasn't enough oxygen to support life, so a mask had been placed over my mouth. I felt for the rubber tubing that I knew must be there somewhere. When I found it, I felt along its length, trying to determine where it went. I discovered that the tube went between my knees, where I encountered a longish narrow tank and realized it was one of the portable oxygen tanks they used throughout the hospital when transporting patients.

I was cold, naked and scared. I wondered how much oxygen was in the tank. I wondered how much I'd used and how long I'd been in there. I felt along the walls of my prison with my hands, trying to determine what I was lying on or in—or whatever. The more I felt around, the more horrified I became. I was getting a pretty clear picture of where I must be, but I didn't want to believe it. Still, the realization of my surroundings surged through me, and I started hyperventilating again. I wasn't positive but I was pretty sure that I was in a drawer in the morgue.

I tried to slow down my breathing and think happy thoughts. At least I was alive—that was a positive. How long would that be the case though? I wondered again how long I had been in there and whether Mendoza and Sherrie were looking for me yet. I was pretty sure they were, but how would they ever find me if I was in a drawer in the morgue? And I was pretty damn sure I was in the morgue.

I strained to see in the dark until my eyes started burning from the effort. I thumped what I thought must be the door of the drawer with my feet. I had little room to maneuver and I wasn't getting any results. The horror of my situation threatened to overwhelm me. I must have passed out again, because the next thing I remember is opening my eyes and being unsure of where I was. What I had surmised earlier quickly came back to me, and I started thumping the door with my feet again.

I heard a voice exclaim, "She's awake. And she's thumping around in there."

I screamed with all my might, but the oxygen mask muffled my voice. My screams didn't reach beyond my prison.

"Let her thump around," I heard another voice say. "It's not going to get her anywhere. Besides, the more she wears herself out, the less energy she'll have to fight us when we bring her out."

The voices belonged to a male and a female, but the barrier between us muffled the voices so that I couldn't recognize them.

I stopped thumping and thrashing and listened intently. I could hear some clanging and what sounded like water running. One of the people outside my prison was humming. Humming? Now that really pissed me off. How dare they lock me up in a morgue drawer and sit out there humming? I thumped again in protest, and the humming stopped.

"I hope she's not injuring herself in there." the male voice said.

The female voice answered, "Who cares? There's only one part of her anatomy we're interested in, and I doubt she'll do any damage to that."

I could feel my whole body suffuse with color as my rage continued to build. I had a pretty good idea what part of my anatomy they were referring to, and that part was mine, damn it! I took a few deep breaths to try to calm down. I continued to listen intently but could hear little else. The two people outside my door had stopped talking, and, other than the sound of water running, I couldn't hear much else.

My head was pounding with the strain of listening, when I suddenly heard a telephone ringing. It must have been a cell phone, because it was a zippy little "doo-dah" tune. Someone answered the phone, cutting off the tune. "Yeah," I heard the male say. "Okay, we'll see you in about 30 minutes then."

"It's time?" I heard the female ask.

I didn't hear an answer, but I did hear a key being inserted into a lock at my feet. I closed my eyes and tried to make myself go limp. I wanted to them to think I was still passed out when they opened the door.

I heard the handle on the door being pulled and could glimpse a crack of light enter my prison as the door swung open. I kept my eyes closed and waited.

"Looks like she's out," the female said. Her voice was very clear to me now, and my heart thumped heavily in my chest. It was Sam's stepmother—Alayna Macgregor.

The male spoke up, "Don't be so sure. She's a sneaky little bitch." I recognized the male's voice, and my heart rate sped up even more. The voice belonged to Officer Stefansky. Who would have guessed it? I wondered if he'd finished my Christmas shopping, but in light of what was happening, I highly doubted it.

I felt myself being pulled from the drawer and continued to play possum. I felt unbearably exposed, knowing that they were staring at my naked body. The metal slab I was lying on was disengaged and I was put onto a portable stretcher. When they'd completed the transfer, they started to wheel me away from the bank of drawers. I took the opportunity to spring to life and sat up quickly. I hurled myself off the stretcher, ripping the oxygen mask off my face as I did so.

I landed on the floor on my knees, and pain shot up my thighs. I briefly glanced at the astounded faces of Stefansky and Alayna and tried to get up and lunge for the doors. What I hadn't counted on was being numb from the waist down. I couldn't make my legs move quickly enough. Stefansky grabbed me by the waist and wrestled me down to the ground. I kicked out and landed a foot in his abdomen, sending the breath whooshing out of him.

I tried to stand up again, but Alayna was in front of me and she kicked me in the face. I saw stars when the toe of her shoe came into contact with my cheekbone, and my head snapped back so hard I was surprised that it stayed attached to my neck. I fell back and landed on top of Stefansky, who was still gasping for breath.

"Grab her arms!" Alayna yelled at Stefansky as she landed another kick, this time to my ribs. I thought I felt one rib crack, and the pain was blinding. It was at that moment that I realized that they probably didn't intend for me to leave alive that night.

I lay there with my arms pinned by Stefansky and watched Alayna secure tethers used for tying uncontrollable patients to stretchers. The floor was cold against my bare skin, and Stefansky's breath in my face smelled of sour milk. My head was spinning from the pain.

When Alayna had completed her task she went to the morgue desk and picked up a gun. She leveled it at me. "Up and at 'em, girl," she commanded, nodding toward the stretcher.

I remained silent and allowed Stefansky to pull me up by my arms. The movement renewed the pain in my ribs, and my head reeled from it. I tasted blood in my mouth and I wheezed with each breath I took.

"Looks like you've got a punctured lung there, dear," Alayna said sweetly. "You should really have a doctor take a look at that," she sneered.

"Bitch," I managed to wheeze out.

Stefansky led me to the stretcher, and Alayna told me to lie down. The gun in her hand brooked no argument. "Strap her down," she told Stefansky. He did as he was told and stepped back when he was finished to admire his handiwork.

"What next?" he asked Alayna.

I lay spread-eagle on the stretcher, and each breath I took sent blinding shockwaves of pain through my body. I knew I was in deep trouble and couldn't see any way out of the situation I was in. If only I had asked Sherrie to accompany me to the rest room, I thought.

"The rules for the ritual state that we need to cleanse her with the ointment," Alayna told Stefansky. She went to the bank of sinks along the wall and brought back a clear jar that held a murky liquid. I could see a finger bobbing in the mixture. At least I knew where Horace's finger had gone.

"Are you sure we need to drink that stuff as well?" Stefansky sniveled. Alayna nodded. Stefansky made a face and went pale.

Alayna took a sponge and soaked it in the liquid, then started to give me a sponge bath with it. The smell was obnoxious, and I wrinkled my nose in protest. She continued with her task, covering every exposed inch of my body with a fine sheen of the ointment. She hummed as she worked.

I was fighting to stay conscious. The punctured lung was making it hard to breathe, and I kept wanting to give in to the blackness that threatened the edges of my vision. I realized that they were preparing me for the ritual that was supposed to take place three days from now—that is, unless I'd been in the drawer for a few days, but I didn't think I had.

"She doesn't look so good," Stefansky told Alayna.

She shrugged in response. "She's fine. We only need her alive for another hour or so, anyway."

Stefansky gave me a look that seemed to show concern. "I still think I should be head regent. I mean, the last time he tried, it he botched it."

"We didn't have the last coin then—or the correct virgin," Alayna answered.

I closed my eyes. My head was spinning and nausea was threatening to overwhelm me.

After Alayna had finished sponging me down, she stood back to survey her work. Apparently satisfied, she made a phone call. "We're ready down here," she announced into the phone then snapped it closed.

Alayna looked at Stefansky and said, "Show time." She picked up two purple robes and handed one to Stefansky. They put them on and pulled the hoods over their heads so that their faces were barely visible. Alayna picked up a sheet and covered my entire body, including my head, and before I knew it, I was being moved again.

I allowed myself to drift off while the stretcher was in motion. I felt the stretcher stop at one point and heard the clinging of an elevator. The noises and the starts and stops told me that I was in the freight elevator and was headed to some unknown floor. When the elevator stopped and the doors whooshed open again, I could feel a gust of extremely cold air flow around me. The stretcher was put in motion again and finally came to its final stop when we reached what I supposed was the intended destination.

The air was frigid and the sheet became extremely cold against my skin. I started shivering uncontrollably and gasped when the sheet was pulled off, and the cold air hit me full force. I could barely breathe as it was, and the freezing air only seemed to suck more of my breath away.

I opened my eyes and found myself gazing at the winter night sky. A full moon floated above me, and wisps of clouds moved gently among the stars. I moved my head to glance around and saw that I was ringed by about eight figures draped in purple robes. I blinked my eyes, hoping I could wake myself up from a nightmare, but it didn't work.

I was freezing, buck naked and strapped to a stretcher spread-eagle in front of eight insane people on what appeared to be the rooftop of the hospital. I tried to scream, but the cold air and my wounded lung wouldn't let me. The only noise that passed my lips was a quiet hiss. I could taste the blood that bubbled on my lips with each breath.

The ritual began, and the robed figures started chanting in a singsong rhythm. I noticed another figure emerge from the shadows. This one was wearing a white robe, but the cowl of the hood hid the person's features, as it did with the others.

The singsong chant continued, and the white-robed figure approached me. I figured that they had to complete the ritual quickly or I would surely die of hypothermia. I continued to stare at the white-hooded figure, and it was then that I noticed that he was carrying an ornate dagger.

"Are you people insane?" I tried to scream, but the words came out in a whisper. I wanted to give up to the cold and go to sleep, but terror kept me from closing my eyes. The man came closer and was at the foot of the stretcher. He removed the cowl from his head, and I found myself staring directly into the eyes of Adam Petrovich. He held the dagger in one hand while his other hand went beneath the folds of his robe. He appeared to be fondling himself.

The chanting was rising and swelling around us, then it suddenly came to a stop. I could hear the electrical whirl of the great fans in the ventilation system atop the hospital and vaguely registered this was the same noise I'd heard on Kimberly's tape.

The purple-robed figures where passing around the elixir I'd been bathed with, each taking a deep drink. I started praying for a miracle. I somehow knew that when the elixir reached Adam I was toast.

Adam himself was clambering onto the stretcher with me. I tried to scramble away from him, but the tethers held me secure. He knelt at my feet, waiting for the elixir. Someone handed it up to him, and he brought it to his mouth.

Just as he was about to take a deep swill of the murky stuff, a door on the roof burst open, and I saw Mendoza was running toward me with a gun in his hand. Sam emerged from the door as well—right behind Mendoza.

A roaring filled the air, and a bright light appeared above us. I stared into the light, which got brighter and brighter, and I finally discovered it was coming from a helicopter. The noise was deafening as it hovered over the small circle of robe-clad figures, pinning them with light. As I watched Mendoza and Sam approach the stretcher where I was lying, one of the robed figures lunged at Sam and pulled him to the ground. Two more purple-robed figures stepped from among the rest and pointed guns. I tried to scream for Mendoza to watch out, but I couldn't get enough air to get the warning out. I needn't have bothered: the robed figures with the guns, trained them on the rest of the purple-robed figures.

Adam glanced up at the helicopter briefly, before turning his attention back to me. He was intent on completing the ritual, and I screamed silently as he poised himself over me, his focus entirely on impaling me, not only with himself, but also with the dagger at the same time. He held the dagger over his head as he moved the rest of himself over me, and I tried to scream again. At that moment, Mendoza launched himself forward and tackled Adam, rolling him off the stretcher and onto the ground. I heard yelling but couldn't see what was going on down there.

The helicopter continued to hover over us, and a voice boomed over a loud speaker. "FBI! Drop to the ground and spread your arms! We have you in our sight. One move and we'll shoot. I repeat. FBI! Drop to the ground or we'll shoot."

I watched as one robed figure after another followed the orders they had been given. I couldn't see what had become of

Sam and his assailant. The two figures that were standing with their guns drawn removed their hoods and waved at the helicopter. One of the two figures was Haley Smith and the other was Officer Stefansky.

Haley came running to my stretcher. She ripped off her robe and threw it over me. "You just don't listen," she screamed at me. "Why don't you listen?" I could see the fear in her eyes and knew that she had been terrified for me.

I felt the tears flowing from my eyes. "Mendoza, Sam?" I rasped.

Haley glanced to my right and grinned. "They're okay," she comforted me. A few seconds later, Mendoza was at my side. The look on his face took away what little breath I had left. His face showed heartbreaking fear mixed with an undeniable love.

"You okay?" He seemed to choke on the two words.

I nodded, unable to speak. He grabbed my hand and tried to rub some warmth into it.

I glanced around, worried about Sam, and saw him approaching behind Mendoza. When Sam reached the side of my stretcher, I saw that his green eyes were hard with anger and fear and his mouth had a grim line. With trembling fingers he gently touched the cheekbone that Alayna had kicked earlier. I looked from Sam to Mendoza, then back again, and tried to speak. My words came out as a wheeze, and I struggled once more for air.

Mendoza noticed my gasping for air, and his fingers tightened on mine. "Somebody get a doctor!" he yelled. "She's been hurt!"

Sam looked at Mendoza incredulously. "I *am* a doctor, you nitwit." Sam quickly began to try to untie the tethers that restrained my arms and legs.

"Well do something then!" Mendoza shouted at him.

"I'm trying to," Sam yelled back. "Help me with these straps!"

Mendoza gazed down at me with fear as my eyes began to close. "Stay with me, sweetie! Oh no, come on, stay with me!" he begged.

I couldn't though. I was done struggling and let myself flow into the darkness.

## Chapter 43

Two days after the aborted ritual, I woke up to the bright fluorescent glare of hospital lighting. I immediately closed my eyes against the glare and opened them again, this time slowly peeking out beneath my lashes, taking in my surroundings. I appeared to be in a hospital bed and I prayed to God that I wasn't at Cedars Memorial, but I figured I probably was. I moved my head a little and saw Mendoza fast asleep in a chair at the side of my bed, his hands resting on his lap. With effort, I moved my right hand and placed it over his. His eyes flew open, and he stared at our two hands for a few seconds before turning to look at me.

"Hey there," he said softly.

"Hi," I rasped out.

"How're you doing?" he asked.

"Been better," I whispered.

"I love you," he said quickly.

"I know," I whispered back.

He sighed and squeezed my hand. "Good."

I think I must have fallen asleep again, because the next time I opened my eyes it was morning and Haley had assumed the vigil and was sitting in the chair Mendoza had been occupying.

"You awake?" she asked.

I nodded.

"Scared us, you know," she scolded.

I nodded again. "Sorry."

"It's okay."

"Who are you?" I asked. I knew she knew what I meant.

She sighed. "Special Agent Samantha Langley, FBI, Paranormal Research Division, at your service, ma'am. I'll tell you more later, but right now you need to rest."

I nodded. My eyes were already feeling heavy again.

The next time I opened my eyes it was evening. I was beginning to wonder why I couldn't stay awake. I decided that I was either really tired or really sick. I glanced around the hospital room and noticed cards and flowers on every available surface. I grinned to myself. Suddenly I was very popular. The room and the chair next to my bed were empty of people. I was hungry and thirsty, so and I looked for the call button to ring for the nurse. I found it, and pressed the button.

About a minute later, a nurse came rushing into the room. She seemed astonished to find me there with my eyes open. "Can I help you?" she asked.

I nodded. "I'm thirsty... and hungry," I rasped.

"Sure, I'll get you something to drink right away. If the doctor says it's okay, I'll bring you a tray." She started to leave, but I waved her back. My heart had started doing a tap dance in my chest when I heard the word "doctor." Although my fear was not necessarily unreasonable, after what I had been through, felt that I had to know who my doctor was.

"Who's my doctor?" I asked in my scratchy voice.

"Why, Dr. Murphy, of course. He's the best pulmonary specialist we have on staff. Aside from your punctured lung, you've got a nasty case of pneumonia. You're lucky to have him."

I started to relax and smiled at her weakly. "Thanks," I rasped, and the nurse left on a mission to find me food and drink.

I found the bedside remote control for the television and flipped it on. I started surfing through the channels and settled on the evening news broadcast. As it turned out, the lead story involved me. The report started with the words: "Continuing story on the clan reenactment." My picture jumped on the screen. It was one of the better photos in the file that Sherrie had found in Alfred's apartment. I knew I had Mendoza to thank for that.

The announcer went on to report on the events surrounding the arrest of the most prominent members of the executive staff at Cedars: Alayna Macgregor, Adam Petrovich, Joyce Petrovich, Mabel Winchester, and several other players whose names I didn't recognize. The name Sam Macgregor, Sr., was not among the names listed in the report. I frowned in confusion. I was positive that he was not only part of the clan but also the head Regent.

The news anchor continued and explained the mythical legend surrounding the sacrifice of a virgin and the belief that great healing powers would be bestowed upon the Trufalic clan member who took the lead in the sacrifice. The pictures on the screen changed as she spoke of the details leading to my rescue. Then I saw a picture of Sam Macgregor, Jr., displayed on the TV screen. The news report stated that the young physician, the stepson of Alayna Macgregor, had been cleared of any involvement and was currently assisting the police with putting together all the pieces of this case, which appeared to span almost a decade.

My picture flashed on the screen again, and the reporter went on to say that I was currently hospitalized, recovering from multiple injuries, but that, from all accounts, it appeared that I was still indeed a virgin. I groaned. Now everyone in the nation knew that I hadn't been laid yet.

The perky nurse reappeared with a bottle of ginger ale, ice water and a tray of gelatin, colorless broth and sherbet. "Doctor's orders, sweetie. Just clear liquids for you today. He said he'd be in to check on you soon." She glanced at the television screen. "You're quite the celebrity around here. We've managed to keep the reporters at bay, but they're requesting a news conference as soon as you feel up to it."

"A press conference?" I asked weakly.

"Sure, everyone wants to hear from the virgin what it was like to be a clan sacrifice. Juicy stuff."

I groaned.

"By the way," she continued. "What do you want me to do with all the other stuff people have been sending you? We've been keeping it at the nurses station but, we'll, we're running out of room to work."

"What stuff?" I asked.

"Fan mail, flowers, gifts. Everyone wants to wish the conquering virgin well and according to some of the letters a lot of men want to marry you. Oh yeah, and a guy named Horace wrote one saying it was okay that you missed your date with him. He said that, after the police told him what the finger was used for, he'd rather not have it back."

"You read my mail?"

The nurse looked sheepish. "It gets boring on the midnight shift."

"Bring it all in here, I guess," I replied. "Except for flower arrangements with carnations. I'm extremely allergic to them."

"You sure?" she asked.

I nodded. She left the room. About 20 minutes later, she and a few other nurses started rolling in carts piled high with mail, bouquets, balloons, stuffed animals, chocolates and so forth. I was overwhelmed. "Oh, my God!" I exclaimed.

The other nurses who accompanied my nurse with all my goodies gawked at me as they unloaded the carts onto every available surface in the room. They had to unload the last cart onto a corner of the floor. I felt like I was in the middle of a flower shop or a gift shop. As they were rolling their carts out, Sam walked into the room.

When he saw that I was awake, a big smile spread across his face, but there were dark circles under his eyes and his hair was mussed as though he'd been running his hands through it. I could only imagine how bad I must have looked. I wasn't even sure how long I'd been there at that point.

He leaned down to kiss my cheek and ran a finger along it. "Did my stepmother do that to you?" he asked.

"Do what?"

"Well, you've got a hell of a bruise there, sweetie."

I remembered Alayna's kick to my face.

"I hate to say it, but she did."

"And your ribs? Did she break those too?"

"Fraid so." I replied.

"I'm so sorry," he said, and his face reflected his sympathy.

"Hey," I said softly. "You didn't know."

"It doesn't help. I feel responsible. I never liked her, but I had no idea what she was capable of."

"What? You mean you didn't know your stepmother was a homicidal bitch? Everyone knows that stepmothers are evil. Remember Snow White? Cinderella?"

Sam laughed. "I remember, and I also know what happens at the end of the each of the stories."

"What's that?"

"This," he said, leaning in and kissing me gently on the lips. Even in my drug and pain-debilitated state, his kiss took my breath away.

When he straightened up, he searched my eyes, and I smiled. "I like happy endings—a lot," I said.

"Me too," he sighed. "I like you a lot. I think I might even be falling in love with you."

"Join the club," said a voice that came from behind him.

Sam and I both turned to face Mendoza. I wondered how long he'd been there.

"Hey, Roman," Sam said without the slightest hint of his previous hostility.

"Sam," Mendoza replied. There was no hostility in his voice either. Actually, they seemed almost friendly toward each other. I was confused.

"You will remember that I saw her first," Sam grinned at Mendoza.

"Yeah, well that was before you and I buried the hatchet. I saw her first when she woke up," Mendoza explained.

I realized that something had happened to make the two men like each other again while I was in la-la land. This was very, very weird and really confusing.

"Umm, you guys want to fill me in on what's going on here?" I asked. "Why aren't you trying to kill each other?"

Sam smiled at me. "I wish I could stay to give you the details, but I have rounds to make. I'm on night shift tonight in the E.R."

He kissed me on the cheek again, right in front of Mendoza. "I'll be back soon," he said, and then looked at Mendoza. "She's all yours ... for now. Don't do anything I wouldn't do. Actually, scratch that. Don't do anything I'd want to do."

Mendoza nodded, and we both watched Sam leave the room. As he swung the door open, my mother stepped in. She gave Sam a quick hug, then rushed to my bedside. Apparently, a lot had been going while I was out.

"Hey there," Mendoza grinned when he saw my mother. "Look who's awake."

My mother took my hand in hers. She was smartly dressed in a wool jacket and slacks accented by a teal blouse. "Are you okay, baby? I was so worried! I've been here for two days, and you haven't opened your eyes for me—not even once."

I took a sip of my ginger ale to clear the dryness in my throat. "I'm fine, Mom. I'm sorry you were worried." I grinned up at her. "How's Mr. Oppenheimer?" I asked.

She flushed and rolled her eyes. "Remind me to never, ever drink Madeline's punch again. As for worrying, that's my job. I'm so proud of you, sweetie. Who would have thought it—my daughter the hero? Why I could just burst with excitement." She took the chair next to the bed and started playing with my hair, which I was sure looked pretty bad about now.

Mendoza sat on the bottom edge of my bed. "I'm sure you have a lot of questions."

I nodded. That was the understatement of the year. What I really wanted to know was what the heck had happened between him and Sam to bring about their reconciliation, but I didn't want to ask in front of my mother. Instead, I asked him, "How did you find me?"

Mendoza frowned. "It wasn't easy. After you disappeared, Sherrie and I were sure you had to be in the hospital somewhere. We started searching every nook and cranny. I wasn't terribly alarmed, because I knew that they had to keep you alive and that the winter solstice wasn't for a few days."

"You weren't alarmed?" I asked. "I was dying of fright, naked in a morgue drawer and you weren't worried?" I felt like punching him.

He saw the look in my eyes. "Of course, I was worried but, as I said, the sacrifice wasn't supposed to take place until Monday. I had also found out that the Santa at the Christmas party was actually Sam Macgregor, Sr. If you remember, we were pretty convinced he was part of the clan."

"Are they sure he wasn't in on it?"

Mendoza nodded. "Turns out, Alayna kept him in the dark about everything, including the fact that she was also carrying on a sexual affair with Adam."

I shuddered, thinking that I had nearly had a "sexual affair" with Adam myself. I pushed back the thought and asked, "Why did they do the ritual early?"

"Well, that's the thing—it wasn't early for them." Mendoza replied. "We were operating according to our modern calendar. I don't know why I missed it earlier, but while we were searching for you, I happened to glance out one of the hospital windows and noticed the full moon—or almost a full moon. It's impossible to tell unless you have a modern calendar. Anyway, the moon was huge just hanging up there. I remembered that the ritual was supposed to take place under a full moon and the moon appeared to be full. It was then that I realized we didn't have any time left."

I nodded. It all made sense. We were going on the basis of the modern date for the winter solstice, along with modern technology for determining the exact date of the moon's zenith. The Trufalic clan must have been using an ancient calendar. "So, how did you find me?" I asked again.

"It was your friend, Sandy."

"Sandy?" I asked blankly. "I don't know anyone named Sandy."

"Sure you do," Mendoza smiled. "The woman you feed occasionally in the E.R. The homicidal schizophrenic, remember?"

My eyes widened. "How did *she* help you?"

"It appears that Sandy pretty much lives full-time in the hospital. I was rushing down a back corridor, and she was camped in one of the doorways. I would have never seen her, except that she called out to me. She said, 'You there! The king and the witch got her!' At first, I was going to ignore her, but I remembered that she'd warned you about a king and a witch, and I didn't think it would hurt to see if she knew something. I stopped and listened to what she had to say. She pointed down the hallway and said that they'd taken you that way. Then she said that you were dead, and they were going to bury you."

"That must have been awful to hear."

Mendoza nodded. His eyes were full of an emotion that I couldn't describe, but I knew that, whatever it was, he felt it intensely and it was coming from his heart. "I thought I was too late. I thought I'd lost you."

My heart warmed at the care I detected in his voice, but I wanted to know more. "What did you do next?" I asked.

"Well," Mendoza went on, "I asked her to take me to you. She said Henrietta didn't want me to. So I told her to tell Henrietta that I'd make it worth her while if she helped me. Sandy considered that for a moment, then got up and started walking. She didn't say anything, but I followed her anyway. She led me to the morgue and told me they had taken you in there. I couldn't get inside, and Sandy watched me as I pounded on the door. Then she pointed to the elevator and said that later, they had taken you to heaven. I realized that the ritual was probably taking place on the roof. At that point, Sherrie and Sam rejoined me. We had split up earlier to search for you. Sherrie stayed with Sandy while Sam I took the stairs at a full out run. When we finally reached the roof, Adam was getting ready to, well, you know."

I remembered them bursting through the door of the roof. I remembered how afraid for him I'd been when I saw Haley and Stefansky draw their guns. "Thank you," I said simply.

"Thank Sandy," Mendoza replied. "We would have never made it in time if it hadn't been for her."

"Where is she now?" I wondered.

"We took her to the station as a witness and we've been doing a pretty good job of feeding her down there. We're in the process of trying to find a good group home for her. She needs to be in a place where she can get the kind of help she needs on a constant basis."

"What about Stefansky?" I asked. "Couldn't he have told you where I was? I mean, he's one of your men right?"

Mendoza shook his head. "Stefansky is one world-class actor. He came aboard my team about four months ago and had us all believing that he was a bumbling oaf. As it turns out, the F.B.I. planted him. He and Haley have been working to bust the remnants of the Trufalic clan for years—ever since Kimberly Hawthorne disappeared."

I shook my head in amazement. "So, you didn't know..."

Mendoza nodded. "I had no idea."

"And Haley? Oops, I mean Samantha? She's known Alfred for years. She's been undercover all this time?"

"Yeah," Mendoza replied. "She had a special interest in the case. You see, she was separated from her siblings at birth. When she became an FBI agent, she started using her resources and her other so-called special talents to try to find her brother and a much younger half-sister, whose name was Kimberly Hawthorne. Haley followed a trail that led her to the Macgregor's. At the same time, Alfred's coin-smuggling activities caught the Bureau's attention. Haley asked for the case so that she could stay in the vicinity. The Bureau let her go deep undercover to explore Alfred's activities. I don't think either the Bureau or Hal ... , I mean Samantha knew the two were connected at the time."

"Wow," I said. My head was spinning. "I don't remember any coins at the ritual. What did they use them for?"

Mendoza smiled. "They used them in advance in order to learn the words of the chant. The first ritual wasn't a success, but they didn't have the correct coins, and their virgin didn't have a birthmark like yours. So once they had the fourth coin and a new virgin, they wanted to try again."

"Who stole the coin from my apartment and the fingers?" I asked him.

Mendoza shrugged. "Haley *did* take the fingers, and she returned all but one of them. She'd received a phone call from Joyce, who told her that you were bringing them home with you. The clan needed a finger for the potion. Because she was working undercover and supposedly a member of the clan, she didn't have a choice. As for the coin, it appears I wasn't the only visitor you had that evening. Alayna stopped by too."

"I don't remember that at all! I'm sure I would have remembered that."

"You probably would have, but she managed to spike your wine with a sedative—much like the date rape drug. According to her, in your tipsy state, it wasn't hard to slip the drug in your wine glass. Not only did you not remember her visit, but when she asked you about the coin, you were eager to be rid of it. She knew you were in the resuscitation room when Tenny was brought in and hoped that you had some idea of where the coin went. She couldn't believe her luck when you answered your door half-drunk as it was."

"Remind me to never drink again," I mumbled.

My mother had been sitting quietly, which was unusual for her. She finally spoke up, "Whatever happened to this Kimberly person?"

"She was murdered the night of her senior prom."

I gasped. "You know this for sure?" I asked Mendoza.

Mendoza nodded grimly. "We found her in the morgue. She's been in drawer number nine for the last eight years."

I gulped. Adam had told me the drawer was locked because it didn't work. All along it had held a ghastly secret.

"And that's not all," Mendoza continued. "Preliminary autopsy results show that she was pregnant."

"Oh my!" She had been telling the truth when she told Sam she was pregnant. "Do they know who the father was?" I asked.

"Yes, several of the clan members state it was Adam Petrovich's child. DNA will confirm it. When they tried to do the ritual with Kimberly, she was actually in on it. According to those we've questioned so far, she was a willing participant. She'd been offered a lot of money for taking part in the sacrifice."

My eyes must have been as round as saucer. "So that's why they didn't kill her immediately. They had her consent."

Mendoza went on, "Do you remember the tape we listened to—the one with all the screaming?"

I nodded.

Mendoza went on, "Well, even though she was a willing participant, she wigged-out at the last minute. Most of the screams were hers. She was trying to get away. Some of the screams were the outraged clan members. They managed to subdue her, and the ritual was performed. Afterward, she'd agreed to stay quiet for an additional amount of money. Everything was hunky-dory until she found out she was pregnant. She started blackmailing Alayna and Adam for even more money. Alayna decided that if she could get Sam to marry Kimberly, she'd keep quiet. But Kimberly didn't go for it, and that's what got her killed. Alayna decided not even to risk trying to pay you off. She decided that you had to die immediately."

I sat in my bed silently. At least now I knew why Sam and Mendoza were friendly again: they finally knew what had happened to Kimberly Hawthorne and could no longer blame each other.

"How did you find out all of this?" I asked.

Mendoza sighed. "Alayna and Adam are rolling over on each other in their confessions in an attempt for leniency. Between the two of them we've gotten most of the story. Alayna told us that, when Sam had come home after his senior prom and told her that Kimberly had turned down his marriage proposal, she had been furious. Alayna had called Adam with the news, and he went looking for Kimberly. When he found her, he injected her with the same poison that he had used to kill Alfred eight years later."

"Adam killed Alfred, as well?" I asked.

"It appears that way. Adam followed Alfred to the deli, where Alfred passed out. He managed to spike Alfred's chilidog during a heated discussion. Alfred wanted more money for his part in the plot—his videotapes of you and the arrangement he'd made for the coin to be stolen from the Smithsonian. He also wanted out of the plot completely once he handed over the coin. Adam decided that he didn't need Alfred anymore and killed him. He knew Alfred had the coin with him the day he killed him and that Alfred would end up at Cedars after he keeled over. Adam's plan was to steal the coin from the ER. But the coin disappeared that same day."

"Into my pocket."

Mendoza nodded.

I wondered how Alfred and Adam hooked up in the first place. I looked at Mendoza and asked him.

"Well, it seems that Adam was obsessed with the Trufalics. Alfred and his knowledge of the coins came to Adam's attention by way of the award-winning article that Alfred had written regarding the coins. Adam arranged to meet Alfred and they hatched the plan to reenact the ritual together. It turns out that Alayna has a rare incurable blood disease that will probably kill her before she's 50 years old. She had a vested interest in creating an ultimate healer, so she used the medical records in her office to identify and locate the virgins required for the sacrifice. The first was Kimberly. That wasn't hard; the girl was dating her son. She had come from a broken family and very poor background and was easily influenced by money. You weren't so easy to trap. When Alayna discovered you, you were working with NERT. It took a good bit of maneuvering to land you in Alfred's apartment building. Do remember how you heard about an apartment that was available to rent?"

I shook my head, no. It had been so long ago.

"The apartment was advertised on the bulletin board in Alayna's office. You had mentioned your apartment search to your gynecologist during one of your office visits. Having read your records, Alayna had already taken an interest in you. When she asked your doctor about your visit, Dr. Reese mentioned that you were stressed out about finding a place to live. Alayna invented a reason to call you back in and made sure the availability of that apartment was brought to your attention."

"How clever and how unbelievable," I said. I felt like a puppet. That gang had manipulated me for a very long time.

"How did Joyce, Mabel and the others get sucked in?" I wondered out loud.

Mendoza shrugged. "Mabel hoped that the so-called ultimate healer could reverse the aging process. As for Joyce, well, she wanted the power that would be associated with whoever had the gift—her daddy. As for the others... I'm not sure."

"What about my job at Cedars?" I asked. "Did they plan that too?"

Mendoza shook his head no. "That was just one of those weird coincidences. Imagine Alayna's horror when she discovered that her son had taken an interest in you."

My head was reeling and I was feeling a little dizzy.

"Oh, honey," my mother piped up, "you look pale. I think all this talking has worn you out."

I ignored her. "So that's why Alayna wanted Sam to take Joyce to the party. Once I disappeared that night, she didn't want him to become a suspect."

Mendoza nodded. "Joyce was desperately trying to keep you and Sam apart throughout this whole thing. Her job was to make sure you didn't get too involved with him. Everyone was pretty upset when I ran you in for a drug test too. They tried to make that go away by having the lab rescind the results of your blood test."

I remembered the concerned look on Joyce's face as I had left the triage office the day I was tested. Her expression had struck me as odd even then.

## Chapter 44

The door to my hospital room opened again, and Sherrie tromped in. When she saw that I was awake, she rushed over and tried to give me a bear hug. My ribs were still tender and I yelped.

Sherrie stepped back quickly. "Oh, God! Sorry, Hoochie girl, but I'm just so happy to see you awake. You look terrible, though. Don't they have shower facilities around here?" She pushed the call button. "We're going to get you cleaned up. After all, your public is dying to meet you."

Mendoza laughed. "Yes, you're quite the star these days. The press has been clamoring for an interview, and there have been inquiries from Oprah and Howard Stern."

"Oprah?" I asked. "Oprah wants to talk to me?"

"And Howard Stern as well. He's dubbed you the 'Hymened Honey,'" Mendoza laughed.

"How flattering," I muttered sarcastically.

"Well, that's going to have to wait," my mother finally spoke up. "She needs rest, and, yes, she certainly needs a shower."

The nurse stepped into the room. "Who let you all in? The doctor's orders say one visitor at a time."

Mendoza stood up. "I have to be going anyway. This whole thing has created a mountain of paperwork, and I'm going to be working overtime for a while." He came over to the side of my bed and kissed me on the forehead. "Get some rest, okay?"

I nodded. I could still feel where his lips had pressed my forehead. The moment he left, my mother scolded me.

"You never told me about the nice, hot detective. Why am I always the last to find out about everything?" She shook her head in mock wonder.

"He is pretty hot." I answered.

"Sure is," Sherrie piped in.

"And the delectable doctor?" My mother wanted to know more. "What about him? We had lunch yesterday and, I'm telling you, that man is too good-looking and too nice to be true."

"He is pretty delectable," I agreed.

"Delectable and most likely delicious," said Sherrie.

"Well, I can tell that you're in trouble with those two up to your eyeballs. Just what are you going to do about it?" Mom pried.

"I don't have a clue."

"I could help you with that," Sherrie said.

"What do you mean you don't have a clue?" my mother asked.

"I really think I may love them both, Mom.'

"Love, shmove, you've known both of them less than two weeks. What you are in, my dear is lust. There's a difference."

I raised my eyebrows. This was, after all, coming from a preacher's widow.

"Well, what would you do if you were in my shoes?" I asked her.

Mom didn't hesitate with her answer. "Heck, I'd do them both.... of course, your biggest problem is figuring out which one gets the goodies first."

"Here, here!" Sherrie concurred.

"Mom! Did you just say what I thought you said?" I was discovering all kinds of new dimensions to my mother.

She shrugged. "Things aren't the way they were when I was your age. You have options I didn't have. I had to marry your daddy, the first man I had slept with, because I had gotten pregnant with you. You, on the other hand, can be choosy. You can try on different men and find out which flavor you like best."

"It's always worked best for me!" Sherrie chimed in.

I stared at my mother with my mouth open.

"What?" she asked. "When I'm right, I'm right."

I grinned at her. "I love you, Mom."

Tears sprang to her eyes. "I love you too, sweetie. Now get some rest, and I'll be back in the morning."

"Where are you staying?" I asked her.

"Why, your place, of course!" she stated. "And you'll just love what I've done with it. You'll see it when you get home."

I groaned, but she ignored me and gave me a quick kiss before leaving.

The nurse came in and busily took my vital signs while talking to Sherrie about how to go about getting me in the shower.

Sherrie helped me get undressed and had me in the shower shortly after the nurse left. My legs were still wobbly, and I was grateful for the handrails in the shower stall. I stood under the hot spray, willing the memories of my ordeal to follow the water down the drain. I had a feeling that the image of Adam with his twin daggers poised above me was going to stay with me for quite some time. I realized how close I'd come to losing my virginity against my will. And I knew also that my mother's words made sense. I had the right to be choosy.

When I emerged from the shower, still steaming from the heat, Sherrie helped me dress in the nightgown that my mother had brought for me. I got back into bed, and Sherrie filled me in on the details that Mendoza had omitted. "I've never seen a man go so crazy nuts," she said. "When he realized you were missing, he looked like he wanted to kill someone. He was the first to notice that Joyce had disappeared as well. When he asked Sam about her, Sam said he didn't know where she was and seemed concerned only about your whereabouts. And just like that, Sam and Mendoza forgot that they wanted to kill each other and went to work finding you."

"I noticed they were different toward each other this evening, but I thought it was because the Kimberly episode was finally laid to rest."

Sherrie nodded thoughtfully. "That probably had something to do with their making up, but they really put their differences aside before they knew that. They went to work together because of you."

I digested that information. If anything, it confused me more as to who was more doable in the deed department.

"So, how does it feel to have two men so crazy about you?"

"Honestly, the idea almost scares me as much as being locked up in a morgue drawer," I answered.

Sherrie laughed, "Well, you know me, I always seem to need more than one man around. If you need any pointers…"

I laughed and immediately winced as my ribs protested.

Sherry sighed and squeezed my hand, "Gosh, Hoochie girl! Oprah! Did you ever think you'd be on her show?"

I shook my head. "Don't forget about Howard Stern. Apparently, I'm the most popular virgin out there."

"Yep," she smiled smugly. "I wonder if you can bring a friend on Oprah's show with you?"

Long after Sherrie had left, my thoughts lingered on Sam. I thought of how we'd met and the sparks that had ensued. I thought of Mendoza and the sparks he evoked. I wondered if I'd ever be able to sort out all those sparks and was still wondering when I fell asleep.

## Chapter 45

I was allowed to leave the hospital on New Year's Eve. My mother, accompanied by Sherrie, deflected the paparazzi, while the orderly assigned to my wheelchair deftly maneuvered my chair to my mother's car. I kept my head down and stayed silent as the lights from camera flashes ignited the dusky air. Really, I thought, the questions bordered on the ridiculous. The assembled media kept asking, "How does it feel?" How does what feel? I asked myself. Being a virgin? Being ignored by the men in your life?

Neither Sam nor Mendoza had come back to see me in the past few days. I hadn't gotten so much as a "Merry Christmas" greeting from either of them. It turned out that Stefansky had actually completed my shopping, though, and he had dropped the gifts off at the hospital on Christmas morning. I was astounded not only because he had done the shopping but also because Stefansky, the bumbling, blushing undercover agent, had completely disappeared and the man who had swaggered through my hospital room door that morning, while resembling Stefansky, had the self-assurance and laid back stature of another hot cop I knew. Sherrie had been in my room at the time, and she and Stefansky had started dating almost immediately.

Sherrie, my mother and I had shared Christmas together in my little hospital room. We enjoyed a nice dinner along with a bottle of champagne that Sherrie had smuggled in. Mom loved her vibrator.

I settled into the car and stared out the window at the passing scenery. It seemed odd that the world looked the same after all that had happened in the past couple weeks.

Once we got to my apartment building, my mother let me lean on her as we entered. She unlocked the door to my apartment, and Sherrie entered first and switched the lights on. Still leaning on my mother, I entered behind Sherrie, and my mouth dropped open in awe. My Charlie Brown Christmas tree was taller, greener and brighter, and I had the feeling that the tree had been a victim of the pod thing. Twinkle lights were draped everywhere around the apartment, and the smell of something delicious was emanating from the kitchen.

Mom and Sherrie settled me down on the couch and handed me a blanket. "Hoochie girl, enjoy!" Sherrie grinned at me with a knowing look and left before I could reply. My mother patted my hand and said, "If you need me, I'll be next-door at Samantha's." Then she left too, closing my apartment door with a quiet click behind her.

I sat on my couch, dumbfounded and feeling abandoned and lost. Enjoy what? I thought. Why were they leaving me alone on New Year's Eve?

I didn't have to wait long for my answer. The door to the kitchen swung open, and Sam emerged with a wine glass in each hand. He stood there with a bemused gaze and stared at me with those amazing emerald eyes. "Did you think I had abandoned you?" he asked with a quirky grin.

'Um, yep," I answered, the beginnings of a smile teasing the corners of my mouth.

"Oh ye of little faith," he replied quietly as he approached and offered me one of the glasses he held.

"Why?" I asked as I took the wine.

"Why haven't I been to see you?" he asked.

Much to my dismay, I felt my eyes tear up. "Yes," I whispered. It was at that moment that I knew how badly I'd missed him.

"I wanted you to be sure," he said quietly.

"Sure of what?" I asked.

"That you really wanted me to be there." He knelt in front of me. "Plus, I have been busily helping the police put my stepmother behind bars. You may remember her as the vicious, evil villain-ness who tried to…"

"You ass," I cut him off.

He took my hands and kissed each finger reverently, igniting fires in my belly that traveled freely throughout my body.

"I want you, Charlie. I want you like no one I've ever known or thought I wanted in my entire life." When he looked up at me his eyes had turned forest green—a color I hadn't seen before.

"But I haven't even been to your house. You could be a slob or a hopeless pack rat for all I know."

"You'll see my house and you'll find out all kinds of endearing, lovable qualities that you didn't know about me before."

I held up a hand. "Whoa, buddy, are you sure that you're not just a victim of my awesome new celebrity status?"

"You're kidding, right? I fell for you the day you hit my Navigator. I've never known anyone with your spunk or your absolute disregard for *my* awesome status as a doctor."

He placed a hand on the nape of my neck and drew me toward him until his lips met mine, as usual, all conscious thought went out the door. This time his kiss was gentle and probing—almost shy. Nonetheless, I felt my entire bone structure melt and fires ignite along the nerve endings throughout my body.

A sudden knock at the door broke the embrace and I sighed. "It's probably Hal ... I mean Samantha on virgin patrol."

Sam sighed, and I went to the door and opened it to find Mendoza standing there. He had a bottle of champagne in one hand and a bouquet of flowers in the other.

Mendoza noticed Sam standing behind me and said, "What are *you* doing here?"

"I could ask you the same question," Sam replied.

Mendoza handed me the flowers. "I can assure you that this bouquet doesn't have a single carnation in it."

The flowers were primarily red roses with daisies and baby's breath intertwined through them. I thought it was sweet and felt my heart melting.

"What's that supposed to mean?" Sam asked, snarling.

It seemed, the men were forgetting that they were friends again. I cringed as I remembered the last time I had to break up one of their fights.

"Have you two forgotten you're supposed to be friends?" I stated loudly. "Behave or else!"

They both turned to me, and both their faces warmed. Green and blue eyes stared at me with the same tender expression. I felt my heart do a little jumpity-jump in my chest and wondered how I could possibly choose one or the other? It didn't seem the least bit fair that I had to. Apparently, the power company agreed with me, because, just at that moment, it made good on the threat to shut off my electricity, throwing everything into darkness.

"Trinity"

Charlie Meadow's adventures continue!

Available December 2013

Visit Angela @ www.angelasherwood.com

www.ingramcontent.com/pod-product-compliance
Lightning Source LLC
Chambersburg PA
CBHW071643090426
42738CB00009B/1411